SLEEPING AROUND

Also by Brian Thacker

Rule No. 5: No Sex on the Bus
Planes, Trains and Elephants
The Naked Man Festival
I'm Not Eating Any of that Foreign Muck
Where's Wallis?

SLEEPING AROUND

A COUCH SURFING TOUR OF THE GLOBE

First published in 2009

Allen & Unwin
83 Alexander Street
Crows Nest NSW 2065
Australia
Phone: (61 2) 8425 0100
Fax: (61 2) 9906 2218
Email: info@allenandunwin.com
Web: www.allenandunwin.com

National Library of Australia
Cataloguing-in-Publication entry:

Thacker, Brian, 1962-

Sleeping around : a couch surfing tour of the globe / Brian Thacker.

978 1 74175 210 6 (pbk.)

Thacker, Brian, 1962- --Travel.
Australians--Travel--Foreign countries.

910.4

Set in 11/15 pt Minion Pro by Bookhouse, Sydney
Printed in Australia by McPherson's Printing Group

10 9 8 7 6 5 4 3 2 1

CONTENTS

INTRODUCTION

I live in a small one-bedroom flat with my wife and 5 children. There is no couch, so you will have to share a room with the kids. I live a long way from the city and there is no public transport. I should also probably tell you that I've only recently got out of prison.
Brian Thacker
Melbourne, Australia

Admittedly, I was perhaps a little sceptical when I initially registered on GlobalFreeloaders.com a couple of years back. According to their mission statement: 'GlobalFreeloaders.com is an online community bringing people together to offer you free accommodation all over the world. Save money and make new friends whilst seeing the world from a local's perspective.' It sounded like a brilliant concept. First of all there was the 'free accommodation' bit—I concede I'm somewhat 'frugal' when I travel and will happily do things like wallow in my own sweat because the air-conditioned room cost a dollar more. But it wasn't just my penchant for penny-pinching that attracted me to the idea of GlobalFreeloading, it was also the idea that you could bypass the standard tourist routes and be assimilated into local lifestyles and cultures. I just tweaked my profile somewhat so no one would want to come stay with me. I mean, exactly what sort of lunatics open their homes to total strangers from the other side of the world at a time when you can't carry a nail file onto an aircraft? Even if they trust me, can I trust them? You certainly couldn't tell if a potential host was trustworthy by looking at a lot of the profiles on the GlobalFreeloaders site. Many gave absolutely no indication of what type of person they were and looked something like this:

> Spare couch. No pets.
> Claudio Hernandez
> Bogota, Colombia

I forgot about the site until a few months later (surprisingly enough no one had requested my 'couch') when, in one of my usual aimless wanderings around the net, I stumbled upon CouchSurfing.com. The website had the same premise as GlobalFreeloaders (their mission statement is: 'Participate in creating a better world, one couch at a time'), but they had taken the concept to a whole new level. The profiles were more detailed and built on a MySpace/Facebook type model with users including their photos, interests, what types of people they enjoy, a list of friends, languages spoken, places travelled and even a comprehensive couch description.

Perhaps the most redeeming feature, however, was that the hosts and guests vouched for each other much like eBay.

CouchSurfing.com began in 2004 when 22-year-old Casey Fenton, a software programmer in New Hampshire who had been working 100-hour weeks for a website he himself had founded, decided he wanted a weekend away. He found a cheap last-minute flight to Iceland, but when he discovered how expensive accommodation was in Reykjavík, he did what any reasonably able, ethically flexible programmer might do: He hacked into the University of Iceland student directory and spammed more than a thousand students asking them if they had a spare couch. In his email he said: 'I'm coming on Friday. I want to see the real Iceland. Will you show me your country?' The overwhelming response—more than a hundred replies from potential hosts all eager to show him 'their Reykjavík'—not only secured Casey a couch for the weekend, it also sparked the CouchSurfing concept and website.

I joined immediately and even penned a more realistic profile—minus a few kids and the prison sentence. A stranger's couch suddenly sounded a whole lot safer. And a whole lot easier to find. To secure a couch all you had to do was search for the city you planned to visit and you would be presented with a list of hosts. Contact any from the list who interest you and the hosts would get back to you if they have a couch available on the dates you need. And after you decide which couch suits you best—*voilà*—you've got a free place to stay and a new friend who most likely knows the city better than any hotel concierge.

Seeing a city through the eyes of a local was actually the thing that attracted me the most to the couch-surfing concept. In my travels I've had a taste of staying with locals and the experience has often been the highlight of my trip. I have been lucky enough to take part in a traditional family feast on the Pacific island of Futuna, as well as a traditional family feast in Kyrgyzstan, and also a traditional family feast in Morocco and . . . okay, I do like family feasts. But really, can you truly say you've experienced somewhere if you haven't had a beer with a local, in their local?

While I was checking out a couple of profiles on CouchSurfing, I noticed that some members were also members of HospitalityClub.org, so I joined that as well. Hospitality Club's mission statement is: 'By bringing travellers in touch with people in the place they visit, and by giving "locals" a chance to meet people from other cultures, we can increase intercultural understanding and strengthen the peace on our planet.'

The HospitalityClub site was similar to the CouchSurfing site, but was founded for an entirely different reason. The site began in 2000 and was set up by Mensa member Veit Kuehne from Germany for Mensa members only. Their mission statement was: 'Mensa SIGHT [Service of Information, Guidance and Hospitality to Travellers] allows members to enjoy the company and hospitality of fellow intellectually gifted people from around this world.' It was only when they got bored talking about quantum physics to each other that they invited the rest of the world to join.

At around this time, I had a couch-surfing brainwave. I decided that I would go on a Grand Couch Surfing Tour of the Globe. What better way to see and experience the world—and purely coincidentally have another idea for a book?

But which countries should I surf in? The world is full of couches. On the CouchSurfing website alone there were more than 200 countries represented, including members in such far-flung and far-off-the-tourist-track nations as Iraq (34 members), Afghanistan (28), Palestine (24), North Korea (4), East Timor (3), São Tomé and Príncipe (2) and one member in the Spratly Islands (wherever that is). There were even five members in Antarctica—although none of them offered an actual couch except Daniel, who listed his occupation as 'Waste Management'. Under 'Accommodation' he had:

> Maybe. I say maybe because IF you're coming to Antarctica I assume you've already secured a comfy bed. BUT if you somehow manage to get here without one, there is always a couch in the lounge.

I figured that if I got a round-the-world ticket and did at least two countries per continent I would get a good cross-section of couches (and their owners). In the end my itinerary was shaped by a preference for visiting places I hadn't been before and the vagaries of international flight schedules. All that was left to do after I'd booked my tickets was to choose a host who was happy to choose me as their guest. My simple criterion was that I wanted to stay with folk who sounded interesting—I had to get a book out of it after all and I guessed that I wouldn't get much of a story if my host got home from work at seven every night and crashed in front of the TV. I wanted people who really lived their lives and were happy for me to live them with them for a few days. And if my hosts sounded just a little odd, then so much the better. Mind you, I did find some profiles that were more than just a little odd:

> *Interests:*
> Beauty and the lust for learning have yet to be allied.
> *Favourite Music, Movies and Books:*
> The very meaninglessness of life forces man to create his own meaning.
> *Personal Philosophy:*
> And new philosophy calls all in doubt, the element of fire is quite put out; the sun is lost, and the earth, and no man's wit can well direct him where to look for it.
> *One Amazing Thing I've Seen or Done:*
> It is amazing how complete is the delusion that beauty is goodness.
> Murat, 33
> Istanbul, Turkey

I sent out all my requests two months before I was due to fly out and sat back and waited for couch invitations. With a week to go before departure, I had all my couches 'booked' with a suitably eclectic mix of people, including folk of different ages and sex; singles, families and couples; and occupations, from an architect and a nurse, to a university student and even someone who was unemployed.

My Grand Couch Surfing Tour of the Globe would be a series of snapshots of everyday life all over the world right now, when technology is bringing us closer together but the politics of fear may be driving us further apart. Can a Muslim in Istanbul and a Catholic in Rio de Janeiro watch the same TV shows? Does someone from Nairobi enjoy the same music as someone from Santiago? Who drinks more—the Belgians or the Canadians?

In an age of cheap airfares and porous borders, where almost every corner of the globe, from Azerbaijan to Zambia, is open for tourism, going into someone else's home is possibly the last authentic travelling experience. And for the growing legion of couch-surfing members, the only way to experience it is by sleeping around.

CHILE

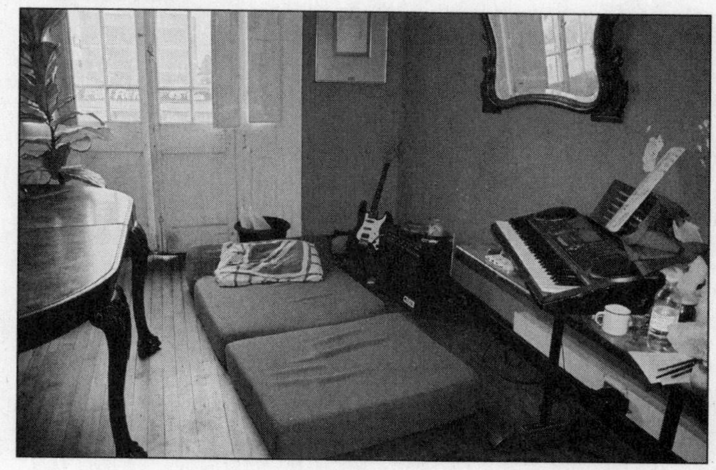

1

'The only rule I have is that you HAVE to shower every day please! (I have had terrible experiences in the past.)
Daniel Ortega, 24, Santiago, Chile
GlobalFreeloaders.com

My Grand Couch Surfing Tour of the Globe didn't start too well. I couldn't find a couch. Or, more precisely, my couch was playing hard to get and wouldn't return my emails. I'd already booked my spot, but it would have been handy if my host Daniel had told me exactly where in Santiago the couch in question was located. Daniel had seemed keen for me to stay when I'd contacted him a month earlier. Well, not exactly bursting-with-excitement keen. He had answered my request for a couch with:

Ok
I would have not problems those days.
Daniel

Daniel was one of a number of people in Santiago I had contacted for a couch. I liked his profile on GlobalFreeloaders because I was intrigued to meet him and hear all about his horrific stories of the unwashed. His brief profile read:

> Spare room in 3 Bedroom apartment close to the Andes (view from the living room). A block from the subway station, and 30 min from the city. I am a uni student so I have plenty of spare time on my hands for going out.

I had confirmed my booking for Daniel's couch and he'd emailed me straight back and said to drop him a line a couple of days before I was due in Santiago. I had sent Daniel three emails in the week before my departure, but he hadn't responded to any of them. I thought that he might have reneged because he was worried about my standards of hygiene, so I even sent him an email to tell him how much I loved taking showers.

With only two days left before I was due to fly out, I gave up on Daniel and sent out a new pile of couch requests. The couch owners I emailed included Ignacio, who 'loves chillies and collects hot sauces from around the world'; Ann Maria, who does not like 'people who walk around nude or half-dressed in front of me'; Claudio, a belly dancer, who said 'I'm physically living in Chile, but my mind is somewhere else'; Mauricio, a financial reporter whose interests included oncology *(the study of tumours!)*, 'the afterlife' and 'being profound'; and Diego, who may just be a friend of Daniel since he says you can bring a pet as long as 'you don't bring anything that might stink'.

I was still checking my emails an hour before I left for the airport, but the results weren't good. Every single one of my requests for a couch drew a blank. Most of my potential hosts totally ignored me, and all the rest were otherwise occupied—three were out of the country, two already had couch-surfing guests and one was rearranging his sock drawer.

I hadn't had any trouble finding a couch anywhere else in the world, so why was I in danger of a total couch wipe-out in Chile? I couldn't understand why I wasn't getting any response. I even resorted to telling Mauricio that I, too, like being profound and assuring Diego that although I didn't own a pet, if I did it wouldn't be a stinky one.

I checked my emails one last time in the transit lounge at Auckland airport. 'Yes, I would love to have you stay,' said Christian Petit-Laurent Eliceiry, film director, 32.

Bingo.

Christian had just finished filming a documentary in Spain and had 'plenty of time to show me around, go bike riding in the mountains and visit neighbours'. Just as I was excitedly rubbing my hands together, I noticed the last line of the email: 'I'll be back in Santiago on the 27th.' That was the day I'd be flying out of Santiago to Brazil.

Okay, be positive. There was still hope. I had all of 23 minutes to send out more emails before the flight to Santiago boarded. And there were still 1672 couch owners left in Santiago I hadn't emailed yet. One thing I wasn't going to do, though, was to send out a 'blanket' email to all 1672 people. I'd already received 'blanket' requests to stay with me in Melbourne from people who hadn't bothered to read my profile or even say 'Hello Brian' and I'd ignored them.

I only had enough time to shoot off a dozen more couch requests. I also decided to cast my couch-surfing net a little further by sending requests to a few people in Valparaíso, less than two hours from Santiago. Although there were plenty of couches to choose from in Santiago and Valparaíso, many of the hosts didn't speak English which was one of my criteria as, unfortunately, I only speak English (a limitation of my Grand Couch Surfing Tour of the Globe, I fully acknowledge).

Ten hours after leaving Auckland we were flying over Chile's coast, which lay below like the front edge of a stage with the snow-capped Andes resembling a long white silk curtain as the dramatic backdrop. I actually didn't know very much about Chile. Amazingly, after all my years of travelling this was my first foray into South America.

Even as I waltzed through the arrivals gate of Aeropuerto Internacional Arturo Merino Benitez, I was still optimistic that I would track down a couch for the night. I'd pop into the airport internet cafe where I was sure there would be a couch offer waiting for me with simple directions to the host's salubrious home and the promise of an ice-cold beer waiting for me on arrival. I soon discovered, however, that my masterful plan had one tiny flaw. There was no internet cafe at the airport.

That left me with very little option. I had to get into the city. A city I knew absolutely nothing about. To gain a true 'local's perspective', I had decided not to take guidebooks with me and to do very little research on my couch-surfing destinations. Which would have been all very well if there had been a prospective local to give me a local perspective.

The centre of Santiago seemed the most likely place to find an internet cafe. I still hadn't given up hope of procuring something that resembled a couch for the evening. I wasn't being totally inflexible, though. At this late stage, I'd settle for a chaise longue, a chesterfield, a divan or even a large ottoman.

Santiago looked like a European city thrown into the middle of the Himalayas. The towering mountains around the city seemed to crowd in almost to the edge of the suburbs, with the snowy peaks shimmering brilliantly white above the city's murky brown haze. Every time the airport bus stopped to let someone out, I would say 'El Centro?' to the bus driver and he would look at me with disdain and say something in Spanish which I guessed meant: 'What do you think you idiot? Does it look like the centre?'

But when we finally got there, El Centro looked nothing like my idea of a city centre. I was dropped off on a wide busy boulevard lined with office buildings and poplar trees. The spot looked identical to the last three stops on the boulevard where the bus had dropped passengers off. I stood for a minute and tried to get my bearings (which is actually quite difficult when you have no idea even where you are supposed to be), then started walking up the boulevard.

Still looking for the heart of the city, I turned down the first side street I stumbled upon. It was lined with shops and sidewalk cafes filled with slim good-looking folk eating large good-looking ice creams.

I found an internet cafe easily enough, but much to my frustration I still couldn't find a couch. I sent out a few more requests as I still had another six nights in Santiago, but I resigned myself to the fact that I was going to be couchless for the first night of my Grand Couch Surfing Tour of the world. It looked like I had to get a hotel—either that or go Park Bench Surfing.

I passed a couple of hotels, but opted for Hotel Foresta, which was only-just-slightly-rundown (read: cheaper). The hotel overlooked Cerro Santa Lucía, a lavishly landscaped park that looked more suited for mountain goats than people. Crammed into a small city block was an impossibly steep wooded hill full of fountains, curving staircases and intricate stone paths.

No wonder I wasn't getting a response to my couch requests. Everyone in Santiago under 30 was canoodling in the park. After checking into my only-just-slightly-rundown room, I decided to take advantage of the balmy late afternoon and climb the park. The steep hill was packed with amorous couples, their arms, legs and lips all entwined. They were sprawled on park benches, lustfully lounging on the grass and there were even parents groping each other while their kids ran around their ankles.

I hiked up the narrow leafy terraces trying to find a lookout, but every time I stepped into one of the small nooks hanging precariously over the rocky edge, I'd bump into a couple with their tongues down each other's throats. The final steep ascent took me up to the tiny Caupolicán Plaza and a sweeping view of Santiago. The suburbs of the city really did stretch out to the very base of the Andes and in some places were creeping up the lower reaches as if the mountains were slowly pushing their way into the city.

'It was on this site that Pedro de Valdivia, the conqueror of Chile, founded Santiago in 1541 for the crown of Spain. The hill was originally called Huelén, which in the local mapudungún language means "pain or sadness". In 1872 . . .' I couldn't read the rest of the plaque because a young woman's bottom was draped across it while her boyfriend fondled it (that's the bottom he was fondling, not the plaque).

The streets behind the hotel were a warren of charming little cobbled lanes and passageways that were packed with restaurants and bars. As a parade of beautiful people wandered around happily spinning out the process of deciding where to eat, I randomly picked the first restaurant with outdoor tables and ordered a beer. My first night of my Grand Couch Surfing Tour may have been couchless, but I was still determined to enjoy myself. Or get drunk. Whichever came first. Getting tipsy proved to be quite easy. First of all my beer was served in a huge Alice-in-Wonderland tea cup. Then, when the waiter suggested I should try the Chilean national drink known as 'pisco sour', he brought out two large glasses. It was two-for-the-price-of-one Pisco Sour Happy Hour. The drink had more pisco than sour and was basically a glass of strong clear brandy with a squirt of lime and a pinch of sugar in it.

I tried to soak up the pisco sours with a plate of fried squid and salad, but the combination of lime-flavoured rocket fuel and jet lag (I wasn't sure if it was 3.30 in the morning or 3.30 in the afternoon in Australia) was definitely affecting my judgement. That's probably why I dropped into a bar on the way back to the hotel for another drink. Bar Berri looked as if it belonged to a past age with its low ceilings and tiny wood-panelled rooms. When I ordered a beer in my clumsy Spanish, the manager asked where I was from. 'Ah, Steve Irwin!' he gushed. 'Crikey!' he said as he handed me my beer.

I'd only been sitting at a table by myself for a few minutes when the manager came over and said, 'I have a friend you can meet'. His friend was the Spanish ambassador to Chile. 'Ah, Steve Irwin!' the ambassador said, shaking my hand. This might work out all right, I thought. My suave new friend would surely have a spare couch. And more than likely it would be a lovely, soft leather one. I soon realised, however, that the ambassador might have other plans for his couch that night. Even as he spoke to me, he was deftly fondling his secretary's bottom.

On the way back to the hotel I noticed that the internet cafe was still open, so I shuffled in to check my emails. I was nothing if not persistent.

'YES!' I blurted out at the top of my rather inebriated voice.

As far as couch surfing goes, I'd hit paydirt. I'd been invited to stay at a ski lodge up in the Andes for two days. Miguel Angel Chacana lived in Valparaíso, but according to his profile he 'wasn't home too much'. Miguel worked as a guide and cook on horse riding tours in the wilds of Patagonia in the summer and 'cooked in a ski lodge when it was busy' in the winter. Miguel was in Santiago for the night and he said in his email that if I wanted to join him I needed to call him before eleven o'clock because he was leaving early in the morning for the 90-minute drive up to the lodge. I looked at my watch. It was five to eleven.

2

'Skiing is the sport I like the most in winter and sleeping later from time to time.'
Miguel Angel Chacana, 45, Valparaíso, Chile
CouchSurfing.com

Miguel looked nothing like Miguel.

'Brian?' he asked as he stepped out of his car in front of the hotel. In the photo of Miguel on his profile, he had a shaved head. This Miguel had a wild crop of grey hair and was at least ten years older.

'Hola, nice to meet you,' I said, reaching for Miguel's hand.

Miguel grunted a quick 'Hola' then grabbed my pack and threw it into the boot of the car.

'Now we go,' Miguel said with an evil grin. Okay, possibly I was being a little paranoid, but it all seemed a little odd. Miguel didn't appear to speak much English yet his CouchSurfing profile was written in perfect English. As we drove away I began to feel a tremor of foreboding. In Miguel's profile he sounded nice enough, but I really knew nothing about him. Why, for example, had he previously shaved his head? Or was he wearing a wig? Then it hit me. No one at home knew where I was or who I was with. If Miguel took me up to a secret hideout in the mountains to torture me, no one would ever know. Maybe that was it. Maybe Miguel was part of some Chilean Freedom Fighter group and he was about to hold me to ransom. Even more worryingly, none of my friends or family have lots of money, so Miguel and his Freedom Fighters would have to kill me to prove a point. Maybe this couch-surfing thing wasn't such a good idea after all.

I looked Miguel up and down to try and figure out where he kept his gun. He looked normal enough. Ah, but that's why he was the perfect choice to lure innocent and naïve couch surfers onto his 'couch'.

'So Miguel,' I stammered, '. . . are you a good skier?'

'I'm not Miguel,' he said, staring at the road ahead.

Oh dear.

I was right. I was being kidnapped.

'We pick up Miguel on way,' the man who wasn't Miguel said cheerfully—almost *too* cheerfully.

I see. In case I tried to put up a fight, there would be two of them to hold me down. Maybe I could jump out of the moving car. There was hardly any traffic, however, and we were moving quite quickly. Still, a few grazes and a broken arm or two would be a darn sight better than getting hung up by my testicles.

When I'd told friends that I was going to be staying with complete strangers in cities I'd never been to before, at least half of them had said, 'But they might be axe murderers!' (Not just plain old murderers, mind you, always axe murderers.) One friend had been right, though. He'd predicted that I'd be kidnapped by freedom fighters.

Just as I was contemplating jumping out of the car, we pulled up in front of a neat line of apartment blocks and a bald-headed man wearing a bright red fleece skipped out and jumped into the back seat.

'Hola Brian, welcome to Chile!' the real Miguel said, with a warm handshake and a beaming smile. After ten minutes in Miguel's company, I was pretty sure he wasn't a freedom fighter (although his surly friend Roberto with the evil grin could still have possibly been an axe murderer). Miguel may have been a stranger, but he seemed truly welcoming and genuine.

I was certainly in for a welcoming surprise when I got to the lodge. I wasn't sleeping on a couch. I had a bed. And not just one bed, I had 28 beds to choose from. It was the end of the ski season and the lodge was empty. Miguel's best friend and fellow guide Jorge was the manager of the lodge and Miguel, who cooked at the lodge during peak ski season, was coming back to help clean up the place.

'I almost didn't make it up to the mountains this winter,' Miguel said.

'Why is that?' I asked.

'I almost got eaten by a puma.'

Miguel went on to tell me that at the end of the summer, the guides help lead more than one hundred horses across the breadth of the country to winter pastures, and each night someone has to guard the horses from pumas who like to 'eat their ears'.

'A puma tried to get into my tent,' Miguel explained casually.

I'd only just met Miguel, so I didn't think it was appropriate to tell him that maybe it was because his extraordinarily large ears did look rather tasty.

Besides having to keep large felines out of his sleeping bag, Miguel certainly had a fun-packed working life. He spent six months of the year in Patagonia leading and cooking for small groups of cashed-up Americans on twelve-day horse treks. The treks were very la-di-da indeed, with the staff often outnumbering the guests. Six packhorses were needed to carry tents, food and spare chaps. Miguel then worked for three months cooking at the ski lodge. He spent the rest of the time in Valparaíso where he liked 'sleeping late from time to time'.

'Would you like to go skiing?' Miguel asked.

'Yeah, that'd be great!' I said with a huge grin.

'We can hire some skis here,' Miguel said as we pulled into the car park of a McDonalds. The ski-hire shop was in a tiny shack next to the drive-thru.

Not long after picking up my skis, we were leaving the suburbs and climbing steadily up the edge of a steep gorge past stone and wooden houses balanced precariously on stilts. As we drove higher into the Andes, the trees disappeared and we started to cross the archetypal South American prairie—albeit on a 45-degree angle. Ahead and above us the washed-out brown mountains were covered with patches of orange and yellow desert flowers and dotted with 2-metre high cacti. To make the prairie picture complete, as we rounded a bend, a cowboy on horseback (or a *huaso* as Miguel corrected me) trotted across the road.

I couldn't see much of the village we were staying in. Farellones was shrouded in a swirling fog, while horizontal sleet splattered against the windscreen. It didn't look at all promising. Particularly when the ski run, which dropped down into the backdoor of the village, didn't have a dollop of snow on it. Maybe I should have hired grass skis. In fact the only snow around was the small piles of grey sludge collected at the base of the village buildings and the wet excuse for snow dribbling down the car windows.

'Where do you, um . . . ski?' I asked.

Miguel pointed up into the clouds. 'Up there!' he said reassuringly.

Up there somewhere were apparently three ski resorts: La Parva, El Colorado and Valle Nevada. Farellones was *only* 2500 metres high (which is still higher than any mountain in Australia), while the main skiing area was up around the 3700-metre mark.

'There are over one hundred kilometres of ski runs and more than fifty ski lifts,' Miguel added proudly.

The village was mostly made up of small but attractive stone and wood holiday homes and lodges. With no people or cars on the dirt roads, though, the whole place looked deserted and a bit eerie in the smoky clouds. But I did shriek with delight when we pulled up in front of Refugio Alemán. We didn't quite have the lodge to ourselves: In the front garden was a small corral housing three very dopey-looking llamas.

The inside of the lodge was very rustic—which is a polite way of saying a little bit the worse for wear. We found Jorge sprawled out on the couch in front of a blazing fire watching a TV soap on a small worse-for-wear television. The main communal area was a long space with a cramped lounge section, a scattering of pine dining tables and, at the far end of the room, a bar and pool table.

'You like?' Miguel said with a wink, motioning towards the bar.

Hanging across the top of the bar was a large Australian flag. Australians are like dogs. Wherever venturesome and patriotic Aussies roam on this planet, they have to mark their newly conquered territory.

The lodge may have had 28 beds, but they were all jammed into tiny rooms. Miguel gave me the smallest room with one bunk bed in it because 'it will be much warmer for you'. The room was so small that there wasn't enough space on the floor to put my backpack. I must have looked a little disappointed because Miguel said, 'Yes, but you have four bathrooms to choose from'.

Jorge dragged out a cardboard box full of odd bits of skiing apparel that guests had left behind. I grabbed a pair of hot pink women's gloves and a pair of ski pants that were too small around the waist (yes, okay, or my waist was too large). There were no hats in the box, so Jorge shrugged, then tugged the rainbow-coloured knitted hat off his own head and plonked it on mine. Miguel and Jorge weren't joining me for a ski. They mumbled something about 'cleaning the lodge', but Jorge looked to me as if he was set for some serious TV watching.

The modern ski village of El Colorado—and I'm talking about that French housing-commission-flats-in-the-snow style of modern—was a 15-minute drive up a steep narrow road with 180-degree switchbacks. As we reached the top of one long section I looked back; a car at the bottom of the switchback looked as tiny as cars do when you look at them out of an aeroplane window. The snow had stopped falling by the time we reached the ticket office, but the mountains were still under the clouds' tender embrace. At least I would be warm. I was wearing almost the entire contents of my backpack.

I wasn't quite expecting donkey-drawn rope lifts, but I was pleasantly surprised to jump on a brand-new detachable high-speed triple chairlift. The greatest surprise, however, came near the top of the lift. Well, there were two actually: First of all there was a good cover of snow on the runs under the chair and then, just when I was thinking that I could almost see patches of blue sky through the clouds, we (the chairlift and I) suddenly burst out into bright sunshine across an enormous blue sky.

I stood at the top of the lift for some time. One of my greatest joys when travelling is that on every trip there is something new to see that leaves me totally awed. The mountains that encircled me were dark brutal hulks iced with wisps of cloud wreathed like suspended smoke across their distant summits. I almost crashed on my first few runs because I couldn't keep my eyes off the growing army of majestic peaks that were revealed as higher clouds drifted in and out. At least there wasn't much chance of crashing into anyone. I just about had the mountain to myself.

I had an unforgettable day. I spent the morning on my own personal ski lift, then skiing back down on soft spring snow. I lunched in the sun on a huge terrace with only four other diners, then spent the afternoon weaving through steep fields past gargantuan boulders. Towards the end of the day the extraordinary views got even better as the clouds slid down the mountains to reveal an overpowering vista of brown rocky valleys and still more jagged peaks.

When Miguel came to pick me up, we adjourned for a drink at the El Alambique pub in the main base building. Over large mugs of Crystal beer I found out more about Miguel's life. Miguel and Jorge had been working for Blue Green Adventures in Torres del Paine National Park in Patagonia for ten years. It seems Miguel had spent most of his life on the go. Before being a guide he was a taxi driver in Valparaíso and before that he was in the Chilean navy. 'The navy was the only way to see the world,' Miguel said. 'No Chileans were allowed to leave the country when Pinochet was in charge, but with the navy I got to go to Argentina, Peru and Uruguay.'

Miguel has an ex-wife and two teenage children (I didn't ask when he actually found the time to conceive) who still live in Valparaíso. I imagined he caught up with his kids when he wasn't sleeping late from time to time.

When I went to the bar to get us another beer, I noticed a couple of computers set up for internet use. I couldn't help myself. I had to have a quick surf to see if I had a couch to surf for the rest of my stay in Chile.

Triple Bingo. I had three offers, including one from a fellow called José who said: 'I would like to take you out drinking and dancing.' I now faced a dilemma that was the opposite of not having a couch: too many couches and a bloke asking for a hot date. I emailed them all back accepting all three offers. After my time in the mountains, I had three nights left in Chile—which would now be three one-night stands. I would go out drinking and dancing with 35-year-old engineer José, then I'd head out to the suburbs to stay a night with 28-year-old graphic designer Juan and finally catch a bus to Valparaíso to stay with 24-year-old journalist Mariano.

Miguel offered to buy another round, but I declined. Not that I didn't want another beer, it was just that I didn't fancy being in the same car as Miguel with three large beers in him as he drove down a narrow, steep, icy road in the dark.

On the way out we picked up a tall, gorgeous girl called Claudia. I wasn't the only bunk-bed surfer staying at Refugio Alemán. Miguel and Jorge's friend Claudia, who had been filling in at the tourist information counter at El Colorado, was crashing in one of the dorm rooms. Claudia was a ski instructor, but when her season had ended two weeks earlier so had her tenure in the ski instructor's apartments.

'I have a ski bum,' Claudia said to me in the car.

I swivelled around and inspected her bottom.

Just as I was about to comment that I wasn't sure what a ski bum actually looked like, but that she had a nice one nevertheless, it clicked . . .

'Ah, you *are* a ski bum!'

'Yes. For the past four years I have been moving from South to North America working and skiing.'

I imagine many of Claudia's ski-school students fall hopelessly in love with her. Claudia was in her late twenties with long black hair, smooth sun-kissed skin, huge brown eyes and, I might add, a very nice ski bum.

Back at the lodge Jorge was slouched in exactly the same place we left him, still watching TV. The place didn't look any cleaner to me. I had a very long shower then grabbed a beer from the bar. Miguel and Jorge were busy watching Chilean *Big Brother* on the box, so I stood at the large window behind the bar in the dark and watched the sun creep down through the clouds into the valley. The colour soon drained from the sky and then, in a matter of minutes, went from yellow to orange to deep red to purple while the surrounding mountains showed off every shade of blue.

'What are you thinking about?'

I jumped.

'I'm sorry.' It was Claudia.

'I was thinking how lucky I am to be here,' I said, 'and trying to decide if this is the most amazing sunset I've ever seen.'

Claudia moved closer to me. 'Do you believe in God?'

'Um . . . no,' I said awkwardly. Claudia suddenly looked sad. 'Well, sort of, but not really . . . um, sometimes,' I back-pedalled rather pathetically.

'God has done something,' Claudia said lowering her voice.

'Oh, really,' I asked uneasily.

Claudia leant in closer and whispered, 'I'm pregnant.'

Although I was pretty sure that God wasn't the father, I hesitated for a second. 'Um . . . congratulations.'

'I don't think it's congratulations,' Claudia said warily. 'Oh, I'm not sure.'

Claudia then went on to tell me that she had only found out five days before and that the father was a coach on the Canadian ski team who had since gone back to Canada after spending three months in El Colorado.

'I don't know what to do,' Claudia sniffed.

'Does the father know?'

'I rang him this afternoon and he was very happy and told me that he loves me and that I should come to Canada, but . . . I don't know if he is the one. I'm twenty-nine, but I don't think I'm ready for a kid and I don't know if I want to be with Bob forever.'

I said nothing for a minute.

'Oh,' I said. I'm not very good at this talking-about-emotions caper (just ask my wife).

'Please don't say anything to Miguel or Jorge,' Claudia said with a tear in her eye. 'No one else knows.'

Claudia hadn't even told her parents yet. She was too scared.

'Abortion is illegal in Chile and if I have the baby by myself then my family and friends will disown me.' Tears were now rolling down her cheeks.

I realised Claudia was telling me all this because she knew she would never see me again and she just wanted someone to speak to, but I had no idea what to say.

We both stood staring as the sun finally dropped below the horizon and thousands of sparkling lights came to life in the valley below like an upside-down starry sky.

'Is that Santiago?' I asked. I *am* good at changing the subject whenever conversations get too heavy (again, ask my wife).

'I don't want to be a single woman in that *fucking* city,' Claudia said.

I just hoped that she wasn't going to ask me what she should do.

'What should I do?' Claudia said, looking at me with wet eyes.

Oh dear.

Because I really didn't know what to say, I covered all bases instead. 'Maybe you could go to Canada and have the baby . . . or not have the baby, and see if it works out with Bob . . . or if it, um, doesn't.'

Gee, that was a lot of help.

'Thanks, that was a lot of help,' Claudia said, squeezing my hand.

Claudia was chatty and chirpy over dinner, but I could tell that she was doing it so Miguel and Jorge wouldn't think something was wrong. Miguel made some traditional Chilean fare for dinner—hamburgers and fries—and I had to restrain myself from saying 'Claudia *is* eating for two' when she had a second burger.

After dinner Claudia snuck off to bed while the rest of us crashed in front of the TV with steaming mugs of hot chocolate. The more I travel, the more I realise that it is indeed a very small reality-TV-obsessed world. After Chilean *Big Brother* came Chilean *Dancing with the Stars* followed by *South American Idol* (which we all agreed the Chilean girl was a shoe-in to win). During the Colombian girl's soppy slow love song, I dozed off. 'What sort of boring couch-surfing guest was I?' I thought when I woke up an hour later. Then I realised that Miguel and Jorge were so engrossed in a reality TV show involving women with large breasts shouting a lot that they hadn't even noticed I'd been asleep.

'I'm really sorry, but I'm going to have to go to bed,' I said with a big yawn.

'You'll probably need a few extra blankets,' Jorge said, handing me a large pile of blankets. 'The heating has been turned off in the rooms and it's like a fridge in there.'

I'm an idiot. When will I ever learn? I worked as a ski guide in the Swiss Alps and I know the weather can change in an instant, so why hadn't I taken any sunblock with me up to El Colorado? Now I looked like Mr Tomato Head.

Jorge was in his usual spot in front of the TV. 'Oohh, your face is red,' he said gravely. Over the next few days I would get that from every single person I met.

It was another gloriously sunny day, so before I left for Vallee Nevada I slapped a thick layer of sunscreen onto my face (yeah yeah, I know it was way too much way too late, but if I got any more burnt, my face would self-combust).

I had to drag Miguel away from TV to come skiing with me.

'I'll start the cleaning then,' Jorge said—without looking up from the TV.

The resort of Vallee Nevada looked as if they had shaved the top off a mountain to put in the parking lot and an impressively monolithic hotel. There was no time for sightseeing, though, as we headed straight up Tres Puntas, the highest lift at 3670 metres, then dropped off the run (actually it was more like dropping off a cliff) into a stash of wind-blown powder. Not only was it wonderful having a local to ski with, but on our long rides on ski lifts we had a lot of time to chat about life, skiing, football, Chilean culture and teenage girls getting their chests slashed open and their innards yanked out. Miguel pointed out the highest peak (El Plomo at 5430 metres), where a few years ago an Inca mummy was found preserved in the ice. 'The Inca princess took two weeks to walk to the summit in bare feet and then she was sacrificed,' Miguel said matter-of-factly.

Later on Miguel told me that there was no culture left in Chile (now that the good ol' days of tearing apart virgins had gone). 'Chilean culture is based around gossip,' Miguel said angrily. 'All we have is gossip magazines, gossip TV shows and TV shows talking about gossip magazines.'

We then talked about Brad and Angelina's relationship problems.

I did find out that I was Miguel's first couch-surfing guest. He'd had a few requests before, but he'd always been too busy. He thought I sounded interesting and he also felt a little sorry for me. 'You sounded quite desperate,' he said.

'Maybe just a little bit,' I said. Okay, maybe it was more than just a little bit. I may have pleaded and begged for a couch in my last few emails.

As usual when you're having such a fabulous day, it ends all too soon. And with it my time in the mountains. Miguel was staying on to 'finish cleaning the lodge'—or more accurately to *start* cleaning the lodge, since Jorge was still glued to the TV when we returned—so I was grabbing a lift back to Santiago with Roberto the axe murderer.

It was going to be a strange feeling popping in and out of people's lives throughout this trip. Miguel and I hugged knowing that we would probably never see each other again. 'Um . . . good luck,' I whispered to Claudia as we hugged. By the time you're reading this, Claudia might have had a baby, might have settled down in Canada or might be living back in that fucking city, Santiago.

3

'Everyone is welcome to stay at my place as long as you do the dishes.'
José Levican, 35, Santiago, Chile
HospitalityClub.com

José's city apartment block looked like an office building and José looked like a clerk. José was a studious-looking chap with neat clothes, neat glasses and an incredibly neat haircut. His apartment was also very neat, but that was because it was so tiny there was hardly any room to fit anything in it. José greeted me at the door with a clerkish handshake and by the time I'd taken two steps into his apartment, I'd already walked through the kitchenette and into the lounge room—which was very light on for lounges. There was only barely enough room for the one-and-a-half seater couch that took up half the lounge room.

Sitting on the mini-couch was Caroline, a pretty and petite couch surfer from France. She already had dibs on the couch, so my 'bed' was to be a few cushions thrown onto the floor. Mind you, I was happy to sleep anywhere.

Apart from the fact that my bed of cushions was free, I was still so excited about staying in a local's home and having the opportunity to experience how other people live. Albeit a tad squishy.

The introductions were barely over when I asked, 'Have you guys eaten yet? Would you like to go out for dinner?' My enquiry was perhaps a little precipitate, but that was because I was ravenous after a big day of skiing and my stomach was making terribly embarrassing loud gurgling noises.

'We have eaten already, but I will make you some dinner,' Caroline said. She stood up to walk to the kitchen, although she could have very easily reached the stove from the couch. This was wonderful: One couch surfer was cooking dinner for another couch surfer she'd only just met in someone else's home.

José poured me a beer from an extraordinarily large bottle of Heineken, and then joined me on the couch. I knew a little bit about José from his HospitalityClub profile. I knew his interests included languages, astronomy, sciences, baroque music, playing the guitar and 'trying to understand the human mind'.

'So, you're an engineer,' I said. That was the other thing I knew about José.

'Yes, I'm designing pipes for making ice-cream at the Nestlé factory.'

'Oh, so you do contract work?'

'No,' José said, shaking his head. 'I have worked there for three years.'

'I see, so . . . why do they need so many pipes?'

'They have to operate under the Swiss system,' José said. 'The pipes are . . . supercalifragilisticexpialidocious . . .' Well, that's what it sounded like to me and it still made about the same amount of sense after he'd dragged out a pile of draft plans and talked for ten minutes about how to limit the vortex on the groove gasket when the zirconium blind flange preferred strawberry to chocolate.

Before starting at Nestlé, José had worked in the States for three years. Just when he was about to fully explain how pipes operate under the American system, Caroline handed me a steaming bowl of beef risotto. I quickly changed the subject to couch surfing and soon discovered that José was a bit of a couch-surfing hosting junkie and effectively had the world passing through his lounge. Folk from Slovenia, the Czech Republic, Poland, Germany, Austria, Spain, Ireland, Australia, New Zealand, Canada and the States had all crammed onto his cramped couch. Some had requested his couch, but a whole bunch of them were headhunted (in the nicest possible way) by José to come and stay. On the HospitalityClub website you can not only do a search for a host by city or country, but you can also search by gender, age, language spoken, occupation and—this is where José hunted down his very own couch surfers—'planned trips'. Every once in a while he would do a search to find out who was planning to visit Chile then he would email them and offer up his place. Yes, it might sound a tad weird, but José just seemed genuinely interested in meeting people from around the world. 'I love people,' José gushed. 'And I love hearing about people's lives.' He certainly did love hosting people and he was also a member of CouchSurfing and GlobalFreeloaders.

José had surfed with a few people, but he had mostly used HospitalityClub because he could use the advanced search feature. By searching under 'occupation' he'd found fellow engineers to surf with in San Diego and Buenos Aires. Mind you, if he so desired he could travel the entire planet staying with people who like talking about pipes. There are 843 engineers on the HospitalityClub website.

I've since done an extensive search under 'occupations' and found that if you wanted to, you could also stay with a taxidermist, weatherman, rickshaw driver, anthropologist, NASA rocket scientist, magnetic fridge poet, chimney sweep, hugger (she runs hugging workshops), roustabout, computer games tester and someone who lists their occupation as a 'watcher of life' (I'm not sure the pay's too good, though).

There seemed to be an inordinate amount of people 'working' as 'bums', including a ski bum, beach bum, world bum, professional bum, part-time bum, cycle bum, social bum, internet bum, poker bum, occupational bum, jazz bum and a 'plain old bum'. If you can handle a few nights of water-squirting novelty flowers and balloon animals, there are 39 clowns to stay with. The Finns account for most of the seventeen stand-up comedians, while all of the five butlers you can stay with are English (including the very butler-sounding Gareth Parry-Jones).

There are 28 professional footballers, with eleven from Nigeria (the national team, perhaps?) and one from Congo who says that he is going to be the next David Beckham. If you feel that the world is no longer a safe place to travel, there are 97 police officers from 38 different countries to look after you. You might (or might not) also feel safe staying with one of 113 military folk from 27 countries. Personally, I'd stay away from Zafar, an army officer from Pakistan who wants to 'melt lots of new people'. You could try getting a couch that's out of this world by sharing with an astronaut. I'm not too sure of their legitimacy, though. One is from Amsterdam, so he's probably in space, but not in this universe. The other is from that world-leading aerospace giant Peru, where they must not pay too well. This 'astronaut' is 36 years old and still lives with his mum and dad.

If you're having trouble with your love life, there are four sex therapists and two love counsellors to help you, while the three exotic dancers/strippers would certainly know how to entertain you for the evening. Lora Cherry from Orlando, Florida, says in her profile:

> I'm a stripper, and I'm a vegan. I'm a vegan stripper. The only meat I eat is man meat!

Exotic dancer Candy from the Gold Coast, Queensland, says that:

> You are more than welcome to stay as long as you share your drugs, be nice to my cat and don't steal my stuff. No perverts please. I am normal.

Last, but certainly not least, is Manuel, a male stripper from Detroit. He says:

My house rules are as follows:

1) If you bring someone home—everyone fucks or nobody fucks. So unless you're into orgies, don't even think about it.
2) Take off your shoes.

(I presume you take off your shoes before the orgy.)

I am one of 48 authors (although none of us has a profile as well-written as Manuel's), while Caroline is one of 286 architects. Caroline had also couch-surfed with a few fellow architects on her 3-month jaunt around South America. 'I've only couch-surfed for half of my trip,' Caroline said. 'It's been fantastic, but I am getting tired of telling every new person I stay with my life story.' I imagine that could become tiring. Maybe I should have prepared a Brian Thacker Fact Sheet to hand out to my hosts to 'read in their own time'.

Then again, I think you'd be more than happy to divulge your entire family's past if you were staying with a multi-millionaire who gave you your very own wing in his sprawling mansion. That's exactly what had happened to Caroline in a town in Argentina. 'I'd sent him an email to ask for a couch and he told me to call him when I got to the town and he would pick me up,' Caroline said. '*He* didn't pick me up, though. His chauffeur did and we drove out of the town to this grand mansion on a hill. A maid met me at the door and took me to my room, which had the biggest bathroom I've ever seen. I even had my own lounge room overlooking the swimming pool . . .'

Let me just pause here for a moment to tell you that I stupidly didn't get the host's name or the name of the town. I've told this story to quite a few people and the first thing they ask is: 'Where do I find him?' Sorry, if I knew that I'd be sitting in that lounge overlooking the pool right now dictating this book to one of the servants. Let us continue . . .

'Dinner was an absolute feast,' Caroline beamed. 'And they even had serving staff. I stayed for three nights and didn't want to leave. His family were just lovely.'

A mansion certainly beats a mini-couch in a smoke field. José's friend, who looked like José's assistant clerk, had turned up and they were alternating playing guitar and chain-smoking. Both José and I-never-quite-caught-his-name played beautiful guitar—well, at least one of them did, I couldn't quite see who was playing through the fog.

At 12.30 José announced that we were going out to do some salsa dancing. We were heading to Bella Vista, which I was told was once a dingy neighbourhood before being turned into an artsy enclave. We turned the corner into the main thoroughfare to find a street of old colonial buildings that were now bars blasting out deafening music. Walking down the street past the open doorways was like spinning the dial on a radio, hearing split-second grabs of music before picking up the frequency at the next doorway. Hordes of young revellers drinking large mugs of beer filled the outdoor tables, but the insides of the clubs were quiet. The first one we tried was almost totally empty.

'Nothing happens till one o'clock,' José bellowed over the booming music.

I looked at my watch. It was two minutes to one.

'We better stand aside for the rush then,' I quipped.

We eventually found one club that had people in it. I was just about to go to the bar to get drinks when José said, 'This is a gay bar. Is that okay?'

'Yeah, that's fine,' I shrugged.

I-never-quite-caught-his-name, who didn't speak a word of English, said something to José.

'He says he wants to go,' José translated. 'He doesn't want men pinching his bottom.'

We headed back to the first club, which had begun to fill up. It did feel a bit like being in a cross between a McDonalds and a butcher's shop, though. There was sawdust on the dance floor and the furniture was mostly bright-yellow plastic moulded chairs. The blaring music was a mix of salsa and hip-hop with a dash of techno. We each grabbed a super-size-me bottle of beer and José immediately dragged Caroline up onto the dance floor. I sat with I-never-quite-caught-his-name and we just smiled at each other and said cheers a lot.

By two o'clock I was fading and ready for bed and Caroline decided to walk back with me. 'It doesn't *really* get going till three,' José said as we got up to leave.

'So, how is the mini-couch?' I asked Caroline as I arranged my pile of cushions back at the apartment.

'Very, um . . . small,' Caroline said.

I nodded in agreement. 'Maybe José could start DwarfCouchSurfing.com.'

4

'Requirements and Restrictions: Be nice.'
Juan Francisco Garrido, 27, Santiago, Chile
HospitalityClub.org

Juan learnt English by listening to ELO records. In his teens he wanted to know what the lyrics meant, so he translated every song into Spanish word by word. Juan had failed English at school and now he was completely fluent. Mind you, I don't think the ELO School of Languages is ever likely to threaten Berlitz. Some ELO songs don't even make sense in English. In my experience 'Zing went the strings of my heart, zing, zing, zing' or 'Pretty pretty, chilly chilly, silly silly, money money' don't come up in conversation all that often.

Juan picked me up from the spotlessly clean El Llano metro station, where the cleaners outnumbered the ticket sellers three to one. I told him that I would be easy to spot. 'Just look for the guy with a bright red head,' I said. Juan was also easy to spot because he looked like a graphic designer. He was wearing groovy clothes and he had groovy facial hair.

Meeting your couch-surfing host for the first time can be a bit like a blind date as you check each other out and try to gauge whether you'll get on. But in this case I knew almost immediately that Juan would become a good friend. I was certainly going to be taken very promptly into the family fold. After dropping my bags off at Juan's house, we were heading straight out to his grandma's house for a big family barbecue (or an *asado,* as I was told it's called in Chile).

Juan lived with his mum and younger brother in the southwestern suburb of San Miguel, which was only a short drive from the metro station. It was nice to see broad and leafy avenues and large family homes instead of the endless ugly apartment blocks that the train had passed on my way out of the city. Juan's mum Nancy, who looked young enough to be Juan's older sister, met me at the door with a big hug. The first thing I noticed when I stepped inside was the couch, which I was happy to see looked long enough to fit an average-sized human. I was happier still when I was led upstairs to my very own room with a double bed that could easily fit three or four average-sized humans.

On the way back downstairs we picked up Han Solo from his bedroom. Juan's brother Luis Alfredo was a *Star Wars* fanatic and his room was a shrine to everything that happened a long time ago in a galaxy far, far away. The walls were covered with *Star Wars* framed prints and posters and a frightening amount of figurines were piled up on shelves, side-tables and on the floor. Luis Alfredo even had a Han Solo haircut.

'Luis learnt his English from *Star Wars* films,' Juan said.

Luis Alfredo didn't say much, but that was probably because 'Use the force, Luke' and 'The stormtroopers have taken over the Death Star' are not things you say to someone you've just met.

Juan's bedroom looked like the headquarters of the Chilean Communist Party. The walls were covered with red and black Russian revolutionary posters. Juan was in the final year of a four-year graphic design degree and he was writing his thesis on Russian revolutionary posters. Juan was also learning Russian through mylanguageexchange.com, a website which pairs you up with a native speaker of the language you want to learn who in turn wants to learn your language. For twelve months Juan had been regularly emailing a girl from Moscow called Katya. After six months of corresponding, Katya decided to visit Juan in Chile for a month. Three weeks into her stay, Juan asked her to marry him. 'When I finish my degree I am moving to Moscow to live with her,' Juan said with a beaming smile.

On the drive to Grandma's house I commented on how patriotic the Chileans were. The Chilean flag was flying from (or out of) nearly everyone's house. 'Last week was Chilean Independence Day and by law everyone has to fly the flag for a week before and after,' Juan said. 'The celebrations go on for a week. That's why we are having the barbecue.'

Grandma's house was a grand old place filled with chandeliers, grandfather clocks, marble fireplaces, elaborate antiques and the usual grandma-the-world-over clutter of knick-knacks, framed photos and lace doilies. Within a minute of walking into the backyard, I had a drink in my hand. 'It's called *Ponche a la Romana con Frutilla*,' Juan said as he downed his drink. 'It's champagne, white wine and strawberries.' Before I'd even had a chance to take a sip, a parade of cheerful relatives lined up for a whirlwind of introductions. At least most of the womenfolk did. The old fellows in their neatly ironed collared shirts were hunched over a small table in the corner playing cards. I'm sure that all the drinking over the years has destroyed the part of my brain that remembers people's names because, as usual, I didn't catch a single person's name. At least they all knew mine—Juan's uncle introduced me to everyone as Crocodile Dundee.

Finally, after I'd met twenty-odd relatives (and I mean that in the nicest way), I had a chance to survey my surroundings. Set in the shade underneath a wide trellis entwined with vines, two long tables had been set up for lunch. In the middle of the long backyard, underneath an enormous lemon tree, was one of the biggest barbecues I'd ever seen. Under a thick cloud of smoke three men were tending to what looked like an entire cow cut up into bits. Rising up behind the backyard fence were the Andes. It was amazing to think that we were sweltering on this hot spring day when less than 24 hours earlier I'd been skiing in those very mountains.

Soon there was a flurry of activity as more guests arrived and more drinks were handed out with more vigorous handshaking and hugs. After I finished the drink with the long name, I was handed a large pisco sour. Just when I was thinking that I'd better eat something soon to help soak up the alcohol, it was time to sit down for lunch. Everyone else on the table immediately began taking part in a rapid-fire conversation where the only words I could understand were 'si' and 'no'.

'What are they talking about?' I asked Juan (who, other than Luis Alfredo, was the only one who spoke English).

'They are talking about what's happening on the TV show *Lost*.'

Yes, it really is a small sad world sometimes.

Uncle Diego* put more bottles of red wine on the table than there were people to drink them while Aunty Claudia* produced large plates of little tasty Chilean savoury pastries called *empanadas*. (*These names are fabricated because of the name-erasing circuit in my damaged brain.)

Aunty Claudia* asked me (with the help of Juan's translation) if I liked Santiago and I told her that I did, but that I hadn't really seen much of it yet. 'Santiago very nice nice city,' Aunty Claudia* said proudly.

When she left Juan said, 'There's nothing to see in Santiago. It's nice but boring.'

After an entrée of steaming jumbo mussels, I was handed a plate that was then piled high with so much meat it would have made a vegetarian faint. I ended up with a slab of pork ribs, a lamb shank, thick juicy pork sausages, chicken legs and beef legs (I think I got two entire cow's legs).

Just when I'd put something that resembled a dent into my mountain of meat, another huge helping of yet more meat was unceremoniously dumped onto my plate. I was already stuffed and my stomach felt like it was going to burst, but Uncle Carlos* and Uncle Eduardo* were still cooking giant slabs of animal on the barbecue.

Fuelled by free-flowing champagne, wine and pisco sours, everyone was becoming increasingly boisterous and loud. Juan tried to translate a particularly heated conversation. 'They are having a philosophical debate about whether nothing exists until humans experience it.'

Fifteen minutes later I asked Juan whether they had resolved their debate.

'Oh no, now they are talking about what is happening on the TV show *24*.'

'Does your family get together often?' I asked Juan.

'Yes, very often. Family is the most important thing to a Chilean.'

I was envious of these folk. The last time that my entire immediate family sat down to a meal together was Christmas day, 1991. I think I now know the secret, though: A family that smokes together stays together. Just about everyone at the table was puffing away like mad when they had finished their meaty feast.

There were a few smoky gasps of horror, however, when I passed around a pack of Australian cigarettes. (I'd just like to add here that I only brought the cigarettes with me all the way from Australia to warn people of the dangers of smoking.) On the front of the box was a large photo graphically demonstrating what happens to you if you smoke. Apparently, after too many ciggies you will look just like the Elephant Man. The photo was of a horribly deformed foot with rotten and missing toes. This is caused when smoking damages your blood vessels and blocks circulation, resulting in gangrene. Or, according to Uncle Miguel*, by working too hard.

Uncle Miguel* stared at the photo and said (well, Juan said as he interpreted for me): 'This means that if you try and work and smoke at the same time you will drop something on your foot and smash your toes. So we should do less work.'

Actually, the graphic warning seemed to inspire everyone to smoke more, because less than an hour later they had all run out of cigarettes. 'We need seven packs,' Juan said as he counted hands. I volunteered to walk up the street to buy them because I really needed a break from drinking. I was getting quite tipsy and I didn't want to tip over that line into tanked and do something embarrassing. Not that I necessarily would, but I once made a total twit of myself on a similar couch-surfing experience.

On my first-ever trip overseas, I was invited to stay with a girl in Dublin who I'd met briefly at a party in Melbourne. When I rang Louise from London, she told me that it was her 21st birthday party the next night and that I was welcome to come. I bet she regretted that later. After catching an overnight ferry, I arrived, without any sleep, on the afternoon of the party, and headed straight to the pub with her boyfriend and his mates. By the time we got to the very swanky party at nine o'clock (Louise's parents lived in a large house in Dublin's most exclusive suburb), I was already pleasantly plastered. I don't remember the exact details of the next few hours, but I do remember spilling a full glass of beer all over the dog, smooching and groping Louise's best friend in the middle of the lounge room, then collapsing in a drunken stupor underneath the pool table. I felt so embarrassed the next day that, after much apologising, I packed up and left.

Back at the barbecue no one had collapsed yet, but many were on their way to getting seriously intoxicated. The wine had run out and they were now drinking a wicked concoction of Drambuie, Johnny Walker, ice and fresh cloves. At least if I did fall over or try to grope Aunty Claudia*, I'd still be in the good books. When I returned with the cigarettes I also had a bouquet of flowers to give to Grandma, who almost hugged me to death and told Juan that I could move in with her.

'You are going to write that Chileans are a bunch of drunks,' Juan said.

'Yes, but nice drunks,' I said, smiling drunkenly.

Six hours after we had sat down for lunch, dessert was brought out. It was dark by the time people started getting up from the table. The children played happily in the garden, the old men went back to their game of cards, the older women cleaned up, and Uncle Diego* and Aunty Claudia* canoodled in the corner like teenagers while their teenage children sat drinking with us.

We finally got up to leave at 8.30, which was just in time. Any longer and I would have nodded off and fallen face-first into my cake. Juan, who had been holding back on the drinks, drove home and said, 'I'm sorry Brian, but I have to work on my thesis tonight.'

'That's okay,' I said, looking at my watch. It was nine o'clock. 'I've still got lots and lots of notes to write as well.'

I was asleep at about eight minutes past nine.

I still wasn't quite sure of the whole couch-surfing protocol. When I awoke at eight the next morning, the house was quiet. Everyone was still in bed. I knew that because I tiptoed down the hallway and put my ear against everyone's bedroom door just to make sure. I really didn't know what to do. Is it considered rude to help yourself to breakfast? I wanted a shower, but did I have to wait till everyone had one before I jumped in? I snuck back into my room and made the bed and packed my bag. Fifteen minutes later I re-packed my bag, then wrote in my notebook that I'd just re-packed my bag, then made the bed again.

It was a bit after nine o'clock when Juan's mum would have had second thoughts about strangers couch-surfing in her home ever again. She stepped out of her bedroom to find a man in his underwear standing on his tiptoes with his ear up against her youngest son's bedroom door.

Breakfast was a little uncomfortable. Juan's mum didn't speak English, so I couldn't explain that I wasn't trying to sneak into Luis Alfredo's bedroom. Breakfast was a veritable feast of warm fresh rolls, giant slabs of ham and cheese, boiled eggs, pickles, jam, tea and orange juice. It was all *muy bueno* (very good), but all the food also meant that I was at the breakfast table for half-an-hour and the only thing I could say in Spanish to Juan's mum was '*muy bueno*'. I said that a lot while trying to smile without looking too much like a deviant.

Juan finally wandered down at 10.30 (he'd been working on his thesis till 3.30). I was in a bit of a rush to leave, as I had to get to the central bus station and catch a bus to Valparaíso, so I asked Juan if he could drive me to the metro station. Juan told me that he was sad to see me go and that I should stay for a couple more days. Although I had spent less than twenty-four hours with Juan and his family they had treated me like one of their own and when Juan gave me a hug it felt like I was saying goodbye to a dear friend. Even Juan's mum was keen for me to stay after I explained to Juan what happened and he told her that I wasn't really a dirty old pervert.

5

'Interesting enough, the historical hull of the city proves for the visitor that it is a cultural patrimony of the humanity by UNESCO.'
Mariano Carlos Cubillos, 24, Valparaíso, Chile
CouchSurfing.com

'This is my place,' Mariano said, pointing across the busy city street to a large grey building. The building was a hardware store. Thoughts crossed my mind of sleeping on a bed of paint tins and eating dinner with a garden trowel before we entered a side doorway and climbed up a flight of steep stairs to a large bohemian pad. I say 'bohemian pad' because it was exactly what I imagined a bohemian pad would look like. The large high-ceilinged open lounge area was sparse, with only a scattering of mismatched lounge chairs that looked just made for some serious lounging about. Leaning against the walls were a series of finished and unfinished paintings and a collection of musical instruments, including two acoustic guitars, a mandolin and what I imagine is a mandatory requirement for any bohemian pad: a set of bongos. There was no TV, only an old turntable. The only other piece of furniture was a small coffee table that had a large ashtray on it filled with joint butts. To make the bohemian picture complete, lounging on one of the chairs was a hip-looking dude wearing a cravat and floral pants.

Even if I really tried I don't think I could invent a better bunch of bohemians to be sharing a bohemian pad. There was Nicolas, the puppet maker, and his boyfriend Sebastian, the cinema studies student; Marcella, the surrealist painter; Leonardo, the musician; Frida, the Asian/Swedish/Chilean silversmith; and my host Mariano, the journalist.

Mariano showed me my bed, which was a bright blue single-seat lounge chair that folded down to became a very short mattress. The chair was totally covered in dog's hair. The hair belonged to Mariano's dog Remedios who, by the way, didn't look too happy about me stealing his bed.

When I arrived in Valparaíso it was Remedios the beagle that I was told to look out for in the crowded bus station. Attached on a leash to that beagle would be my host Mariano. Mind you, if Mariano had told me to look out for an incredibly tall, handsome-looking beatnik with a goatee, I think I would have found him easily enough without Remedios.

The bus had arrived bang on the scheduled 1.30 arrival time after a 90-minute journey through verdant hills dotted with orange and purple flowers, vineyards, lakes, orchards and pine forests. The most impressive leg of the journey, however, was saved for last as we dropped spectacularly into Valparaíso. Ringing the bay was an immense natural amphitheatre and the chain of surrounding hills was covered with a chaotic tumble of vibrantly coloured houses that were wedged precariously in every fold of the steep hillside. The city itself looked decidedly rundown, but I liked it.

Mariano's flat also looked decidedly rundown—although I think any sort of renovation would have spoilt its charm. Remedios wasn't exactly charmed with me, however. After having his bed stolen, he was now going to be stuck inside while Mariano took me out to the city's main market, El Mercado Cardonal, for lunch. 'Remedios was a present from my ex-girlfriend,' Mariano said as Remedios gave us that pathetic sad dog look as we left. 'I'd been very sick for a week and I was feeling miserable, so she gave me a cute puppy as a remedy. So that's what I named him.'

'There is a bottle shop on every other corner,' said Mariano as we passed our sixth bottle shop in two blocks. 'Chile is the fifth biggest drinking country in the world,' Mariano said proudly. I was quite surprised that Chile is only fifth—after my day with Juan's family, I would have thought Chileans would at least be on the podium (albeit in danger of losing their balance and toppling off).

El Mercado Cardonal was on two floors. The bottom floor was all produce, then some rickety wooden stairs led up to a rough-and-tumble jumble of restaurants or *cocinerías*. It looked like a clichéd Hollywood movie-set version of jaunty seafood restaurants, with fishing nets strung up on the ceilings and filled with plastic lobsters, red-and-white-checked tablecloths and old men sitting around in striped shirts and captain's hats.

As soon as we sat down, we were given a bowl of *pebre* (a Chilean salsa dip made with tomato, chilli, coriander and chives) and bread.

'Chile is the second biggest consumer of bread in the world,' Mariano said with a mouthful of bread.

Of course, it was no accident that I chose Mariano, a journalist, as a couch-surfing host. It was obvious, even to me, that a journalist would be an easy source of local knowledge. Mariano had worked as a political reporter for Chile's largest national daily newspaper, *La Tercera*. I say had worked, because Mariano had given it away. 'Most days I would work twelve hours and it was just too stressful,' he said with a sigh. 'I'd had enough of politics anyway. It's all the same. We vote one fucker out then vote another fucker in.'

Mariano was now studying part-time for his Masters and writing a thesis called 'Untouchable Paradise in Valparaíso'. It may have sounded more like a novel of bohemian life, but it was actually philosophical in a more literal sense. He explained the argument to me, but I have trouble saying philosophical, let alone understanding it. Mariano was very passionate about the project and believed the thesis would be very well received.

'What do you want to do when you finish?' I asked.

'I'd like to open a bar,' he mused.

Mariano recommended that I have a local dish called *chupe de locos*. 'It means full of craziness,' Mariano told me after I had ordered it. (It also means 'suck like crazy', as I discovered when I went to check the exact spelling on the net and was taken to a series of rather interesting photos on a Spanish gay porn site.)

It may have been full of craziness, but it was also full of scrumptiousness. It was similar to a clam chowder and the massive bowl was chock-full of sizzling chunks of abalone, fish and shrimps and topped with cheese.

Mariano had a meeting about a freelance journalism job ('I do some jobs because I have to eat!' he said), so I went to walk—or, more accurately, waddle—off my lunch. I headed down to the port because Mariano had made it sound mightily impressive. Valparaíso was, until the opening of the Panama Canal, the most important port in South America. In the space of less than a hundred years from the early 1800s, the population of the city rose from 5000 to more than 100 000. In the process it attracted wealthy foreign merchants who helped make Valparaíso Chile's financial and cultural capital.

I walked for ages next to a high cyclone-wire fence that separated the docks from the city. Although the area was certainly impressively large, I was largely unimpressed. The port, like most ports the world over, was grey and dirty and all I could see were lots of large ugly cranes, large ugly shipping containers and considerably larger ugly rusting ships. The entire bay was closed off for the docks, which meant that you had to leave the city to actually get near the water. I wish I'd known that before I'd walked for more than an hour looking for a break in the cyclone fence.

I returned through the centre of town, which had the feel of a Mediterranean port city. The narrow, congested streets were lined with solid, classic buildings that had once been colourfully painted but were now faded and crumbling. Some of the buildings looked admirably grand, but I didn't get much of a chance to admire them. I was too busy avoiding the large packs of roaming dogs. I had never in my life seen so many stray dogs. They were everywhere and they were loping through the city—and, curiously, stopping dutifully at traffic lights—as if they owned the place. Each gang seemed to have a leader, but it wasn't necessarily the biggest pooch. One gang, which was mostly made up of large nasty-looking brutes, was being led by an extremely cocky cocker spaniel.

I gave a wide berth to one mob that was milling about the front of a bottle shop as if they were waiting for someone to go in and buy them some beer. I was steering well clear of the packs because—and for the life of me I wish I knew why—whenever I make eye contact with a dog, it suddenly feels a pressing need to tear me into teeny-weeny bits. I spent most of the walk back with my shoulders hunched and my eyes fixed firmly on the ground. Just to prove my point, I accidentally glanced up at a lone dog sitting nonchalantly on the footpath. As soon as our eyes met, its muscles tightened, its eyes took on a satanic glow and it lunged at me as if it had been waiting patiently all day for me to turn up. I swung my bag at the beast while screaming every swear word I know and running backwards. When I got to the other side of the road, I stood and watched as hordes of people wandered past the dog without it giving so much as a slight grimace to a single one of them.

I needed a drink, so I thought I'd stop at one of the bottle shops that are on every other corner. Only I happened to cross all the *other* corners that didn't have bottle shops. After six blocks I finally found a supermarket instead. It was dark when I got back to the apartment, but I was still a little shaken by my meeting with the Mutt of Satan.

'The dogs around here are fucking crazy!' I barked to Mariano.

'Oh no, they never bother anyone,' said Mariano serenely. Mariano was looking very serene because he was lounging on the couch with Sebastian and Marcella sharing a whopping joint and listening to the soothing tones of Chilean jazz. I declined a puff (I've never been into marijuana because it just smells too much like incredibly whiffy socks) and opened the bottle of wine.

To be honest I thought that the ensuing conversation might include lots of impenetrable hippy ramblings and prolonged bouts of helpless giggling, but we had an absorbing discussion about art (Marcella was, like myself, a big fan of the Belgian surrealist artist René Magritte), music (Mariano's previous job as a journo involved interviewing musicians for a jazz magazine) and cinema (Sebastian only watched independent and art house movies, because Hollywood films were 'full of much fucking shit'). I was really enjoying their company and everyone was so sweet that at one point they were talking amongst themselves about whose turn it was to clean the toilet (or some other domestic chore), and they all kept speaking in English for my benefit.

My stomach was rumbling and it wasn't because I had the munchies—suddenly it was ten o'clock and I hadn't had any dinner. 'It's Sebastian's turn to cook tonight,' said Mariano, showing me the cooking roster. Each flat mate had a designated cooking night every week (with a cooking-free day on Sundays). By eleven o'clock, Sebastian's dinner still wasn't looking too forthcoming, so I helped Mariano make a stack of cheese rolls. We couldn't find any clean plates, though. As in shared houses the world over, the sink was piled high with dirty dishes. And just as in shared houses the world over, everyone seemed to think they would be cleaned by some magic fairy.

I had to move a guitar amp and a collection of foam puppets off the floor in the dining room to clear a space for my couch-cum-mattress. As I lay in bed I decided that I should rate the rest of the couches on my couch-surfing trip, starting with Mariano's couch:

Couch rating: 7/10

Con: The couch was covered in dog hairs

Pro: The dog hairs were extra insulation against the cold

'Oh, my God!' Mariano shrieked when he saw me in the morning.

I shrieked as well when I looked at myself in the mirror. I looked like I had leprosy. My formerly red face was now peeling off in great big ugly grey chunks.

Mariano must have felt sorry for me because he volunteered to take me on a tour of the city even though he had work to do. Our trek began in the dark empty side streets. Mariano assured me we were taking a 'shortcut', but I actually think he was worried my post-nuclear face might send the local populace running for the hills—or running away from the hills in this case, because that was where we were heading.

At the end of one of those dark dead-end streets, we came across a lift built into a cliff face. This was one of Valparaíso's famed *ascensores*, 38 'elevators' that were built mostly in the nineteenth century to transport folk up to their mansions in the hills. The *Ascensor El Peral*, which was more of a funicular than an elevator, coughed and spluttered its way up through a jumbled maze of multicoloured weatherboard homes and weather-beaten Victorian mansions that clung to the sheer cliffs. I was not at all surprised when Mariano told me that in 2003 the entire area had been declared a UNESCO World Heritage Site.

Our first stop was the grand Palacio Baburizza, which I liked very much even if it was a rather odd mix of Art Nouveau, Tudor and Hogwarts with its green tiled spires. In front of the Palacio was a wide terrace with fabulous views of the city and bay—which really was *all* docks. We spent a couple of hours exploring the maze of narrow cobblestone alleyways and sinuous streets that snaked down ravines and around the hillsides. Every now and again we stopped for a rest in impossibly tiny parks. Each park had a massive tree in the middle, usually surrounded by canoodling couples and canoodling dogs.

We stopped for lunch at the precariously perched Restaurant La Colombina, which used to be a private mansion, and were escorted to a table on the bougainvillea-adorned balcony overlooking the entire city. (I noted that the waiter, who was staring at my leprosy, seated us as far away from other diners as possible.)

'Santiago is shit,' Mariano said as we sipped our pisco sours. I had asked him if he would ever live in Santiago. 'It is too cold in winter, too hot in summer and too polluted—Santiago is the third most polluted city in the world, you know.' Mariano looked out across the city. 'Valparaíso is my home, now.' Mariano was born in Argentina, but when he was fourteen his parents separated and he moved to Valparaíso with his mother. His mother had recently moved back to Argentina, but Mariano had decided to stay because he said that he felt more Chilean than Argentinean now.

Mariano recommended that I order the *camarones frescos sobre lechuga, limon y mayonesa*, which was a king-sized plate full of exquisitely zesty king-sized prawns. I raised my pisco sour and toasted couch surfing (and the restaurant which I would never have found if I hadn't been staying with a local) and we both agreed that couch surfing really is quite a wonderful innovation in the way we travel. I told him that I had learnt more about Chile and its people in the past six days couch surfing than I would have if I'd stayed for six weeks in a hotel. I had been Mariano's first couch guest and he was looking forward to hosting more people. 'I'd do something about the dog's hairs on your couch, though,' I said. In the space of two days we had become friends and good friends should be honest with each other.

Mariano and his flat mates must have really liked me because, even with my leprosy, they all gave me great big hugs when I left. I was back in Santiago by nightfall, but I had time for a quick bite before I headed to the airport. I found a little restaurant with a nice dark corner to hide in. I didn't think it was very fair to send other diners screaming out in horror—my face was such a mess of peeling skin that I now looked like Freddy Krueger.

As I was waiting for the airport bus I noticed an internet cafe across the road and I suddenly thought I should probably pop in and send an email to Pedro, my first couch-surfing host in Rio de Janeiro.

Olá Pedro
I'm looking forward to meeting you tomorrow, but I thought I'd better email you to tell you not to slam the door in my face when you see me. I don't have leprosy or any other type of contagious skin disease. I just got badly sunburnt and my face is peeling.
Oh, and you probably should warn the neighbours as well.
See ya
Brian

BRAZIL

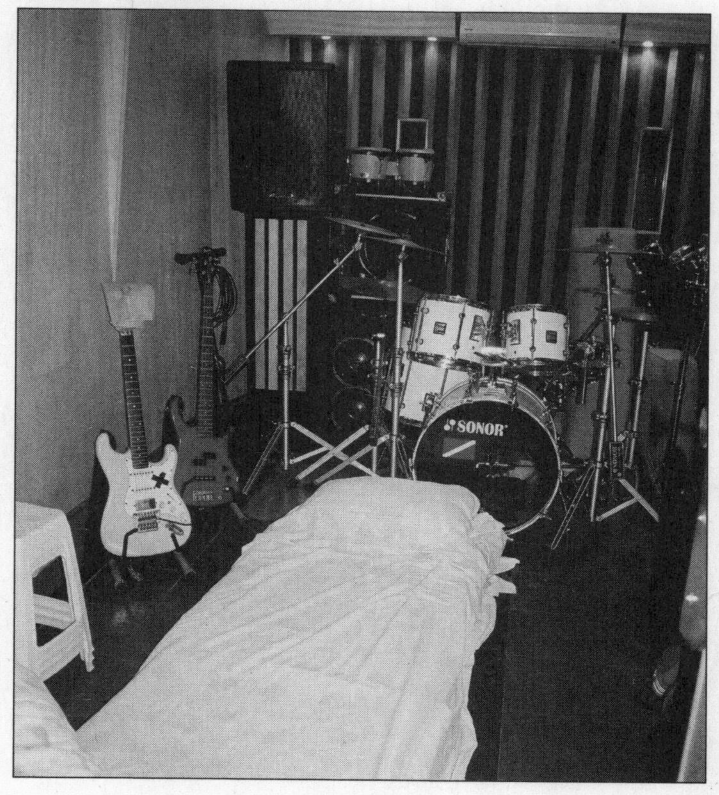

6

'Types of people I enjoy: Drunks and party crashers.'
Pedro Conforti, 29, Rio de Janeiro, Brazil
CouchSurfing.com

In my current state it was just as well I wasn't planning to stay with Amado in Rio. He would definitely have slammed the door in my face. On his rather direct GlobalFreeloaders profile, he wrote:

> Small room with a comfortable single bed. The only people I would be reluctant to accommodate are angry, un-polite, dirty, or extremely fat people. Also I cannot accept people with serious dangerous illnesses as of the heart, skin, nervous, circulatory or digestive body systems, and all that can suffer sudden crisis requiring emergency professional attention. I like to drink a lot and I drink wine and beers with meals.

I suppose all that worrying about rushing people to the emergency ward had driven him to drink. Mind you, Rio is often regarded as the hedonism capital of the world and, if the profiles of some of the other potential hosts were anything to go by, then the city has its fair share of drunkards. I could have requested a couch from Maria Luiza, a 25-year-old molecular biologist who had listed only one thing under Hobbies and Interests: 'I love to get drunk'; while 27-year-old Vidal was 'just a regular guy who likes to party all night till I fall over'.

I decided to follow the 'when in Rome' strategy and found a couch with 26-year-old architect Mariana, who was 'unique and wild and loves to party'. I also chose Mariana because I figured that it would be quite a privilege to stay with 'the coolest girl in *all* of Rio'. Mariana couldn't host me until the weekend, by which stage she had warned me in an email to be prepared: 'Get ready to party hard because we hardly ever sleep.' I decided to go into training by finding another lively type to stay with for my first two nights. Pedro Conforti was a 29-year-old 'colourist for cinema and music videos' and like myself had graduated as a graphic designer and played in a band. He also liked 'drunks and party crashers'. Me too.

Pedro had given me clear and concise directions to his place, but I was a little worried about where he actually lived. In his email he said 'I live in a small alley' and that it was 'in between a bar and a Dominos Pizza shop'. But not even the prospect of dossing down on an old mattress next to rubbish bins could dampen my excitement at driving into one of the most famous cities in the world. And as soon as the taxi left the airport, I spotted the famed silhouetted statue of Christ on the top of Corcovado Mountain, which then kept appearing and vanishing as we drove in and out of the tunnels that wind their way under a series of lush green hills between the airport and the city.

Pedro did live down an alley that was off a busy commercial street, but his home was quite a step-up from a cardboard box. The narrow lane was a private alleyway and Pedro's humble abode was an architect-designed, glass-fronted, four-storey house jammed between older, comparatively dilapidated, buildings.

Pedro met me at the grey metal gate that separated the alley from the street. He had jet-black hair and sideburns (he was also my third couch-surfing host in a row with groovy facial hair) and was wearing mirror shades and a T-shirt with 'I really feel alright' on it. After a welcoming handshake Pedro said, 'Oh, before I forget, here's a key to the house so you can come and go as you please.' It felt a bit odd taking a key to Pedro's house. Apart from two very short emails in which I had requested and confirmed his couch, we didn't know each other at all. Was this the level of trust that couch surfing created or was it that I just looked like a very trustworthy person? Either way, it was nice to feel so trusted.

'Gee, that's a nice Fender Stratocaster,' I gushed. The first thing I noticed on my tour of Pedro's house was how much stuff there was worth stealing. The ground floor was mostly taken up with a state-of-the-art recording studio that was crammed full of musical equipment, including a full drum kit, a 'stack' of Marshall amps, four electric guitars, one bass guitar, three keyboards, a collection of microphones and stands, and a mixing desk. 'I'll set your bed up in here,' Pedro said, pointing to a space in front of the drum kit. 'The walls are totally soundproof, so you can snore and fart as much as you like.'

A wrought-iron spiral staircase wound its way up from the ground floor through an open space to a lounge room/ kitchen, master bedroom and a roof garden. The second-level lounge room was full of more great stuff to pilfer. There was a wide-screen television, an elaborate stereo system and, on a long desk at the end of the room, the latest Mac computer and another mixing desk bursting with leads of all sizes and colours. A very long and very comfortable-looking black leather couch took up almost another entire wall. 'The couch wouldn't be very nice for you to sleep on,' Pedro said when he noticed me eyeing it off. 'I have two cats and they would try and sleep on your head.'

Past the large bedroom on the third floor was the white-tiled roof garden, which was half-enclosed, with a lounge area and bar. High up above, looking down over the roof garden as if guarding the barbecue and kitty-litter tray, was the statue of Christ the Redeemer.

It was somewhere up towards Christ the Redeemer that Pedro was taking me for lunch and he was in quite a hurry to get there. He drove, or rather raced, up steep cobblestone streets while engaging in an animated conversation and somehow evading oncoming cars, pedestrians and yellow tramcars with scores of people hanging off the side (if you 'hang off' the ride is free, Pedro told me). We were heading to

Santa Theresa, which had become hip when local artists had taken over the crumbling nineteenth-century hilltop villas that were sandwiched between squatter slums. The area was now full of antique shops, handicraft shops and restaurants offering, I was told, 'the best Brazilian seafood in Rio'.

It was after three o'clock by the time we sat down for lunch and we scored a great table overlooking the street at Restaurant Sobrenatural, which was an intimate place with exposed-brick walls covered with bright cheerful paintings. 'I don't know if I'm the right person to stay with,' Pedro said as we sipped our *caipirinhas* (Brazil's national drink made with *cachaça*, a sugar cane liquor, and lime). 'I'm probably not your typical *Carioca* [citizen of Rio],' he shrugged. 'I don't really like football. Or the beach.'

'But don't all Brazilians love football?'

'My family is crazy about football,' he said. 'And for years they tried to get me into it. On my eleventh birthday, my parents hired a full-size football pitch and gave me a World Cup Football Party. After playing a match we watched the Brazil–France quarter-final on TV while we ate a Brazilian flag birthday cake with "WINNER" on it. When Brazil lost, everyone went home and the party was over. On my fifteenth birthday, which was during the next World Cup, Brazil lost to Argentina and since then if Brazil play on my birthday, no one in my family says a word to me or even says happy birthday just in case I bring bad luck.'

We started with a traditional Brazilian entrée, but thankfully not Pedro's favourite traditional Brazilian entrée of boiled chicken hearts. Our *pastel de siri e camarão* were delicious little pockets of shrimp and crab with a spicy chilli dipping sauce. Over our superb main course of *bobó de camarão* (prawns with manioc cream) and crunchy *farofa de dendê* (manioc flour and dried shrimps cooked in palm oil), Pedro told me that I could thank the rain for him having the day off. Because it had rained over the past few days, there had been no film shoots, which meant that there was no new film coming in for him to grade. Pedro was one of only a handful of film graders in Rio (most of Brazil's film work comes out of São Paulo), so he was in such high demand he could determine his own hours. 'I usually go in around lunch time,' he said. 'And work till eight or nine.'

After lunch there was more frenetic (at times verging on maniacal) driving further up towards the looming Christ statue. Without warning we swerved off the main road down a dirt track through a forest that ended suddenly, breathtakingly, at a helipad hanging out over the edge of a sheer cliff. Pedro had been in a frantic hurry so we wouldn't miss sunset. Although the helipad afforded one of the most spectacular vistas I have ever seen, it obviously wasn't on the tourist route. We were the only ones there.

I had an almost eerie sense of familiarity as I gazed down on the city, transfixed. It was the same feeling of déjà vu I had when I first went to London or New York or Paris. I'd seen so many photos and movies of Rio de Janeiro that it felt like I'd stood on this very spot before. I stood on the helipad in awed silence taking in the whole sweeping magical view, which spread out in all its double-edged beauty. On one side was the glamorous white sand of Copacabana and

Ipanema beach and the expanse of white apartment blocks and lush rainforest that spikes up in the form of fairytale mountains and then tumbles into the water with specks of islands adding the exclamation points. Then, below us, the virtual deluge of slums, or *favelas*, tumbled down the mountains like a hellish scene from a Breughel painting. The First and Third Worlds come together here, and the clash is spectacular and compelling.

'They scar the city,' Pedro said, waving his arm towards the *favelas*. 'The government is not interested in fixing them and more and more people from around the country are moving in. The land is owned by the government and the church, so people can build wherever they like.'

'BOOOMMM!'

'What the hell was that?' I gasped. It sounded like a bomb had gone off.

'That comes from the *favelas*,' Pedro explained. 'It's to announce that drugs have arrived. Because of the drugs, the *favelas* are not as poor as they used to be. There is electricity and they even have cable TV.'

After seeing the film *City of God*, it was one place I was happy to keep away from. That film is about the spiral of violence and terror in Rio's *favelas*, with drug runners blowing up cars and murdering scores of people. I also remember reading that the murder rate in Brazil is close to one hundred a week and that the thousands of violent deaths every year fall within the parameters of the United Nations' definition of a low-intensity civil war.

'We can go for a look if you like,' offered Pedro.

Although a good mugging, kidnapping or even a not-too-serious shooting would make a great story for my book, I declined Pedro's kind offer.

By the time we left the helipad, lights began to flicker on around the city at the same time as early-evening stars appeared in the deep-blue sky.

As soon as we walked through the door back at Pedro's, he was making us large *caipirinhas*. In Pedro's profile he said that he made the 'best *caipirinhas* in Rio'. He forgot to add 'the strongest'. Then again, he did say that he liked drunks.

Pedro played me the demo CD from his band *Surfista Pratedo*, which he had recorded in my soon-to-be-bedroom. It was a catchy guitar-rock sound with a female vocalist singing in Portuguese. 'I like doing the film work,' Pedro said. 'But music is my passion.' While we sipped our drinks, Pedro was 'editing' a new song he'd written. I say editing, but he spent the entire time pulling plugs in and out and cursing a lot. I watched as he tried one plug in the same hole eight times. I had a shower (and managed to scrub off most of the dead skin, so I looked almost human again) and when I came back Pedro was still plugging and un-plugging leads and scratching his head.

Pedro was also quite a computer boffin. I commented on the pile of old Mac computers shoved under a desk and he said that his uncle was one of the first people in Rio to own a computer. He also explained that he learnt his English from US computer magazines—which would explain why, when I got out of the shower, he said 'So, did you successfully re-boot your operating system?'

Pedro's girlfriend Nathalia turned up at ten o'clock and we headed to Ipanema for dinner. Even though it was after eleven when we got to the open-fronted restaurant, which was two blocks back from the beach, we had to queue to get in. The restaurant/bar was full of young, beautiful, groovy people. Waiters carrying trays filled with plates of delectable little goodies brought the food around yum-cha style. We had Lebanese meat balls, freshwater crab chowder and prawn pies. When I say we, I mean Pedro and I—the very slim and petite Nathalia made do with a large serving of rich chocolate cake and profiteroles.

'I don't like football or the beach *or* Carnaval,' Nathalia said with a shrug. 'I don't like football because if I'm at home when Brazil plays, my dad makes me stay in the bathroom.' A few years back Nathalia was watching a World Cup game with her family and when she went to the toilet, Brazil scored. While she was in the toilet during the next match, Brazil scored again. 'So now they keep pestering me to come around during a match and sit in the toilet,' she explained.

Pedro said that for a while he was turned off Carnaval and would leave the city when it was on. 'It became too formal,' he said. 'But in the last few years it has come back to the people and the parade now winds all the way up to Santa Theresa like it used to.'

'I hate it,' Nathalia sniffed. 'There's too many people and it takes twenty minutes just to walk across the street. Everyone is too happy and everyone wants to touch you and kiss you.' Nathalia did have a funny story from the last time she went to Carnaval, though. Nathalia studied for a year in Sydney as part of her architecture course and three years ago Nathalia had a girlfriend from Australia staying with her at Carnaval time. After the parade they ended up at a party on the beach. Her girlfriend, who was a bit drunk, picked up a nice-looking fellow and danced with him until the early hours. She really liked him and wanted to go back to his place, so she asked, 'Where do you live?'

'Here!' he said.

'Yeah, I know you live in Rio, but where?'

'Here!' he said pointing to the sand. 'I sleep on the beach.'

Maybe he's now one of the beach bums on CouchSurfing.

I woke up late and with a bit of a fright. Not only was the studio-cum-bedroom pitch black, but the soundproofing also made it perfectly silent. The only sound I heard all night was a purring cat trying to get through the narrow gap under the heavy studio door so it could sleep on my head. Having no cats sleeping on my head, though, did help lift the couch rating:

Couch rating: 7/10

Pro: So dark and quiet that I slept well

Con: So dark and quiet that I slept through most of the day.

When I got upstairs Pedro was on the computer. 'I have to work today, so I've printed you a map of the city and the

Events Page for September from the Rio Tourist Guide website,' he said. That was very nice of Pedro but, besides the Rio Film Festival, most of the events listed didn't sound very enticing and, to be frank, one just sounded like shit. The 'tourist website' list included: The 55th Brazilian Congress on Colon Proctology; the Brazilian Congress on Concrete (sadly, I would just miss that one as it started the day I left Rio); The 9th International Conference of the Stability of Ships and Ocean Vessels; and The International Symposium on Improving The Mammary Health of Brazil's Population. Actually, the last one could be interesting.

Pedro had already planned my itinerary, though. He was going to drop me off at Copacabana beach and his mapped-out walking tour led me to Copacabana Fort, Ipanema beach and then on a particularly long walk around *Lagoa Rodrigo de Freitas* (the large lagoon that separates the beach from the mountains) back to his house. Pedro had a haircut appointment in Copacabana. 'Nathalia set it up,' he grunted. 'My whole life I have gone to a barber, not a hairdresser. She made an appointment! Who makes an appointment for a haircut?'

On the fifteen-minute drive from Pedro's to Copacabana we passed lines of people standing on the side of the road holding up election placards and posters, including massive billboards that needed two or three people to hold them up. 'The presidential election is this Sunday,' Pedro said. 'It is illegal to advertise political parties on billboards or to stick up posters, so the candidates pay people from the *favelas* about a dollar to stand all day holding signs.' By the time we got to Copacabana we would have passed close to five hundred people holding up signs.

I have always wanted to go to Copacabana. I've always wanted to go so I could experience the area's rich cultural melting pot through its diverse and historical neighbourhoods, its grand colonial churches and splendid neo-classical buildings.

Okay, I'm lying.

I've always wanted to go to Copacabana so I could hit the beach and look at Brazilian girls' bottoms.

Sadly—just from a research point of view, of course—Brazilian girls' bottoms were a bit light on. Pedro told me that Copacabana was the place to be from the 1940s to the 1960s, but the beachfront buildings are now mostly full of little old ladies in large old apartments. To my surprise the beach was quite empty. Not only was it a gorgeously warm day, but I'd seen lots of photos of Copacabana and the beach was always chock-full of people. Maybe eleven o'clock was too early. I didn't fancy hanging around waiting for the old ladies to come out in their G-string bikinis, though, so I decided to head straight to the fort.

Copacabana doesn't get good press. I'd read and heard many stories of people getting held up at knifepoint and everything you read warns you not to take anything valuable with you when you walk around. As I stepped out of the car, I asked Pedro if I would get knifed. 'Just don't walk down a dark alley and ask a thief for a light,' Pedro said with a grin.

I felt very safe in the fort. As soon as I stepped through the gates I was surrounded by a hundred soldiers dressed in full camouflage. I had a lovely if rather expensive breakfast (or brunch or possibly even lunch) at the imaginatively named Café do Forte and sat at a table under the shade of an enormous tree right next to the sea wall, overlooking an army of surfers riding the crashing waves directly below. I ordered my food in Portuguese, and was pleasantly surprised to get exactly what I'd ordered. It is such a difficult language to get your tongue around that I couldn't even pronounce the name of the country's currency, the *reais*. 'It's easy,' Pedro had said to me earlier. 'Like this . . . *hayweeeshayiys*.' I tried it a few times before Pedro suggested that I should just call it 'Brazilian money'.

Weighed down with omelette and cake, I wandered past the whitewashed army barracks then ducked into a small park that ran along the rocky shoreline before stopping dead in my tracks and exclaiming 'Wow!' But it probably should have been 'Ahhh!' Directly in front of me was a sea of tall and tanned and young and lovely girls from Ipanema spread out on the beach or strolling along wiggling their bare bottoms. Most were wearing the bikini that shows everything without quite showing everything: a sliver of a thong downstairs and a spaghetti strap upstairs—vermicelli, really—anchored by a pair of nipple badges. I'm no expert, but I didn't think there was too much need to improve the mammary health of Brazil's population.

The only downside to my arrival at Ipanema beach was that I couldn't get *that* bloody song out of my head. I did manage to eventually stop singing it, but then I began whistling it between my teeth as I climbed a narrow dirt path that wound its way up to a bluff and a stunning vista over Ipanema beach. I was sitting on a bench soaking in the view—while still dementedly whistling away—when a young lady in a long white cotton dress sat next to me and began stripping off. When she'd got down to her tiny white bikini, I noticed a small tattoo on her lower back just above her bottom (well, where else was I supposed to look?). It looked like a rubber stamp and written inside was: 'Made in Brazil'.

I spent most of my time strolling along the beach dodging balls. It seemed that the straight guys, who favoured board shorts, were kicking soccer balls to each other, while the gay guys, who preferred their shorts tight and tiny, were playing dainty games of paddleball. The busiest part of the beach was the area surrounding the lifesaving tower Posto 9. There were lithe, fit, bronzed bodies everywhere playing volleyball, kicking footballs or languidly reposed on the beach, while the smell of old socks (marijuana) and music filled the air. Compared to the locals I felt (and looked a bit like) Mr Bean on holiday, so after tramping along almost the entire stretch of beach I headed to the busy back streets of Ipanema.

I spent the next few hours sauntering back to Pedro's house, pausing to gaze in shop windows or at some church or a lovely square or lively cafes full of groovy young people. Most of my return journey, however, was spent circumnavigating *Lagoa Rodrigo de Freitas* as I strolled lazily along the narrow park on the water's edge past joggers and lovers. I stopped for a beer in a waterside cafe and, as the sun dipped behind the mountains, I decided that after only 24 hours I had fallen in love with this marvellous and stunning city. And no, it wasn't just the bare bottoms and healthy mammaries that swayed me.

Pedro had told me that he would be home at eight o'clock, but by 9.30 he hadn't shown and I was getting very hungry. Although I was very tempted, the 'How to be a good guest' section on the couch-surfing website recommends that you 'Do not raid your host's fridge'. Other ways to be a good guest include: Do not ignore your hosts; Do not whisper; Don't be derogatory, impatient or dismissive about your host's children; Do not insult your host's cooking; and Do not party without your host except if he tells you to party.

I was eyeing off the tasty-looking biscuits in the cat bowl when Pedro finally turned up at 10.30. We had dinner at a Mexican restaurant in Cobal market, which was only a short walk from Pedro's house. In the evening the entire market is turned into a huge restaurant precinct and the passageways are filled with tables and noisy diners.

While we were eating our fajitas, I asked Pedro what it meant to be Brazilian. 'Brazil is . . . surrealistic,' he said. 'It has the most amazing mix of natural resources, biodiversity and a history like no other country, because races have mixed together from the very beginning. This cauldron of cultures gave birth to a new sort of place with very few preconceptions and many crossed influences that make the whole bigger than the sum of the parts, and that shows. I am really, really proud of being Brazilian, and not just because of our natural resources, but because we have real freedom—and not the American-way-of-life twisted concept of freedom by money—and a cultural kaleidoscope that truly exists only here.'

I was very impressed. Not only with Pedro's obvious love for his country, but that after a couple of beers his English was better than mine when I'm sober.

'Would you like to go to a nightclub?' Pedro asked after we'd finished dinner.

'Um, yeah,' I said rather unconvincingly. It was already after midnight and way past my bedtime.

'You did say that you want to experience Brazilian life,' Pedro said. 'And that's what we Brazilians do. We go clubbing.'

'I won't get in,' I said, looking down at my cargo shorts and thongs.

'No, you're okay. That's what everyone wears.'

What a wonderful country. Brazil is very proud to be the home of Havaianas, the world's largest and best-known brand of thongs (the ones also known as flip-flops, rather that the ones also known as bum floss), so they consider their humble thongs suitable footwear for any occasion.

We queued for 40 minutes to get into Casa da Matriz nightclub, which was down one of those dark alleys that Pedro told me to keep away from, and when we finally got to the doorman he grunted at me. 'He wants to see your ID,' Pedro translated.

I scoffed, 'He's kidding, right? Tell him that although I often think and act like I'm a teenager, I'm actually close to retirement age.'

Mr Neanderthal refused to budge, though, so we had to drive back to Pedro's to get my passport. When we returned to the nightclub, there was no queue and Mr Neanderthal didn't even bother looking at my ID. The nightclub, which was chock-full of heaving bodies, was in a large old house and the former lounge room was a dance floor while the former kitchen was a bar and the former master bedroom upstairs was another dance floor. I liked it, but I did have to wait ten minutes for a piss; they still only had the three former toilets. Being the old bugger that I am, I preferred the music downstairs where they were playing, as a radio DJ would say, 'the best music from the 60s, 70s, 80, 90s and today'.

We were handed a 'Drink Card' as we stepped inside. All drinks purchased at the bar were marked on the card and you paid at the end of the night. I imagine that after a big night you could be in for quite a surprise. 'What happens if you go crazy at the bar and don't have enough money to pay?' I asked Pedro—or actually screamed over the music.

'They won't let you leave, so you have to get money from a friend,' he shouted back. 'I had to ring up my mum once at four in the morning to bring me some money. What's worse, though,' he continued, 'is if you lose your card and then find it later on the bar after people have bought drinks for everyone on it.'

Around two in the morning I was sitting quietly enjoying my fifth or possibly eighth beer when a gorgeous Brazilian girl asked me for a dance. Well, when I say dance it ended up being more of a stumble. She was blind drunk. 'Would you like to fuck a Brazilian girl?' she bellowed in my ear.

'Pardon?'

'Not me!' she slurred. 'I don't really like you, but I can find someone for you if you like.'

When we left at three o'clock, she had found someone she did really like and was busy trying to get her tongue down into his lungs.

Pedro lit up a joint when we got back to his house. 'My first step-father liked cocaine,' Pedro said in between puffs. 'That was the main reason why they split up.' Pedro was an only child, but his mum had remarried twice and he now had four half-siblings and two step-siblings. 'My real dad is an art teacher at university, but he is also a very famous illustrator of children's books,' Pedro said proudly. 'The only problem with illustrating, though, is that he'd spend months on a job putting his heart and soul into it and get paid hardly anything. One book he illustrated has been a bestseller for thirty years and he only got a one-off payment.' He showed me the book, which—with its fantastically psychedelic illustrations—looked as if he was the one who had sniffed some cocaine, not the first step-father. Or was it the second? It was getting very late.

Sometime after 4 a.m. I staggered off to bed, leaving Pedro playing with his chords again. My couch-surfing trip was slowly turning into a flaking-out-on-a-couch-in-a-drunken-stupor trip.

Ah ha, so that was why Pedro had stayed up! He was waiting for someone. I might not have 'fucked a Brazilian girl', but Pedro obviously had. When I stumbled upstairs at midday, I found a young, and somewhat large, woman in the kitchen cooking something on the stove with a cigarette dangling from her mouth. Pedro's 'friend' spoke no English, so we smiled at each uncomfortably for a minute. Then she started washing the dishes. Gee, that's all right, I thought. Most pick-ups just leave in the morning.

Pedro eventually tottered down the stairs looking, not surprisingly, rather sheepish. 'I didn't get to sleep till six,' he said warily.

'I bet,' I said with a sly wink.

Pedro said something to his lady friend and she stopped washing the dishes and went upstairs.

'The kitty litter needs changing,' Pedro said matter-of-factly.

Boy, maybe I should have picked up as well. I needed my laundry done and there was also that tear in my shorts that needed sewing.

'Um, she seems nice,' I observed cheerfully.

'Yeah, she's great,' Pedro said. 'Rosângela has been my maid since I moved in here. She comes once a week and cleans the entire house and makes me meals as well.' Oops.

They should add 'Don't make assumptions about your host' to the 'How to be a good guest' list.

Pedro paid his maid US$30 for ten hours' work and she also worked for Pedro's mum and two of his aunties. 'Maids are always found through someone you know,' Pedro told me. 'Often people will try to "steal" someone's maid, because a good one—an honest, skilled and hard-working one—is hard to find.'

'Do many people have a maid?' I asked.

'A lot of middle-class people have one and it's usually a black lady that lives with a white family. Many apartments have a small room off the laundry or kitchen, which is the maid's room. It goes back to the *casa grande e senzala*, or the landlord's house and slave's house tradition. Back in the old days the husbands or teenagers would have sex with the maids. Now you can see why most Brazilians have mixed blood.'

Rosângela was making my 'couch' when we left to go to the market for brinner (we were eating so late that breakfast had almost become dinner). We ate at Restaurante do Mercado, a small traditional Brazilian buffet restaurant where you paid according to the weight of the food on your plate. There was an array of delectable-looking salads and meats, but apart from choosing a tiny salad and a small piece of grilled chicken, I got a bit carried away with the chips—I could thank my hangover for that. Pedro scoffed down his food because he had to get to work. It was also time for me to say goodbye to Pedro who had become, after just two days, a good friend. I only hoped I had got drunk enough to qualify as one of the people that Pedro enjoyed.

I devoted most of the afternoon to walking, or more like plodding, to *Pão de Açúcar,* Rio's famous Sugarloaf Mountain. Pedro said that it would take me an hour to walk there. It took me two. I was tired (yes, okay, and a little hungover) but I also did stop twice to buy a pair of Havaianas. They were on sale just about everywhere. I saw racks of Havaianas in a chemist, a video hire shop, a juice shop, a newsagent and even a florist ('It's my wife's birthday, so I'll have a bunch of pink and white Havaianas please').

I can now tick off another location on my James-Bond-filming-sites-of-the-world tour. It was the cable supporting the Sugarloaf Mountain cable car that Jaws tried to bite through in the film *Moonraker*. Bond might have been fighting the forces of evil, but I bet he didn't have to fight his way through a gaggle of tour bus groups just so he could take a photo of yet another [insert superlative here] view of the city.

It was 7.30 by the time I got back to Pedro's house, which didn't leave any time for my planned, and much-needed, nap. Mariana had said to 'get ready to party hard because we hardly ever sleep' but, to be honest, I was more ready to sleep hard and hardly ever party.

7

'I'm the coolest Carioca in Rio and the happiest girl you'll ever meet.'
Mariana Violante, 26, Rio de Janeiro, Brazil
CouchSurfing.com

'I've invited my friend to stay as well just in case you are a rapist or a mass murderer,' Mariana said casually as she greeted me at the door.

'Well, I'm not!' I said quickly and in the process sounded, even to myself, like I very much was.

Mariana's friend, who had been hiding behind the door, popped her head out and gave me a nervous smile. 'This is Paula,' Mariana said brightly. 'She is my best friend and the *second* coolest girl in all of Rio.' Mariana did live in one of the coolest parts of town, in a swanky apartment block which even had a swanky doorman in full uniform in the foyer. The apartment was only one building back from Copacabana beach, which you could see from the lounge-room window. Well, you could glimpse a sliver of it. There was a thin strip of water and sand just visible in a gap between buildings. On my tour of the small apartment we bypassed the couch and I was shown to my very own tiny bedroom with a tiny bed and an even tinier ensuite (so tiny in fact that you could wee in the toilet while standing in the shower—not that I tried to, I hasten to add).

Mariana told me that I was her first couch-surfing guest and that she was a little nervous. It didn't show. She was incredibly bubbly and excited about showing me 'the best time in Rio'. The girls were dolled up in readiness for a big night out. Mariana's long, straight, jet-black hair was perfectly coiffured and she was wearing designer jeans and a white halter-top showing off her deep golden tan, while Paula, who had long wavy mousey-blonde locks, looked ravishing in a stunning floral dress.

'Is it okay if we just stay in tonight and eat at home and watch a DVD?' Mariana asked apologetically.

'That's okay,' I said, trying not to sound too overjoyed.

'Are you sure?'

Oh yeah, I was sure. And so was my liver. I was still sure even when Mariana held up a DVD and gushed excitedly, 'We're watching *Pride and Prejudice*.'

Mariana worked as an architect/interior designer in a business that she'd set up with two other friends from university after they'd graduated three years previously. 'I've had a real busy week, so I need to rest tonight. Then tomorrow I can show you why I'm the coolest girl in all of Rio,' Mariana said with a beaming smile. 'I've got our entire itinerary planned out.' Our itinerary went something like this: beach—lunch—beach—disco dancing—sleep—beach—lunch—beach—samba dancing. 'I'm a true *Carioca* girl,' Mariana said. 'I love the beach and samba dancing.'

'I hate the beach and I hate samba dancing,' Paula retorted.

'We have nothing in common,' said Mariana, giving Paula a hug. 'But we are still best friends.'

We wandered across the road to the supermarket, which overlooked the beach, to get some chocolate. 'You can't watch a movie without a little bit of chocolate,' Mariana said. The 'little bit of chocolate' turned into four large blocks of chocolate.

Mariana loved chocolate so much that she had become a member of the 'Chocolate Lovers' group on CouchSurfing.com, which I later discovered has 1017 members from 38 different countries. Chocolate Lovers is just one of a few thousand diverse groups that have been set up by couch-surfing members. Mariana told me that the members of the Chocolate Lovers group discuss chocolate, have lengthy debates about which country makes the best chocolate and organise chocolate meetings.

By far the largest group on CouchSurfing, apart from specific country or city groups, is the Queer Couch Surfers, with 10 680 members. Other large groups include Photographers (2668 members), Cyclists (2198 members), Beer Lovers (1641 members), and the Tattooed and Pierced Club (1148 members).

Most of the groups have relatively small numbers, although I still found some of them surprisingly popular.

The Masturbators group has 179 members (so to speak). The welcoming spiel to the Masturbators group page reads:

> *Have you jerked at work? Played with the fun dot in the wrong spot? Handled your meat in an airplane seat? Got a fever and played with your beaver? You are not alone! Cum on in.*

I imagine some of those masturbators are also among the 106 members of the Virgins Club. One or two of them may also be among the 18 Gay Cyclists, the 15 We Love Panties Group or the 11 Gay Vegetarian Nudists.

Some groups are just plain weird. There are 165 Dumpster Divers, 11 members of the Midget Tossing Society, 29 in the Ikea Couch Club, 9 Lovers of the Pickle, 9 Mayonnaise Experts, 8 Marmite Lovers, 5 in the Anti-Marmite Movement, 5 Kitchen Cupboard Organisers, 87 International Party Girls Seek Toy Boys, 101 in the David Hasselhoff Appreciation Group, 41 Atheists with Biblical Names, and 163 in the Church of the Flying Spaghetti Monster.

What's a bit of a worry, though, is that only 4 of the 150 000-plus couch surfers are members of the 'Nice People' group. Some groups have an even lower membership—as in only one member. These exclusive groups include: Irish Dancing; Pakistani Bi Men; Well-dressed; People against War; Radical Feminists; Gay Chefs and Perverts.

When I got home I decided to start my own group called The Karaoke Club—our slogan is 'Karaoke is everything'. There are currently eleven members who hail from such places as the Netherlands, Bulgaria, Canada, Australia, Iceland, Denmark and the US.

I'm a member of six clubs (I've also since joined Chocolate Lovers), but some people get a little carried away. Mark from Melbourne, Australia, is a member of 242 groups including: Surfing for Peace; The Church of Lasagne; The Moderate Non-alarmist Socialists; Food not Bombs; I Joined Too Many Groups; and How Do You Delete Groups?

Mariana obviously wasn't one of the the 337 People Who Like Cooking because as she rummaged through a pile of plastic containers in the fridge she said, 'I can't cook. I'm terrible.'

Mariana had a maid who came twice a week and cooked *all* of her meals. 'Tonight we're having . . . um, crumbed chicken and pasta . . .' Mariana was checking the neatly marked labels on the plastic containers to see what tonight's fare was. '. . . And salad and quiche.'

The food was delicious, although the crumbed chicken was only lukewarm. 'I'm not even good at *heating up* food,' Mariana explained cheerfully.

'I was told that Copacabana was full of old women,' I said to the girls over dinner.

'I'm an old woman,' Mariana sighed. 'I turned twenty-six last month.'

At 26 years old, Mariana is the average age for a couch surfer. In fact, the website is mostly surfed by folk in their twenties, and 72 per cent of couch surfers are aged between twenty and 28. Mind you, it's not all young folk. There are some antediluvians like myself on it as well, with more than

30 000 aged between 40 and 49. At the last body count there were even 146 registered couch surfers over the age of 80.

We tried to watch the movie, but the phone kept ringing. Mariana was a popular old woman. One of the callers was Paula's boyfriend. A boyfriend, incidentally, who she'd never met. Paula had 'met' him through wayn.com (Where Are You Now), which is similar to CouchSurfing.com, but without the couch. Fellow travellers chat online and meet up if they are in the same city. Paula had been 'chatting' to Dave from Sydney for a year and they had started 'dating' four months ago. 'I hope to meet him soon,' she beamed.

'My boyfriend hasn't called me all week,' Mariana sniffed.

'That's because he's an *arsehole*!' Paula cried indignantly.

Mariana rolled her eyes. 'Paula calls him "The Arsehole".'

Mariana had been dating 'The Arsehole' for seven months. Nunoo was from Portugal and had been working for Shell in Rio for the past twelve months.

'I saw him last Saturday night,' Mariana said. 'I went to a nightclub and he turned up. We had a lovely night and we had breakfast together and everything. He said he would call me, but he hasn't called all week. Is that strange?'

'No, he's probably just using you for sex,' I wanted to say, but instead I said, 'Yeah, a bit strange.'

'It's not strange,' Paula said musingly. 'It's because he's an arsehole.' Except Paula pronounced it 'asshole' with an American accent. In fact, Paula said everything with an American accent. 'I learnt English from watching the TV show *Friends*,' she drawled. 'I watch it *every* day.'

'I learnt most of my English from *Sex and the City*,' Mariana declared.

I thought 'The Arsehole' might have called when Mariana started crying during one of her many phone calls. 'It was my mum,' Mariana said afterwards. Mariana's mum worked as a doctor in a small village five hours' flight north of Rio. 'She calls every day and she misses me so she cries and then she makes me cry. I'm the only child and I'm her princess.'

When both girls started getting teary during a scene in the movie with the rather droll Mr Darcy, I made my excuses and snuck off to bed.

'I'm so sorry about the weather,' Mariana said sadly as she looked out the window at the drizzling rain. 'I feel terrible about it.'

'I don't think it's your fault,' I said. 'We can do something else. What does a Carioca girl do if she can't go to the beach?'

Mariana's face lit up. 'We go shopping of course!'

We had planned to catch a bus, but once we'd started walking to the bus stop we kept on walking the 6 kilometres to Ipanema. The rain had stopped and, although it was overcast and gloomy, it was still warm and we just about had the whole of the Copacabana beachfront to ourselves as we shuffled past deserted restaurants and cafes. On our two-hour hike we talked about Mariana's job (she not only did the designs for refurbished apartments, but also did the interior design, including choosing all the furniture), we talked about her family (her parents divorced when Mariana was two years old and her dad had only recently got in touch with her 'because I'm now successful') and we talked about Nunoo: 'He goes back to Lisbon in five months and I keep thinking that he is the one. But maybe Paula is right. Maybe he is an arsehole.'

'I have a Havaianas addiction,' Mariana said as she stopped to buy a white pair with 10-centimetre high heels. My addiction wasn't coming along too badly either. I bought another two pairs of Havaianas, making it four pairs in just two days.

Mariana did love to shop. I lost count of how many clothes shops, jewellery shops, hat shops, belt shops, handbag shops and shoe shops we went into. 'Are you bored?' Mariana asked me in a lingerie shop full of stunning women trying on bras. 'No, not really,' I said, wiping the dribble from my chin.

'I go to this church most Sundays,' Mariana said as we passed a small church in the middle of some fashion boutiques. 'I pray for more money, so I can do more shopping.'

Just when I thought that I'd finally got *The Girl from Ipanema* out of my head we stopped for a late lunch (as in starting at 4.30) at The Girl from Ipanema restaurant (or the *Garota de Ipanema* in Portuguese). It was at this very restaurant that Tom Jobim and Vinícius de Moraes wrote the song that has come to be Brazil's most iconic soundtrack (as well as the second most recorded song of all time after the Beatles' *Yesterday*).

We grabbed a table by the window and I very quickly figured out why Tom and Vinícius wrote the song there. I said 'aaahh' a number of times as tall and tanned and young and lovely girls from Ipanema went by in the street. The restaurant was packed with locals and loud American tourists, but the service was efficient and friendly and we shared a main course of *Picanha a Brasileira,* which was a generously laden sizzling plate of superb, thinly sliced rump steak with rice, chips and *farofa*.

We caught the bus back to Mariana's because she had to get home for a 'beauty' appointment. 'I'm going to get my fingernails and my footnails done and get my hair blow-waved,' she explained. 'Brazilian women spend a lot of time and money to look beautiful.' Mariana went to the beauty salon at least once a week and saw her personal trainer three days a week. 'I have to look good for the beach!' she said brightly.

'If my boyfriend rings when I'm out,' Mariana said, 'tell him that I'm busy and that I'm going out tonight with a nice boy from Australia.' I wasn't too keen on getting her boyfriend jealous. Mariana had shown me a photo of Nunoo standing on the beach in little white bathers, showing off his muscles. Muscles that were a hell of a lot bigger than mine.

Mariana came back from the salon looking suitably gorgeous. 'Now I have to get ready,' she said. 'It will take me at least an hour,' she added before disappearing into the bathroom. I tried to watch TV. Mariana had cable TV but, as with cable TV the world over, there was nothing on. We left for Melt nightclub with two of Mariana's leggy cousins at eleven o'clock—at which time on a Saturday night at home I'm either in bed or dozing off in front of the television.

Melt nightclub looked very chic and hip, just like the people standing in the queue to get in. It was so chic and hip that the drink cards were credit cards and the doorman wore a three-piece suit. 'I come here *every* Saturday night,' Mariana said as we were ushered to the front of the slow-moving queue—which was handy because as well as meticulously checking IDs, they were punching everyone's name and details into a computer.

Two more of Mariana's leggy cousins were waiting for us inside at one of the candlelit tables in the ground floor bar. The bar was full of so many glamorous and beautiful people that it looked like the final of *Search for a Supermodel*. I don't speak Portuguese but I could tell that some of them were looking over at me and saying: 'Who invited the ugly bloke?' I was doing all right for an ugly bloke, though. I was surrounded by a gaggle of gorgeous girls who were all chatting rapidly to each other in Portuguese. 'They are saying that *all* Brazilian men have a screw loose,' Mariana's Amazonian cousin Roberta told me.

Just before midnight Nunoo turned up. Mariana spotted him in the crowd and waved him over. 'My heart is beating *so* fast,' she gushed while her cousins all shot him filthy looks. Mariana went all giggly and girly when he gave her a peck on the cheek, and when he went to the bar to get a drink she said, 'He told me that he didn't call me because he wanted to come here and surprise me. He's *so* lovely.'

The disco, which was upstairs, started at midnight and all the groovy and hip people headed up to dance to the groovy and hip *Don't Go Breaking My Heart* by Elton John and Kiki Dee. Mariana and Roberta dragged me up to the dance floor, but when the Doobie Brothers came on I skolled my drink so that I had an excuse to go back downstairs. 'Ask Nunoo to come up for a dance,' Mariana yelled in my ear as I left.

Nunoo was busy. He was busy flirting outrageously with a blonde girl at the bar and playing with her hair.

'I couldn't find him,' I shrugged when I got back upstairs.

'I'll find him,' Mariana said.

This should be interesting.

I stayed on the packed dance floor with Roberta who bent down and hollered into my ear, 'It's like dancing in a barrel of fish!'

'More like a barrel of giraffes,' I said to her right hip.

I told Roberta about Nunoo and the blonde and she said that we should go down to see if Mariana was all right. She was more than all right. We found Mariana and Nunoo draped on the bar with their tongues down each other's throats.

Fifteen minutes later I found Mariana slumped on the stairs in tears. 'He's left me and now he has broken my heart,' she whimpered. 'Why doesn't he want me? I'm beautiful, smart and funny.'

'He doesn't know what he's missing out on,' I said.

'He told me that I was perfect . . .' Mariana sniffed as mascara trickled down her cheek, '. . . but not perfect enough.'

I then reeled out all the rest of the old clichés to try and console her:

'He's not good enough for you.'

'There's plenty more fish in the sea.'

'You'll find someone new, someone better.'

'He's a fucking arsehole!' Roberta summed it up rather more succinctly when I dragged Mariana upstairs. 'She needs to drink and she needs to dance,' Roberta added. When I came back with a Cosmopolitan (Mariana drank Cosmopolitans because that's what Carrie drank on *Sex and the City*), she was dancing while bawling her eyes out. I left her with Roberta and went downstairs to the bar and chatted to a fellow from Australia, because no matter where you travel in the world you'll usually find another Australian to chat to. 'I think I've found heaven,' he said as two stunning girls threw themselves all over him.

By 3.30 I was ready for bed. And it seemed Mariana was ready to take someone to hers. I found her upstairs making out rather zealously with a new Nunoo. When I'd told her that she would 'find someone new', I hadn't meant within the hour. 'Come sit with us,' Mariana said brightly.

I sat and watched a replay of some local football game on the big-screen TV while Mariana and her new beau sat next to me exchanging tongues. In fact, half the crowd seemed to be making out with a boyfriend, girlfriend, friend-friend or possibly just a random stranger. 'I'm sorry, Brian,' Mariana said in between kisses. 'I'm still the *coolest* girl in Rio, aren't I?'

I finally dragged Mariana away from the nightclub at five o'clock just as the first traces of morning appeared in the sky. The entire city still seemed to be up and the kiosks along Ipanema beach were full of late-night (or early morning) revellers drinking from large coconuts and eating sandwiches. It had taken only four days, but I'd finally become one of them. I was now officially nocturnal.

Mariana might have to change the bit in her profile where she said 'I'm the happiest girl you'll ever meet'. She spent most of the morning in bed sobbing and howling into the phone. She eventually crawled out of bed at one o'clock for breakfast.

My meal times were now totally out of whack. We had breakfast at 1.30, which meant that I'd probably be having lunch at seven and dinner sometime the next day. I went to wash the breakfast dishes and Mariana said, 'Don't do that! My maid has to have some work to do.' She wasn't going to be happy with me then. I made the bed.

Although I hadn't actually seen too much of the bed, I gave it the highest couch rating so far:

Couch rating: 8/10
Pro: A *real* bed plus an ensuite
Con: The bed was a bit short (if I'd brought home one of the Amazonian cousins—and I'm only talking hypothetically here of course—I would have needed to fold her in half).

'Would you like to come and watch democracy at work?' Mariana asked. 'I have to vote today.' Voters could choose the venue where they wanted to cast their vote (school, local hall, etc.) and Mariana chose the very exclusive Leme tennis club, which had a restaurant and pool overlooking the beach. 'I'm, how you say?' Mariana said, turning up the tip of her nose with her finger, '. . . a snob.'

On the short walk to the tennis club we were both handed a dizzying array of flyers promoting candidates. 'We have to vote for six different positions, including the president,' Mariana explained. Some of the candidates looked a bit creepy. Luiz Sérgio looked like Borat wearing his grandma's glasses while João Pedro looked suspiciously like Charles Manson. The creepiest one of all, however, was a fellow in an ill-fitting business shirt, beard and a grey wig who hadn't done himself any favours for the photo by wearing his smarmiest smile and sticking his thumbs up in the air.

'Who'd vote for him?' I chortled. 'He looks like a used-car salesman.'

'That's Lula, our president!' Mariana said. 'He's okay compared to some of the other politicians we've had.' Those 'other politicians' included President Fernando Collo de Mello, who won the 1989 presidential election by promising to fight corruption. Then in 1992 he was thrown out of office after being accused of siphoning off more than US$1 billion of public funds. Another was Congressman Hildebrando Pascoal, who was arrested for making cuts, not to the budget but to a man's arms and legs with a chainsaw.

Although we were in an upmarket area, the city's poverty was painfully apparent in everyday scenes: men and women sleeping in the street; destitute boys juggling for spare change at a major intersection; and tiny girls peddling gum outside chic restaurants. The poor were also queueing with the wealthy to vote.

Tables inside the tennis club were set up for voting according to age group. The folk manning the tables were volunteers—well, volunteers in that they would have been sent a letter from the government telling them that they were volunteering. Mariana had 'volunteered' twice before.

'Who did you vote for?' I asked Mariana when she'd finished.

'The used-car salesman,' she said with a grin.

Deciding the fate of the nation takes its toll and we both concluded that we needed a good lie down. I was getting used to this nocturnal caper.

By 7.30 we were showered and changed and on our way to a brothel. Well, a former brothel at least. Casa Rosa (The Pink House) was now a samba club and Sunday night was the *roda de samba* party. The seven-dollar entrance fee included dinner (or lunch in our case) and a perpetual parade of girls wiggling their perfect bottoms. Most of the action was taking place in the large and very pink outdoor area. Mariana described it perfectly: 'It's like a party in someone's backyard.'

The band were all sitting around a table that was covered in bottles of beer and the musicians were singing while thumping drums (*surdos*) and bongos and swinging their *cavaquinhos* (the diminutive guitars that give samba music its characteristic tink). The music was contagious and I couldn't help but wiggle my not-so-perfect bottom. This is what couch surfing is all about. I really felt like I was in Brazil. I was with a local in a local samba bar eating authentic local food.

The languid and tanned locals were still dancing even while waiting in line for food, which was a typical Brazilian dish called *feijoada*. The plate was piled high with *arroz e feijão* (rice and black beans), *farofa*, *linguiça* (slices of spicy pork sausage) and a surprisingly tasty salad made with cabbage and oranges.

I could barely move after all the food. Well, that was my excuse for constantly stomping on Mariana's toes while she attempted to teach me how to dance the *forró*, a fast-paced dance originating in the country's northeast. We were in the *forró* room, which was one of three other dancing rooms in Casa Rosa. The rustic accordion-driven music seemed a tad folksy for a city hooked on glamour, but the Cariocas transformed the tiny room into a sweaty pit of sensuality. Sadly, though, my dancing was more nonsensical than sensual. The dance is 'performed' in pairs and the couple dance very close together. The man's left hand holds the woman's right hand as in the waltz, with his right arm around her back and her left arm around his neck. The man's right leg then stays in between the woman's legs. The dance somewhat resembles a dog trying to have sex with a person's leg.

I really am quite a terrible dancer and I just can't get the whole rhythm thing going. Everyone else was in a perfect groove and doing fancy spins while I stared at my feet, mumbling to myself '1, 2, 3 turn 1, 2, 3 turn 1, 2, 3 stomp . . . oh sorry!' Mariana was incredibly polite. I must have stood on her toes a dozen times, but she was very patient. Mind you, when I suggested that we go outside, she did agree rather too enthusiastically.

We went to another room where a band was playing a jazz samba fusion. I loved it. So did Mariana. I think Mariana particularly liked it because it was the type of music that you danced solo to. 'It's a happy place,' Mariana said, smiling serenely. It really was. Every person in the room was dancing. And it was really joyous exuberant dancing, not the usual stand-in-one-spot-around-the-handbag-waving-your-arms-now-and-again type you see in most nightclubs.

We had a very early night. We left at 1.00 a.m. But not before Mariana walked up to a good-looking guy she'd never met before, said 'Don't I know you from somewhere?' and gave him her telephone number.

I awoke early. Well, in my new nocturnal life, ten o'clock was early. 'I'm so sad that you are going,' Mariana said before leaving for work. 'You are my new best friend,' she added, squeezing me tightly. This was what couch surfing was all about (and I don't mean getting squeezed tightly by gorgeous Brazilian girls). Mariana had taken me into her life and treated me like a dear friend after only a few short days.

And it was because of that generosity and friendship that I was given opportunities to see and do things that wouldn't have happened if I wasn't couch surfing.

I still had a few hours until my flight to the States, so I had a bit of a lie down on the couch when Mariana had gone. I was only a quarter way through my Couch Surfing Tour and I was already exhausted. I needed a break from partying (and drinking). But I had no hope that Bob, my couch-surfing host in Chicago, was a teetotaller and liked nice quiet nights in front of the telly. Not when he lived above a liquor store and, according to his profile, liked to 'drink beer and loot and pillage'.

USA

8

'ABSOLUTELY NO REPUBLICANS!

Sorry, I am firm on this rule. I'm sure there are some good ones out there but they aren't staying here.'

Bob Fields, 31, Chicago, USA

GlobalFreeloaders.com

'What's the name of the person who are you staying with in the US?' the surly American security officer asked me at Rio airport.

'Bob.'

'Bob who?'

I shrugged. 'Err . . . I don't know.'

'Well, where did you meet him then?'

'Um, we've never actually met.'

'So, how do you know him?'

'I met him through Global Freeloaders and I'm staying on his couch.' I tried to explain the concept of couch surfing, but it was all too much for the security guy and he waved me through.

The only problem with visiting the States nowadays is, gee whiz, it's a nuisance to get into. I got asked exactly the same questions again at security check No. 2—and bewildered another security officer. At security check No. 3 they made me take off my belt and checked my Havaianas for nuclear warheads. At security check No. 5 the security officer grilled me about my iPod. 'Where did get your iPod from?' the security goon asked me.

'It was a Christmas present.'

'Who from?'

'Um . . . my wife.'

I was getting my first taste of the whole post 9/11 security blitz and I was still more than 7000 kilometres away from the land of the free and the home of the brave, but I couldn't do a Couch Surfing Tour of the Globe without the good ol' US of A on my itinerary. It is, after all, the centre of the universe—well, according to a lot of Americans, at least.

'Are you seeking to engage in criminal or immoral activities?' Although Bob had told me we were going looting and pillaging, I didn't tick the 'yes' box on the Security Immigration Form at Chicago airport. I can't really imagine too many criminals ticking it either, to be honest. Mind you, if people were honest, 9/11 would never have happened because the hijackers would have ticked the 'yes' box next to 'Are you a terrorist?'

The plan for my couch-surfing jaunt was to go to places where I hadn't been before and, although I'd been to the States a number of times, I'd only been to ten of the 50 states. Even so, I still had plenty of couches to choose from.

Out of the 217 countries represented on the three websites, the USA has by far the most couches with more than 100 000 people registered. Incidentally, on CouchSurfing.com the countries with the smallest membership—with only one member each—are Antigua and Barbuda, Turkmenistan, Guinea, Palau, Burundi, Central African Republic, São Tomé and Príncipe, and Vatican City (I checked, by the way, and the couch in Vatican City didn't belong to the Pope).

So why did I choose Chicago? Simple really: Jake and Elwood. I'd seen the city in so many movies (including, off the top of my head, *The Blues Brothers*, *The Fugitive*, *Risky Business*, *High Fidelity*, *Home Alone* and *Ferris Bueller's Day Off*) that I felt like I'd been there already and wanted to finally see it in the flesh. And it's not just celluloid that makes Chicago famous. It is (or was) home to everything from Jerry Springer to Oprah, *Playboy* magazine to Pullman, McDonalds to Kraft, Frank Lloyd Wright to Hemingway, Al Capone to Walt Disney, Miles Davis to Muddy Waters, and the Cubs to the Bulls.

During my search for a couch, I soon discovered that it wasn't just the city that was intriguing. So were some of the profiles I found on GlobalFreeloaders.com. Jonathon's was rather short and blunt:

> You can stay in my backyard. It's all right, not very comfortable, but whatever, you're a freeloader, what do you care?

I can't imagine what Ron had in mind for entertainment when you stayed with him:

> Plenty of room for travellers. Limited tools available.

If you came from Venus or Saturn you'd be welcome to stay with James:

> We'll consider hosting anyone, but please be considerate (i.e. don't bring a lot of drugs and don't come in totally plastered at 4am, puke loudly on the carpet, and then snore and sleep until afternoon). I don't have any preferences, male, female, bi, les, gay . . . as long as you're not from the planet Mars or Pluto.

And I'm not sure what planet Daniel is from:

> I like lemurs and three-toed sloths. I like waterparks, especially the long twisty slides when they don't require you to be in a frikken innertube. I own a minivan, but don't hold it against me. It hauls a lot of gear. Blue Ice Vodka is my drink of choice. Or water, if I need to operate heavy machinery. I am addicted to shopping for office supplies and I own a parrot, so no cats allowed.

Bob's profile seemed relatively normal compared to some of the others:

> We're generally fairly quiet during the week but drink and swear and talk like pirates most every weekend. We ride bicycles drunk and wear lampshades on our

heads. I like sleeping in the back of trucks and peeing from high places.

Bob lived in Humboldt Park (well, not actually in the park itself), located on the northwest side of the city. The direct train I caught from the airport was the movie-star one that travels high above the street and has featured in more movies than Mel Gibson.

There was no doubt that I was in America. On the ten-minute walk to Bob's place I passed two McDonalds, a Dunkin' Donuts, a Pizza Hut, a KFC and lots of Americans with huge butts. Bob wasn't due home for another hour (he was an elementary school teacher and finished at three o'clock), so I grabbed a beer from Bob's very own ground-floor liquor store and sat on his doorstep on the street. It was hotter and more humid than it had been in Rio and I soon discarded my shoes and socks and peeled off my shirt. When people walking by kept giving me a wide berth, I suddenly realised that it wasn't just the sight of my pasty bare chest. Here I was sitting on a doorstep surrounded by plastic bags, drinking a bottle of beer from a brown paper bag and in desperate need of a wash and shave.

Twenty minutes later Greg Kinnear pulled up in front of me on a bicycle. It wasn't the Hollywood actor, though. It was my host Bob, who shared the same clean-cut, blue-eyed, American-as-apple-pie look, complete with matching dimpled smile. The GlobalFreeloaders site doesn't have profile pics, so I really had no idea what to expect. I certainly didn't expect a man who likes sleeping in the back of trucks and peeing from high places to look like a handsome Hollywood star.

Bob's second floor, three-bedroom apartment was not too shitty at all (on his profile he said that he lived in a shitty apartment). He shared it with Carl ('he does some sort of shit with computers') and his brother Jason ('he does some sort of shit with wood'). 'We've got a sweet-ass deal,' Bob beamed. 'We only pay two hundred and sixty dollars each a month rent.' The reason Bob got such a sweet-ass deal was that less than a decade ago Humboldt Park was considered a ghetto. Gang activity, crime and violence dominated the area. 'A few years ago all the hipsters moved in and it became cool,' he said. 'But now all the fucking *Sex and the City* wannabes are moving in.'

My couch looked very comfortable even though it was in the middle of a barren and desolate desert. The walls in the lounge room were floor-to-ceiling panoramic poster prints of the vivid red spires and stark landscape of Monument Valley. Except for one wall, which was draped with a huge American flag.

Over a couple of beers I learnt that Bob earns $45 000 a year teaching English as a second language to Puerto Ricans and Mexicans at Cicero Elementary School. I also learnt that he was counting down the days until his contract ended (he had 154 days to go), when he planned to buy a van and earn money driving backpackers around the country. Finally I learnt that his obsession with 1970s Schwinn bicycles had turned out to be rather lucrative.

'I buy old ones from classified ads in the newspaper, then do them up and sell them,' Bob explained as we stepped into a long, drafty storeroom off the lounge room. Inside at least twenty Schwinn bikes were in various stages of deconstruction and reconstruction. 'They don't make 'em like this anymore,' Bob said as he pointed out the solid and heavy-framed Black Phantom, Stingray and Scrambler. 'And now they've become cool again, I can make good money,' he said. 'The money I make will help finance my next big trip.' Bob went on to tell me about one of his early entrepreneurial schemes, which had paid for a twelve-month jaunt around the States. In his senior year at high school he made $20 000 by selling dope to his fellow students.

While we were chatting, the phone rang. It was a potential buyer. Ten minutes later a fellow turned up looking to buy a bike as a birthday present for his wife. He rode the vibrant green Scrambler across the road and back again, then said, 'I'll take it'. Bob had bought the bike for $35 and, after 'fixing it up a little', had resold it for $150.

'I only put the ad on Craigslist this morning,' Bob beamed.

'What's Craigslist?' I asked.

'I'll show you.' Bob opened up the site on his computer. Craigslist.org had links for cities all over the world and had everything from Cars for Sale to Lost and Found, Houses for Sale to Positions Vacant, and travel deals to personals, including an incredibly explicit 'Casual Encounters' section. 'Check this out!' Bob said with his trademark cheeky smile. He showed me the Women seeking Men section, which was more like Women Desperately Seeking Men RIGHT THIS VERY MINUTE! Many of the women who had posted requests were after an immediate response:

> ***Petite girl wants to play***
> *Can't host, but my boyfriend is asleep and I want to head out. He passed out drunk. I want to suck a big cock. Only reply if you are hung.*

'Let's go cruising,' Bob purred. He didn't mean for horny girls on Craigslist, though. Bob was pointing to his two most prized Schwinn bicycles. Bob snagged the very hipster-looking Schwinn Chopper (complete with gear stick) while I had the menacing-looking Black Phantom. We cruised to a Middle Eastern restaurant, where we ate falafels and talked about Americans in the Middle East. 'The US defense policy is fucking ridiculous,' Bob bellowed through a mouthful of hummus. 'This country could be a paradise. We could use the money those idiots spend on invading countries on social services and education.' Bob didn't like George Bush much either. 'That fucker is responsible for everyone in the world hating Americans,' he spat.

After dinner we went on a pub crawl, or pub pedal in this case, and stopped at one of the outdoor bars on West Division Street. Although it was a Tuesday night, the place was packed. 'Everyone is out because it's usually freezing this time of the year,' Bob said.

The next pub we stopped at was a bordello-styled pub, all dark pillars and heavy purple curtains. Just when I was telling Bob that I was getting a bit peckish, a scruffy-looking Mexican chap strolled in with a bag full of hot *tomale*. Although Bob's description of *tomale* didn't sound too appetising—corn leaves wrapped around corn mash and lard—it was pretty tasty as far as lard and mash go. We grabbed the last few before the guy sold out. 'He's really popular,' Bob explained. 'But not as popular as the Muffin Lady.' The Muffin Lady went from pub to pub with a basket full of delicious baked goodies. But instead of blueberry muffins, hers were Moroccan black. 'You'd be stoned after one muffin,' Bob said. 'She's not around anymore, though. She got busted with ten thousand dollars' worth of cannabis in the back of her car and now she's in jail.'

On the ride home Bob had another go at George Bush and the Republicans. 'If they get in again,' Bob barked as we trundled down the street, 'I'm going to strap a bomb on and go to the biggest church in South Dakota and blow the fuckers up, because they're the one's voting them in.'

'Yo bro! Whassup?'

No, too ghetto.

'Ey, 'ow ya doin'?'

No, too New York.

'Howdy partner.'

No, too cowboy.

I had to get my American accent right because I was about to be Bob for the day. Bob had given me his teacher's photo-ID card, which granted free entry to 54 Chicago museums and galleries. Bob didn't seem to think there would be any problem with my total lack of resemblance to Greg Kinnear.

Bob lent me one of his bikes, but not one of his Schwinn classics. 'The city is full of bike thieves,' he grunted.

'You'll need to take a couple of these,' Bob said, opening a drawer that was filled with an array of bike locks. Bob grabbed two different locks then demonstrated how to put them on. It was all rather complicated and involved wrapping a thick steel cable around the wheels then fixing a clamp through the cable and around a bike rack. 'Take the seat with you when you lock it up,' he said. 'Those fuckers will steal anything.'

Bob told me that it would take 30 minutes to ride into the city. It took me ten, but I may have cheated a little. While I was having breakfast it began raining and I readily concede that I'm a lily-livered wimp when it comes to getting rained on, so I put the bike on the train.

I came up out of Jackson station and all around me the city's workforce was streaming in and out of the 'L' trains and swarming away along a dank State Street underneath the bulky steel elevated train line. It was all eerily familiar, but there was something missing. Ahh, that was it. There were no high-speed car chases or cops having shoot-outs with nasty crime gangs. Pity, really.

It was only a five-minute ride along to my first foray into a life of crime as an ID fraudster. Still, even with the prospect of a prison sentence hanging over my head, I was looking forward to visiting the Art Institute of Chicago.

Being a devoted habitué of art galleries and a great admirer of the French Impressionists, I knew that it housed the largest collection of French Impressionists outside the Musée d'Orsay in Paris. Plus it would get me out of the rain.

'Hey dude, I'm a teacher,' I blurted out as I flashed Bob's card to the young hipster behind the ticket desk.

What was I saying? No normal person says 'dude'.

'There you go, dude,' he said as he handed me my ticket.

Seeing paintings in the flesh after studying them in books for years is like meeting your favourite Hollywood star face-to-face. The Art Institute of Chicago is full of 'celebrity' paintings including *A Sunday afternoon on La Grande Jatte* by Georges Seurat; Van Gogh's *Bedroom in Arles* and *Self-portrait, 1887*; Grant Wood's *American Gothic*; and more than 30 paintings by Monet. There weren't nearly enough famous paintings for some people, though. An old lady tottered up next to me while I was admiring a Pissarro painting and she said to her friend, 'Is this famous?'

'No,' said her friend.

The old lady, who didn't even bother looking at the painting, then said, 'Can you tell me when we get to a famous one?'

I wandered around for three hours and what amazed me the most was that not a single person even batted an eyelid at the fact that I was waltzing around cradling a bicycle seat. I soon discovered, however, that Bob wasn't being paranoid after all and that someone was going to be in for a mighty surprise when they went to ride their bicycle home. All that was left of the bike that had been chained next to mine was the frame, which was the only thing secured to the bike rack. Both wheels were gone. And so was the seat.

Next stop was the third-tallest building in the world—the 110-storey Sears Tower had been the tallest building in the world until 1996, when it was usurped. At least it was easy to find. The third-tallest building on earth is always there, wherever you look. Telescopic in design, its square shoulders fall away at certain points, relieving the monotony of its huge black surface. It's amazing to think that this immense, hi-tech building was built as a monument to the old-fashioned mail-order business that brought anvils, gravestones, wigs, steam engines, girdles and entire kit-houses into people's homes across America.

From the 103rd-floor Skydeck, Lake Michigan looked like an ocean and the city's vast grid of streets were as plain as a map with little silver glints of river and canal, and tiny toy railroads snaking away to the prairies. The other giants of the skyscraper world looked tiny in comparison—including the John Hancock building, which, at 100 storeys, is no skyscraping slouch. Then my absorption in the newfangled world of steel and glass was interrupted by the oldfangled world of straw hats and white bonnets. A family of Amish folk were wandering around the Skydeck looking totally dumbfounded, eyes wide open with childish wonder. The men had Abraham Lincolnesque long pointy beards and bowl haircuts, while the women—all of the women—were wearing aprons. Both the men's and the women's clothes were held together by pins. I'd seen the film *Witness*, so I knew that they couldn't use buttons because they are deemed a 'modern convenience'. It seems soap and deodorant are also deemed a modern convenience, because boy oh boy did they smell. This family may well have scorned buttons and soap, but there was one modern convenience they were more than happy to fully embrace. Dad was slurping on a McDonalds thick shake while the kids were fighting over a bag of McNuggets and fries.

Bob told me that it would take 30 minutes to ride back to his place. It took me more than an hour. But that was because the grid layout of the city was so ridiculously easy to follow that I somehow managed to get lost. When I got back Bob was already home from school and busily pulling apart a bike in his 'workshop'. 'I do most of my bike repairs here,' Bob said as he sipped a beer. He certainly had plenty of space. Bob's workshop was out the front of the apartment on the footpath. Sorry, in America it's a sidewalk. Or a pavement if you're English. I love the fact that even though Americans, English and Australians speak the same language we can have three different names for the same thing.

When I came back from the dunny, I mean the loo, I mean the john, Bob was chatting to his 'friend' Bruce, who went to the liquor store at the same time every day to buy his two cans of beer. 'All the drunks in the area know me,' Bob said, 'because they pass me on the way to the liquor shop.' Most of Bob's 'friends' were, as Bob called them, 'black dudes'.

'They love me,' Bob grinned. 'Because I chat to them and buy them a beer now and again.'

'Hey Bob, you got a dollar?'

This was Robert who, according to Bruce, was 'as old as shit' and 'as dumb as shit'. Robert did look a bit worse for wear. 'See his fingers?' Bruce chuckled, pointing to Robert's lack of fingers on one hand. 'He got 'em stuck to a pole.' Robert had flaked out drunk on the street one night in the middle of the bitterly cold Chicago winter and had tried to get up by grabbing a pole. His hand froze against the post and three fingers had to be amputated to get him off.

I asked Bob to take me to an authentic Chicagoan restaurant for dinner, so we got in his truck and drove to Azteca Tacos Restaurant in Little Mexico. It was at least very authentic Mexican. The restaurant was hot and steamy and the tables and chairs were cheap and tatty. Bob ordered in Spanish. 'No one speaks English here,' he shrugged. We were served enough food for four people—or the immense lady who was the only other diner. As we gorged on homemade guacamole and corn chips, beans, rice, fajitas and an entire fish cooked in lime juice, I asked Bob about Chicago's notorious crime rate.

'We're currently ranked number three for murders,' Bob said proudly. 'After Miami and Orlando.'

Chicago did make it to number one in 2001, Bob told me, but the mayor wasn't happy so he demanded that there be a recount on the basis that the 9/11 deaths should have been included in the New York figures.

'Are there many gangs around this area?' I asked Bob.

'A few, but Southside is where most of the crazy-ass ghetto motherfuckers are.'

After dinner we drove back to Bob's, jumped on the bikes and went for a ride to see some crazy-ass ghetto motherfuckers. Southside is the 'The Black Metropolis' of Chicago and, with an African–American population of around 90 per cent, a couple of whiteys on pushbikes stood out somewhat. It also became quite obvious that we were entering a dodgy part of town. Monstrous concrete housing blocks covered in graffiti loomed over streets littered with abandoned cars, old refrigerators and burnt-out couches.

There was some serious loitering going on, including kids walking in the middle of the busy road while cars swerved around them. 'They've got such a shitty life,' Bob explained. 'That walking on the road is just a way of saying "fuck you" to everyone.' Most of the kids were doing the whole hip-hop look, i.e. they looked as if they were wearing their older (and much larger) brother's clothes.

'Don't look at them,' Bob said gravely. 'And whatever you do, don't stop!'

'Is it safe?' I asked warily.

'Not really. Friends say I'm crazy riding through here,' Bob said matter-of-factly. 'I had a bottle thrown at me once.'

I stared at Bob in dismay.

'They've got those now, though.' Bob pointed to a pole on the corner with a blue flashing light on top. The flashing poles were set up on just about every corner and Bob explained that these recently installed anti-crime cameras were capable of pinpointing gunshot sounds, calculating where the shots were fired, and pointing and zooming the cameras in the direction of the shots within a two-block radius. That's all very well, I thought, but all it meant was that the police would get some nice footage of a bullet passing through my head.

When we got back, I finally met Bob's flatmate Carl, who was an African–American but not, Bob assured me, a crazy-ass ghetto motherfucker. Carl was heading out to a friend's buck's party. 'We don't call it that!' Carl chuckled. 'We call it a bachelor party. A buck in America is a BIGGGG black man!'

I felt a little guilty about appropriating the couch when Carl told me that his good friend Chuck from out of town was also staying the night. 'It's okay, he'll sleep on the Lazy Boy,' Carl shrugged.

Carl wobbled in at three in the morning with a tottering Chuck in tow. I offered Carl's friend the much more commodious couch because Chuck was one hell of a buck. He was about twice the size of the Lazy Boy lounger. He declined my offer, but although he had to lie on a 45-degree angle with his feet dangling off the end, he looked surprisingly comfortable. If Chuck had actually remembered his night's sleep, he'd probably have given the Lazy Boy a good score on LazyBoySurfing.com. Chuck's snooze did, however, have a knock-on effect on the below-average score I gave Bob's couch:

Couch rating: 7½/10

Pro: Bob's long and capacious couch

Con: Chuck's long and cacophonous snoring

Everything in America is big. I spent most of the day surrounded by immensity. In the morning I went to a colossal laundromat where huge black ladies were throwing enormous pairs of underpants into gargantuan washing machines. The laundromat had 82 washing machines and 68 dryers (I was a little bored, so I counted them all). There were also six large-screen televisions playing former super-sized and now super-rich Oprah.

After washing my normal-sized underpants I rode into town to the Field Museum of Natural History, which was so big that I spent three hours wandering around before I even got out of the stuffed-birds-in-glass-cases section. The museum has 6 acres of display area and more than 20 million exhibits. Besides 65-million-year-old Sue, 'The biggest and most complete Tyrannosaurus Rex ever found', which was in the entrance foyer of the museum, all I saw were lots of blue-footed boobys, duck-billed flibbets and an impressive bugeranus.

After the birds I only had enough time to quickly stampede through the jungles of Africa and skip around the totem poles of Native America, because I was meeting Bob for a beer by the shore of Lake Michigan. We met at the front of the Adler Planetarium, which was easy to locate with its domed roof bulging like a blister on a fingertip at the end of a peninsula reaching into the lake.

Getting down to the shore wasn't so easy, though. A belting wind coming off the lake kept forcing us back. The eye-watering gale was so strong that it was creating 2-metre high waves on the lake. When I could actually see through my teary eyes, the view was spectacular. Ranks of huge, granite skyscrapers soared skywards and towered over Lake Michigan, which stretched out steel-grey and steel-cold like a Chicago skyscraper turned on its side.

It was taking all my strength to stay upright against the buffeting wind. 'This is great, isn't it?' Bob squealed over the shrieking wind. Even the beer in my can was swirling around as if in a storm.

'Yeah, fantastic,' I hollered back.

We lasted three minutes before we gave up and jumped back on the bikes.

Bob rode like a maniac through the Gotham-like business district, weaving in and out of traffic, nipping in front of buses and playing chicken with taxis. We zoomed past the gleaming-white Wrigley Building (as in the chewing gum company), zipped past the oddly striking *Tribune* building and broke the two-minute mile down the Magnificent Mile, which glittered like most places where great wealth is spent and displayed.

By the time we reached the John Hancock building, I had learnt three important facts: Chicago's name comes from a local Indian language meaning 'skunk', Chicago produced the world's first pinball machine, and Rudolph the Red-Nosed Reindeer is a Chicago native because a copywriter from a local department store created him for one of its promotions.

We made our way up to the Observatory Bar on the 94th floor of the John Hancock Building, but we didn't stay long. Bob, sounding very much like Jake Elwood, said: 'We're not staying here. The fuckin' beers are ten dollars!'

On the way home to Bob's we stopped at a super-sized supermarket so I could buy the ingredients to make a risotto. I certainly knew I was in America when we walked down an entire aisle devoted to Jell-O.

'Shall I get enough food for Carl and Jason as well?' I asked Bob while I searched for a packet of risotto rice that wasn't 'ready-to-serve, looks-just-like-vomit premixed risotto'.

'Jason doesn't do dinner,' Bob explained drily.

I was yet to meet Jason. I'd only heard him coming in late at night banging doors and stumbling about in the kitchen.

'There's something going on with him,' Bob said. 'He gets trashed just about every night. I don't know whether to be annoyed or worried.'

Like all good Americans, Bob and Carl ate their dinner on the couch in front of the TV. But totally unlike all other good Americans, they didn't have cable. 'We're probably the only people in America without it,' Bob said. 'Even poor white trash have cable.' While Bob and Carl watched some political news show, I flicked through the *Chicago Tribune*. Hidden away on page seven, next to a story about a cat caught up in a tree, was the headline: 'America's population about to reach 300 million'. I pointed out the small article to Bob, who said that when America's population reached 250 million, the entire country had celebrated and the papers were filled with pictures of America's 250 millionth resident: a nice white American baby from somewhere like Idaho. The *Tribune* article pointed out that the 300 millionth American would most likely be born in Los Angeles to a Mexican mother, or was even more likely to be a Mexican walking across the border.

At around 12 per cent of the population, the Mexicans now made up the largest group of US immigrants from a single country. The census bureau predicted that by 2050 Mexicans (and other Hispanics) will make up more than 25 per cent of America's population.

'I'm not racist and my best friend is Mexican,' said Bob when I read him the figures. 'But they have to do something about all the Mexicans pouring in or this country's gonna burst.'

'Maybe we could send them to Australia,' Carl said. 'You've got plenty of space.'

One of the major drawbacks of couch surfing is that you have to wait till everyone in the house goes to bed before you can jump in yours. There's also the danger that you could surprise the hell out of someone who doesn't know you're there. After three days I finally met Bob's brother Jason when he staggered in and almost fell on top of me. I was just as surprised as he was, not least because with his long unkempt hair and dimple-less smile, he looked nothing like his clean-cut brother.

'Whoth HELL are you?' he slurred while rocking from side to side.

'I'm Brian from Australia.'

Jason stared hard at me for a minute. 'Right.'

He then collapsed in a heap on the floor.

'Let's go canoeing and drinking!' Bob urged excitedly. Bob had a day off work, so we jumped in his 'truck' and drove south for an hour to Bob's hometown of Elgin to pick up his canoe. I would also get the chance to notch up another couch, because we were going to stay at Bob's mum's house.

Not long after leaving the sprawling suburbs of Chicago, we were rolling through a quintessential mid-western farming landscape with low wooded hills, green pastures, cornfields, large farmhouses and even larger barns. On the way into Elgin we picked up 21 Buds: a box of twenty bottles of Bud Light, plus Bob's friend Bud. 'Bud doesn't work,' Bob told me. 'He's white trash and he lives with his drunk dad.'

After picking up our collection of Buds, we grabbed Bob's large aluminum canoe and a fold-up bike from his mum's house. She lived in a street full of grandiose houses with neat lawns and oversized American cars parked in the driveway. Bob's dad had passed away and his mum was visiting her sister, so we had the house to ourselves.

Not far out of Elgin we turned off the main road—which was called Sleepy Hollow Road—and drove deep into a forest of silver maples, sycamores and willow trees before stopping right on the edge of the slow-moving Kishwaukee River.

It was a perfect day for a paddle. And to drink beer, Bob and Bud assured me. Although the day was cool, the sun was warm and the only sounds were the gentle gurgle of the river and the frequent click and hiss as Bob and Bud opened another bottle of beer. While we floated merrily down the stream, Bob and Bud began talking about their old school friends. 'Hank was making five thousand dollars a week selling grass, then he went on to crack cocaine and now he's fucked,' Bob said.

Bud had asked another old school friend Ryan to come canoeing with us, but he couldn't because he had an AA meeting. 'He's the funniest guy after a few beers,' Bud said. 'But by his seventh beer he just sits and stares at you, then pisses himself. He's pissed on all his friend's couches.'

'Remind me not to couch surf with him,' I said musingly.

'Everyone had enough of finding their couch wet and smelly,' Bud continued. 'So at a party one night we decided to get him back. When he collapsed drunk in the backyard, six of us pissed on him.'

For long periods we sat in silence simply enjoying the view. Now and again Bob or Bud would point out local fauna including geese, beavers, herons, kingfishers and a particularly quiet screeching owl.

With all the beer being consumed, Bob and Bud kept having to stand up to pee out of the canoe. At one point Bob was letting loose a rather impressive stream into the river when we floated around a bend into the full view of a couple fishing on the bank. 'You better put that little worm away or I'll put it on my hook,' the woman called out cheerfully.

Three and a half hours—and seventeen bottles of beer—later we came to a stop at a deserted picnic area. I'd had three beers while Bob and Bud had downed seven each. 'I'll be back real soon,' said Bob before he headed off on the clunky-looking fold-out bike to get the car. I grabbed a beer and settled in for a long wait, but Bob was back in twenty minutes. We'd basically done a big loop and the car was only 2 miles away.

After dropping off Bud, we picked up a famous Chicago deep-dish pizza from Pappa Saverio's Chicago Deep Dish Pizza House. When we got back to the house with the ominous-sounding Meat Locker Pizza and opened the box, I burst out laughing. It wasn't a pizza. It was a 10-centimetre high monolith of food with thick geological layers of cheese, tomatoes, minced beef, piles of bacon, more cheese, salami, onion, ham and a thick crust stuffed with even more cheese. 'This should be called a Cholesterol Locker!' I chuckled. The pizza was cut into eight slices, but I was full after just one. I had to force myself to have a second slice. I was so bloated that I couldn't get off the couch, so it was lucky it was also my bed. Mind you, I could have chosen another one. There were four couches in three separate living areas. Before I considered a move, however, I had a question for Bob. 'Has Ryan pissed on any of them?'

On the way back to the city we stopped and picked up 300 beers. Bob was throwing a party at his apartment and he was providing two kegs of beer. 'What's the party for?' I asked as we loaded the kegs into the back of the truck.

'To try and get laid, man,' Bob enthused. 'Why else would anyone throw a party?'

'There's no theme or anything then?'

'Sort of,' Bob said. 'It's a pre-Halloween party.'

Halloween was still more than three weeks away.

Bob was expecting around 80 beer-drinking friends to his pre-Halloween party. 'It's mostly thirty-year-old school teachers, a few hicks from Elgin and a couple of hipsters,' Bob said.

We spent most of the afternoon stringing up faux cobwebs, hiding ghoul faces in the toilet and placing black candles into dark corners. Then Bob turned one of the kegs, rather impressively I thought, into a skeleton with the beer hose coming out of its mouth and its arm as the pump. Bob dressed up in a very suave 70s chocolate-brown three-piece pinstriped suit with magnificently wide lapels and even wider flares. He topped off his dashing ensemble with a super-wide brown- and cream-striped tie and big 70s sunglasses.

Most of the party guests, and a few vampires and ghouls, had turned up by nine o'clock and by ten the party was in full swing. The DJ blasted out '60s and 70s underground funk' and the lounge room heaved with dancing demons. The party was like the United Nations as I chatted with folk from France, Germany, Bangladesh, Mexico, Puerto Rico, Argentina, Morocco and a rather intoxicated fellow who wasn't quite sure where he was from. He started to tell me the story four times. 'I was in Dubai and . . .' was as much as I got out of him before he fell asleep on the couch. Like a protective father, I'd been hanging around the couch making sure no one spilled any beer or cigarette ash on my bed.

Bob was the life of party as he danced, flirted and threw himself into heated and deeply analytical arguments about politics. 'The Democrats are fuckers,' bellowed one of Bob's friends.

'Yeah, but we have to vote for one of them,' Bob argued. 'And the Republicans are a lot bigger fuckers.'

Bob was in the middle of another political debate when his best friend Marco interrupted. 'You need to go to the front door,' he said. 'There's a gang of hoods who say they're coming into the party.'

The 'gang of hoods' was four twenty-something Puerto Ricans and one of them claimed that they could come into the party because his mum owned the building. Bob politely told them to shove off.

Five minutes later there was a piercing scream from the street and moments later a couple stumbled up the stairs. The girl, who was whimpering in shock, had blood pouring out from her nose. They had just arrived at the party and the hoods had jumped on the girl's boyfriend and began beating him. She tried to drag one of them off and he swung around and hit her in the face. Bob shouted something about 'dirty motherfuckers' then, looking fervidly around the room, grabbed a frying pan and ran downstairs. Carl and Marco bolted out after him—minus any large cooking implements.

Almost the entire party (except the drunk Dubai fellow) raced to the window to see a bellowing Bob tearing towards the hoods as they clambered into their old brown Chevy

Caprice. They were all in the car except one, who turned around and reached into his jacket.

'He's got a gun!' someone gasped.

The entire party dropped to the floor and I spun around to see dozens of people feverishly stabbing out 911 on their mobile phones.

'It's okay, he doesn't have a gun,' someone else yelled. 'And he's getting in the car.'

No he wasn't. Bob was dragging him out of the passenger window. Everyone in the party was now watching what looked like a scene from the TV series *Mod Squad*. Bob in his pinstripe suit and glasses was wildly punching through the window of the old brown Chevy while 70s funk music was still playing loudly in the background. The mild-mannered real estate agent Marco had pulled another hood from the car and was sitting on top of him and punching the now squealing gang member in the side of the head.

Meanwhile the driver decided that he'd had enough and he was getting out of there. He would have too, if he hadn't hit the accelerator too hard and careered into the side of a parked Volkswagen then slammed into the side of a dumpster. Carl was standing behind the car now, so he had nowhere to go. Well, that's what we all thought until the car suddenly reversed and thundered into Carl, throwing him into a sprawling heap on the road.

A bunch of us ran downstairs and by the time we got to the street a wailing police car with lights ablaze was pulling up in front of the Chevy. Now it was really like a TV police drama as two police officers jumped out and, with accompanying shouting and gesturing, pointed their guns at the hoods. Within a few minutes two more police cars and six more police officers were at the scene, and bundling the hoods into police cars.

Carl was still lying on the road and clutching his leg in pain. Then I saw why. A broken bone was poking out of his trousers. 'I don't want an ambulance,' Carl moaned. An ambulance was quickly on the scene because there was a hospital two doors up from Bob's place. 'I don't want to pay for the ambulance. I can walk there,' Carl said, trying to get up. Not surprisingly, the ambulance officer wouldn't let him move and hoisted him into the back of the ambulance for the 50-metre drive up the road. You have to hand it to the Americans, though, they're great motivators. What other country has a health system that motivates people with broken legs to get back on their feet straightaway?

I found Bob sitting on the back of his truck nursing a bleeding finger. 'The fucker tried to chew it off,' he sniffed as he showed me the large gash on his finger.

The party fizzled out rather abruptly after that brief interlude of pandemonium. I didn't mind, though. After I'd thrown Mr Dubai off the couch, I was in bed by 2.30.

'Thanks for organising the gang violence last night,' I said to Bob as we drove to the airport.

'You did tell me that you wanted to get to know the locals,' Bob said with a wry smile.

'Do you normally have trouble with the gangs?' I asked.

'Nothing like this has ever happened to us before,' Bob said. 'The gangs don't usually hassle us, they just fight other gangs.' The police told Bob that the gang was part of the Young Latino Cobras (which is not to be confused with the Spanish Insane Cobras).

'They have all sorts of weird-ass names,' Bob said. Other weird-ass Chicago gang names include the Looney Toon Crew, the Krazy Getdown Boys and The Insane Popes.

When I spoke to Bob a few months later, he'd just been talking to a friend who he hadn't seen since the fateful night. His friend said, 'The last time I saw you, you were running out the door with a frying pan in your hand screaming bloody fucking murder!' Until then, Bob had forgotten all about his choice of weapon, which had mysteriously vanished.

'My brother and I have been speculating ever since that night,' Bob told me, 'wondering what kind of asshole steals a frying pan from a party.'

CANADA

9

'On the weekends I let my beard grow, fix cars, cut down trees, drink beer and get out of control with my buddies.'
Jeremy Ribbinck, 27, Kitchener, Canada
CouchSurfing.com

You may very well wonder why I chose Kitchener as my Canadian couch-surfing destination. I could have elected to surf in vibrant Toronto, the centre of Canadian culture and media; or rugged Calgary, nestled in the foothills of the Rocky Mountains; or European-flavoured Québec City, bristling with historic buildings; or even charming Montreal with its old-world atmosphere. The couch-surfing hosts of Kitchener weren't exactly glowing with praise:

Kitchener really isn't all that great I must admit but hey, for all you odd birds who want to come here—my place is open. :)
Natasha, 27

> I would love for you to come, as I love meeting travellers, but I'm warning you that there is absolutely NOTHING to do in this poor excuse for a town.
> Caroline, 23

But despite the locals' lack of enthusiasm, there were two things that drew me to this somewhat nondescript provisional city in the middle of nowhere: sausages and beer. Kitchener is home to the second largest Oktoberfest in the world after Munich and my visit just happened to coincide with the week-long celebrations. Caroline might have said that there was absolutely nothing to do in Kitchener, but she obviously wasn't a fan of doing the chicken dance and eating Kartofelpuffers.

And anyway, Kitchener couldn't possibly be that bad. After all, it's by no means the only city that gets a bad rap from its own residents. Even my own beloved country has its mud-slinging critics:

> I live in Canberra, which is the capital of Australia, but unfortunately it's a really really boring city and there's stuff all to do.
> Lynn, 22

Peter from Telford in Shropshire, UK, was a bit more blunt:

> This town is a shithole, but maybe you like visiting shitholes.

I can't imagine many couch requests pouring in for Hutchinson, Kansas, either:

> I have lived here my entire life and it sucks. Hutch is a trash hole infested with lazy non-working money sucking users.
> Ben, 24

Then again, some aspersions are probably close to the truth:

> Welcome to Hell
> Firas, 38
> Baghdad, Iraq

Although most of the couch-surfers in Kitchener were a bit more complimentary about their town, there really didn't seem to be much to do if some of the hosts' interests were anything to go by. I didn't even understand what Susan's list meant:

> Interests: transpersonal and intrapersonal psychological phenomena

At least 32-year-old Ryan liked to mix it up a bit:

> Interests: dancing in grocery stores late at night (when they play the really good music), television and food (especially baked goods)

No one listed their interests as sausages and beer, but 27-year-old Jeremy's weekend pursuits of beard-growing, car-fixing, tree-cutting and beer-drinking sounded good to me.

When I emailed Jeremy to request his couch he wrote back with a detailed itinerary mapped out for me. He also wrote:

> *I am a bit of a con man, so my personality may be less interesting than it appears. I also don't know if I am fit to represent Canada on the world stage. I am currently half-drunk and reek of strippers so if this makes no sense say so and I will try again later :)*

Jeremy had kindly offered to pick me up from Toronto airport, two hours east of Kitchener, and when I finally found him in the crowded arrivals hall I said: 'Sorry, I didn't recognise you with a shirt on.' In his couch surfing profile picture Jeremy is striking a bronzed Adonis-on-the-beach pose.

We trudged to the furthest point in the car park past hundreds of vacant car spaces till we stopped at a lone red beaten-up Volkswagen hatch. 'I took out the starter motor,' Jeremy said. 'I had to drive around till I found a car space on an incline, so I can roll-start it.'

Jeremy seemed quiet and a bit shy, particularly after being with boisterous Bob and his friends. I've met a lot of Canadians in my travels and, although they are often incredibly friendly, they are mostly a subdued lot. I guess that when you live next door to a brash and loud neighbour all your life you are always vulnerable to looking and acting a bit boring in comparison. After only five minutes in the car Jeremy told me that Canadians don't like Americans. 'American culture rules our lives,' he said. 'We're more interested in them than our own country sometimes. There is more on the news about US politics than there is on Canadian politics.'

'That's because American politicians like to start big important wars and give big important speeches about saving the world from terrorists,' I said.

'We know everything about the States, but they know absolutely nothing about us,' he continued. 'On a TV show last week a Canadian comedian walked through the streets of a US city collecting donations. He told them that because of global warming the Canadian parliamentary igloos were melting, so they needed money to rebuild them. Almost every person he asked said that it was very sad and gave him some money.'

Not long after leaving the airport we were driving through rolling green farmland and cornfields. It looked just like America. Jeremy was brought up on a cattle farm an hour out of Kitchener and his parents, who still lived there, were now retired and leased the land to another farmer. The only livestock they had left was their pet horse.

We stopped at the farm because Jeremy wanted to 'find' a starter motor. His parents' two-storey red brick farmhouse was on top of the biggest hill in the county and was surrounded by giant oaks and elms (Jeremy told me that in winter up to 50 cars park on the side of road and use the hill to go sledding). We drove past the house and straight into the barn. Inside, amongst a collection of rusted farming equipment and a couple of bales of hay, were five old Volkswagens in various stages of disrepair. 'I keep all my old cars,' Jeremy said. 'I've had seven Volkswagens and I've kept them all for spare parts.'

After pulling out a considerably corroded starter motor from one of the considerably corroded cars, Jeremy crawled underneath his current car and started bashing things. I stood back as sparks flew out from the top and bottom of the engine. 'Don't worry!' Jeremy barked over the loud cracking noise. 'I'm always fixing things.' I stood back a little further when he told me that the week before, while trying to install a dimmer light in his lounge room, he zapped himself and almost set the flat on fire.

After almost two hours during which Jeremy had tried three different starter motors from three different cars, we drove off again without one. Twenty minutes later there was an incredibly loud clicking noise from the engine and we pulled over into the car park of The Beer Store (they have a huge sign with a photo of a glass of beer on it just in case you're a little confused about what they sell).

'Can you buy rum or vodka at The Beer Store?' I asked while we waited for Jeremy's friend Jeff to pick us up.

'No, you have to get that at The Liquor Store,' Jeremy explained.

He wasn't making it up. The government runs both 'stores' and they are the only place that you can buy beer or liquor (and never the twain shall meet).

Jeff arrived in a new sleek black Pontiac. 'For God's sake buy a decent car,' Jeff said, shaking his head. 'Jeremy's cars break down at last twice a week,' Jeff remarked smugly as he loaded my bags into the boot (or trunk as the Americans—sorry I mean Canadians—say).

Jeff looked even more clean-cut than Jeremy and it only took him two minutes to mention Americans. 'Do Australians hate Americans as much as we do?' he asked as we drove through the outskirts of Kitchener.

It also took Jeremy only two minutes to sum up everything there was to say about Kitchener. Set between Lake Eyrie and Lake Ontario, the city has a population just over 200 000 and is the home of Schneider Foods, which is famous all across Canada for its sausages.

Kitchener looked just like an American city, but neater. We drove past neat conservative houses, neat conservative shops, neat conservative people and the neatest lawns I've ever seen. Every blade of grass was mowed to perfection. Most houses also had Halloween decorations strung up on their porches and pumpkin heads in the garden. 'Isn't Halloween American?' I asked.

'That's why we love it,' said Jeremy sardonically.

Jeremy lived close to the city centre and he worked in a building that was, at all of eight storeys, the city's tallest. He told me what he did for a job and I nodded and said, 'Oh, yeah.' I knew what he'd said, but I still had no idea what he did. He worked in the IT department of MCAP—the largest independent mortgage lender in Canada—where he 'upgraded the underwriter's software compatibility'. He also did casual lumberjacking on Saturdays.

Jeremy lived in a neat (I'm sorry, I have to stop saying neat, but I just can't help myself) one-bedroom apartment with his cat Bentley and a very impressive couch. The couch folded out to a queen-size futon bed. Not long after Jeremy had showered and cleaned off the grease a crowd of people, including Jeremy's girlfriend Danika, arrived in a convoy of taxis en route to the Oktoberfest festival.

Kitchener does have a legitimate claim to hold 'Canada's Great Bavarian Festival' because up until 1916 Kitchener was called Berlin (they didn't want to be associated with those nasty Germans after the war) and more than 25 per cent of the population have German heritage. The festival began in 1969 and now attracts more than 700 000 visitors to such very German venues as the Heidelberg Haus, Altes Muenchen Haus, Hubertushaus, Oberkrainer Haus, Ruedesheimer Garten and the Schwaben Club. We were heading to the very un-German sounding Queensmount Ice Skating Arena for a Rocktoberfest event. There were also events called Hip-Hoptoberfest featuring Canadian hip-hop acts, Pridetoberfest celebrating the Gay Pride of Kitchener, and Dogtoberfest with games and competitions for families with dogs.

'There are lots of ice-hockey rinks in Canada,' Jeremy told me as we marched towards the entrance. 'They outnumber hospitals three to one.'

I had no doubt the Canadians took their ice-hockey rinks seriously. Two stern-faced security guards performed a methodical and ponderous examination of my bag and its contents before I even stepped inside. When I did get inside, however, I have to say I was suitably impressed. The ice-skating rink, minus the ice, had been totally transformed into an authentic German beer hall, complete with long trestle tables lined with fellows wearing lederhosen and Bavarian felt hats and frauleins in dirndls and plaits. Up on the stage Walter Ostanek, the 70-year-old Polka King (and winner of five Canadian Grammys for Best Polka Player, Jeremy told me), was bouncing around doing the chicken dance. This really was just like a Bavarian beer festival and I couldn't wait to get to the bar and grab myself a large frosty stein of German beer.

Except that I did have to wait and they didn't have any German beer. There was a queue just to get to the very orderly queue at the bar, which was being closely guarded by two security gorillas in bright yellow shirts. That's when I realised that the security men outnumbered the drinkers two to one.

When I did get to the bar, they seemed to be only serving Molsen in pathetically small white plastic cups. 'Do you have any German beer?' I asked.

'Yes, we have Heineken,' the barmaid said cheerfully.

'Um, Heineken is Dutch.'

'Same thing,' she chirped.

I grabbed my great Bavarian plastic cup of Canadian Molsen and joined the rest of the group who had procured a table near the queue for the bar. I looked around and spotted lots of large signs being closely guarded by the army of yellow-clad security buffoons.

NO LEANING OR STANDING ON
TABLES AND CHAIRS

DRESS CODE IN
EFFECT—CLEAN LOOKING APPAREL ONLY

NO ALCOHOL BEYOND THIS POINT

NO SMOKING

NO RUNNING

They could have had a 'NO HAVING FUN' sign and it wouldn't have surprised me. I went up on to the dance floor for a bit of polka-ing with Danika's cousin Karen and as we passed a group of lads one dropped down onto the dance floor to do the worm. Twenty seconds later three security guards surrounded him, ordering him to 'calm down.'

'Canadians are a bit paranoid,' Karen told me.

Back at our table the conversation turned to couch surfing. I asked Jeremy if he'd had any other couch-surfing experiences.

'I've had two German girls stay, but that's it,' Jeremy said. 'Kitchener isn't really a tourist hotspot.'

'They were probably lost,' said Jeff.

Jeremy had also couch-surfed his way down to Florida. 'I stayed with two girls in Florida and there was a guy from New York already couch surfing there,' Jeremy said. 'He was only supposed to stay for five days, but he'd been surfing their couch for three months. The girls were too nice to ask him to leave.'

By late in the evening most people were drunk and rowdy. Jeff was certainly drunk enough. He was standing by the dance floor with his arm around a cute girl when a huge bloke walked up. Jeff introduced himself, then said 'Who are you?'

'I'm her boyfriend,' the huge bloke grunted.

Jeff was probably only using the girl for support because we had to almost carry him out when we left. Six of us all piled into Karen's tiny car and, after dropping off a very tall girl who had been lying across our legs in the back seat, we stopped at a neat (stop it!) house in somewhere called Hagersville. Karen had three small children, but they were at their father's house for the weekend. That was a good thing because, boy, did we make a ruckus. As we drank bottles of overtly sweet vodka/pop mix I played Karen's guitar and belted out some tunes while Jeff belted out the contents of his stomach into the toilet.

Once Jeff had finished his yodelling, Jeremy carried him upstairs to bed. Well, when I say 'bed', it was actually more of a cot than a bed. Jeff's feet were hanging over the edge of Karen's baby daughter's bed, which came complete with a Princess Jasmine quilt and Snow White pillow. Jeff was just like a little baby, too: He was gurgling, he had vomit in his hair, he couldn't talk and he couldn't walk.

When I finally crawled into bed (I got the matching Cinderella quilt and pillow set), Karen tucked me in and said, 'I'll leave the Princess Belle light on in case you get scared'.

Late the next morning we had a oh-my-head-hurts big greasy fry-up breakfast at Fireside Family Restaurant & Grill. As I hoed into my mountain of food I asked, 'Is there any "Canadian" cuisine?'

There was an awkward pause.

'Hamburgers?' Jeff suggested.

'Um, I'm pretty sure they're not Canadian,' Danika said.

'I know,' Jeff beamed. 'Bacon and eggs!'

After much deliberation everyone decided that there was probably only one thing that could be classed as Canadian cuisine.

'Maple syrup,' Jeremy said. 'I think that's it.'

After picking up Jeremy's car from The House of Beer (and after Jeremy bashed a few things around in the engine), we drove out to see some Indians on the warpath. Not far from Jeremy's parents' farm was the Six Nations of the Grand River Indian reserve. All of the six nations—Mohawk, Cayuga, Oneida, Onondaga, Seneca and Tuscarora—were in the middle of a major uprising over a land claim dispute. The Indians helped fight the British in 1784, so the government gave them all the land for six miles on either side of the Grand River. There were only a few hundred Indians, so they said it was too big and gave it back to the government. Two hundred years later, and now with a population of more than 20 000, they decided they wanted their prime real estate back. In the past few months they'd gone to all the big houses on the riverfront and handed them eviction notices. They had also taken over a subdivision for a new residential development, blocked major roads and were throwing bottles at cars and people.

'It doesn't matter if they throw bottles at this car,' Jeremy shrugged as we drove into the residential development. There wasn't much sign of the uprising, though. The restless natives had hoisted their protest flags up next to the 'Display Suites Now Open' flags and a group of non-bottle-throwing Indians in jeans and T-shirts were milling about the entrance, but that was about it.

I could tell when we'd entered the reservation. We drove past the 'Red Indian Mini Mart' and a billboard for 'Mohawk Flooring—Check out our lamination'. The most obvious indication that we were in the reservation, however, was the large blinking neon signs advertising discount cigarettes. Because the Indians don't have to pay tax, selling cheap cigarettes is their biggest source of income. We drove through the reservation's main 'town', which had two totem poles, one tipi and a large drive-thru cigarette shop called Red Indian Cigarette Heaven. The rest of the town was made up of modern houses with large American 'trucks' parked in the driveways.

'They also make money from stealing cars,' Jeremy said when I commented that the locals seemed to be doing all right from selling cigarettes. 'People find their cars a week later burned out in a field and stripped of parts,' he explained.

As we drove out of the reservation we passed a truck abandoned on the edge of the road. Painted on the side of the truck in big red letters was: 'YOU STEAL OUR LAND SO WE STEAL YOUR TRUCK'.

Imagine inviting a stranger you'd only met the day before to your family's Christmas dinner. That's essentially what Jeremy had done when he invited me to join his immediate family for Thanksgiving dinner. As with Juan's family barbecue, I was amazed that these kind couch-surfing folk didn't think anything of inviting a virtual stranger to such an intimate family occasion.

Even though Jeremy's family were incredibly welcoming when I arrived at the farmhouse, I did still feel a little awkward about intruding into their Thanksgiving celebrations. Well, everyone made me feel welcome except for Jeremy's older brother Rob. When I said hello to him, he just grunted at me. Everyone was in the living room, including Jeremy's mum and dad Janey and Albert, brother Steve and his wife and three kids (to three different fathers, Jeremy told me when I commented how different they all looked) and Rob the grunter.

We had only sat down for a few minutes when we were ushered into the dining room, which had large windows affording spectacular views of the surrounding hills. The table was already laden with huge bowls of mashed turnip, green beans, red cabbage, mashed potato, sweet potatoes, stewed apple, cranberry sauce and a giant jug of gravy. There was a round of applause as Janey brought out a massive roast turkey, which Albert dutifully carved up, and by the time my plate had completed its tour of the table I had a mountain of food.

I was sitting next to Albert, who was quick to tell me that the first Canadian Thanksgiving preceded the American

Thanksgiving by 40 years (Canada's first Thanksgiving was in 1578). 'It's a celebration of being thankful for what one has and the bounty of the previous year,' Albert said. Rob wasn't being very thankful, though. He didn't even look up from his food when Albert raised his glass to propose a toast.

After our somewhat gluttonous feast, the family kept chattering away while I struggled to stay awake. I was not just tired. I'd picked up a dose of CSFS (Couch Surfing Fatigue Syndrome). I was trying really hard to stay awake, but my eyes kept drooping and my head kept dropping, then snapping back up again. Finally, after a considerable struggle with the weight of my eyelids, I dozed off.

I woke with a fright as a huge plate of pumpkin pie was plonked down in front of me. How long had I been asleep? Thirty seconds or ten minutes? Rob seemed to be the only one who'd noticed that I'd nodded off, but he wasn't talking to anyone so I was okay.

As soon as Rob finished his dessert he said 'I gotta go', stood up and left. He hadn't said a word the entire meal. We all sat around the table for a while after dinner, but I think that was mainly because we were all too bloated to get up out of our seats.

'Rob doesn't say much,' I said to Jeremy on the drive back to his place.

'Talking to him is like pulling teeth,' Jeremy said. 'And I haven't seen him for four months!'

'Does he have a girlfriend or a wife?' I asked.

'No, he's gay. Everyone in the family is fine about it, but he's not.'

'When did he come out?'

'He told my parents when he was nineteen, but Steve and I didn't find out until a few years later. We only found out because when Steve was leaving home he was having a heated argument with Mom about whether he was sleeping with the girl he was moving in with. He said: "She's just a friend. What about Rob? He lives with two girls and you never hassle him." "That's because the two girls are lesbians and Rob is gay," Mum said.'

When I told Jeff that I was planning to go to Niagara Falls, he told me to 'push all the American tourists over'. There was one small problem with his request. I couldn't see any American tourists. Or any other kind of tourist for that matter. Niagara Falls might get 18 million visitors a year, but I imagine not many of them get there via the three-hour local bus service from downtown Kitchener.

The North Niagara Bus Terminal was in the middle of several blocks of derelict buildings on the edge of town and I had to walk through the somewhat shabby suburbs to get to the falls. At least they were easy to find: I just headed for the source of the rising mist that was drifting languidly over the town.

Oscar Wilde described the falls as 'simply a vast amount of water going the wrong way over some unnecessary rocks', but I can't see how he couldn't have been even a little impressed. Once I had conquered my inexplicable desire to hurl myself over the railings, I stood watching the cascade for ages, as if hypnotised. It was only after the gushing gallons prompted a very urgent desire to pee that I was able to drag myself away.

I eventually found the tourists. They were all joining me in wearing identical bright-blue plastic ponchos on the Maid of the Mist boat tour. As the boat approached Horseshoe Falls the buildings above faded in the mist, the roar of the cascading water grew deafening, cartoonishly perfect rainbows appeared in the enormous curtains of water falling above us and I was busting to go to the toilet again.

Perhaps Oscar Wilde would have been mightily impressed with the centre of town. Or blinded. Only a few hundred metres away from the falls was a mini Vegas, but tackier. The main drag, which was full of fairy-floss-eating children, was lit up with a dazzling jumble of bilious neon signs advertising a whole universe of worlds including Lego World, Super Hero World, Hot Dog World, Fun World, Dinosaur World (incorporating Dinosaur Mini Golf), Criminal World, Frankenstein World and WWF World. Perched on top of most of the 'Worlds' were monolithic effigies of monsters, super heroes and a rather gross-looking hot dog. I was impressed. The Canadians had somehow managed to even out-crass the Americans. I thought I might check out one of the Worlds, but when I got closer to Frankenstein World I realised that it was actually just a Burger King masquerading as a World with a colossal Frankenstein on the roof eating a giant whopper.

I had my own private bus on the way back to Kitchener. I was the only passenger, but that didn't stop the bus driver stopping for long spells in deserted bus stations along the way. It was 9.30 by the time we crawled into a wet and windy Kitchener and I put my electric-blue Maids of the Mist poncho on to walk back to Jeremy's. As I was trudging through the rain, someone honked their car horn at me. 'Yeah, yeah, very funny,' I mumbled to myself. 'I know I look like a giant blue jellybean.' They honked again. I turned around and was just about to abuse them when I saw that it was Jeremy. What a lovely fellow. He'd looked up the bus timetable on the net at work and had come to pick me up.

'I thought I'd take you to see some real culture,' he said as I hopped in.

We drove out into the suburbs and pulled into the car park of a large and somewhat unremarkable building called RoXXanes.

'What's this?' I joked. 'A strip joint?'

'Yep,' Jeremy said matter-of-factly. 'And tonight's amateur night.'

The place was jumping (or rather sliding up and down) as men, including two fellows in lederhosen, ate their dinners while girls flashed their fannies in their faces.

'The winner gets fifteen hundred dollars,' Jeremy explained. 'Anyone can enter, but it's mostly uni students and a few tellers from the bank.'

As we sat down with our ludicrously priced beers, a girl in skin-tight jeans jumped up on the stage and began her striptease act. Except there was a lot more teasing than stripping as she clumsily squirmed and squeezed her way out of her tight jeans. While she was finally frolicking naked across the stage, Jeremy casually said, 'I used to date a stripper'.

'What was that like?' I said, staring at bouncing breasts.

'She was nice, but my mates used to go to her club and watch her spread her legs and play with her clitoris. I couldn't handle it.'

As Tight Jeans Girl struggled to get her pants back on I said, 'There must be a few drunk girls who wake up in the morning and say "Gee, I had this weird dream last night that I danced naked in front of a hundred men."'

We didn't stay to see who won. I couldn't afford to buy another beer.

I lost a few years off my life in the middle of the night. While I was slumbering away peacefully, Bentley (the cat) leapt from the top of the bookshelf onto my chest. I jumped so high out of bed that I sent Bentley bouncing off the ceiling and onto the television. And just when I had been about to give Jeremy's couch the highest rating so far. Instead, he got:

Couch rating: 8/10
Pro: Comfortable and cosy couch
Con: Confounded and crazy cat

Bentley was giving me a wide berth at breakfast while Jeremy got ready for work. When I asked Jeremy what I could do with my last day in Kitchener, he suggested I could go gawk at some god-fearing Mennonites, who Jeremy described as a bit like the Amish but without the pointy beards. Five miles out of town in the village of St Jacobs is Canada's largest Mennonite community.

I started the day at the Kitchener farmers' market, which, although it had been operating since 1839, had moved recently to a modern building in the centre of town. Jeremy said that I would find Mennonites there selling homemade bread, jams, cheese, sausages and vegetables. Unless Mennonite farmers grow junk jewellery, Miss Loo's Scottish soaps, cheap shoes or emu oil, there wasn't much produce for sale. Admittedly, only about a third of the market was open, but the only Mennonite I found was a skinny fellow with a table full of turnips.

When I arrived at the market, the heavens opened and the torrential rain hitting the market's roof sounded just like Niagara Falls. I grabbed a cup of tea from one of the food stalls and picked up a copy of *The Echo*, the local weekly newspaper. The lead story was headlined 'Welcome to Dullsville', and the first line of copy read 'Was this the most boring week in the history of Kitchener?' They were so short on news that on the second page they had rehashed a story that happened twelve months previously. It was a good one, though, in a very ghoulish way. A local man who had committed suicide by hanging himself from a tree in his front yard was left hanging in the breeze for four days because passers-by thought the corpse was a Halloween decoration.

When the rain subsided, I wandered through town to the bus station. The folk of Kitchener sure did love their Oktoberfest. There were people doing normal daily errands like going to the bank and picking up dry cleaning dressed in lederhosen and dirndls. There was also a dizzying array of lederhosen for sale at the Hans Haus Oktoberfest shop—which was open all year in case you had a pressing need for novelty beer mugs. Oktoberfest was being celebrated in other shops as well, with German-inspired displays in butchers, clothes shops, banks and, my favourite, the Stag S&M leather shop. The mannequins in the window had huge breasts and were wearing 'mini-skirt' leather dirndls. A sign underneath read: 'Whose pretzel will you straighten this Oktoberfest in your dirndl of desire?'

There were no buses to St Jacobs. Of course there wouldn't be. No need really. Not when everyone plods around in horse-drawn buggies. I caught a bus to a mall at the edge of town and went the rest of the way in a taxi.

I'm guessing the traditional Mennonites must live out of St Jacobs, because most of the houses in town had a truck in the driveway instead of a buggy. The main street was mostly Ye Olde Arts-and-Crafts Shops selling quilts and maple syrup. In the centre of town was the Mennonite Museum & Information Centre. The curator seemed surprised to see me. Actually, I think he was surprised to see anyone at all and he had to turn off the lights and plug in the projector in the theatrette so I could watch the 'Mennonite Story'.

The start of the film showed gawping tourists taking photos of Mennonites in their old-world attire. Personally, I think the Mennonites were at least equally entitled to gawp at the tourists' attire. The film was shot in the 1970s and the camera-wielding cats were all wearing outrageously flared pants, platform shoes, body-fitting floral shirts and boofy haircuts that made the Mennonites' bowl cuts look stylish.

The film described the Old Order Mennonites' way of life. They don't date and only meet the opposite sex at Sunday evening sing-alongs; weddings only take place on Tuesdays and the entire wedding meal is prepared by the bride; phones must be black (with no accessories or call waiting); they don't use hairdressers and the 'young men' have 'haircut parties'.

Sadly, the Maple Syrup Museum was closed, so I dropped into a Mennonite bakery for lunch where girls in traditional handmade outfits and bonnets were selling homemade bread from wicker baskets. The bakery also had a bar and a large plasma TV playing MTV pop videos.

There were no taxis in town, so I decided to hitchhike back to Kitchener. I didn't have much luck, though. Cars zoomed by without even looking like slowing down. When a fellow in a horse and buggy plodded past me, I smiled at him and stuck out my thumb in jest. He pulled over.

My new Mennonite friend was Matthias Brubacher and he was on his way to the mall. He explained that there's a 'high-rise' horse-and-buggy park at the mall for the convenience of low-tech shoppers like him. It's a barn. Matthias, who was in his early twenties, lived with his parents and his seven brothers and sisters on a farm where they made and sold butter, apple butter and maple syrup.

'We go to bed at eight and get up at five-thirty,' he told me proudly.

I was tempted to ask him if he had a spare couch. An early night was just what I needed.

'Is there a traditional Canadian restaurant?' I asked Jeremy as we drove around later looking for somewhere to eat. It was my last night in Canada and I wanted to go somewhere truly Canadian.

'Chains,' Jeremy said. 'Canadians love restaurant chains more than anyone in the world.'

'Really?' I said.

'They like to be able to go to another town and eat somewhere familiar, ordering off the same menu.'

'What about that one?' I asked, pointing to the Swiss Chalet Restaurant.

'Yep, all over Canada,' Jeremy said. 'Whatever cuisine you can think of, we have a chain of them.'

The largest chain in Canada is truly Canadian, but I didn't fancy it for dinner. When ice hockey star Tim Horton retired in 1964, he decided to open up a doughnut and coffee shop and called it, wait for it, Tim Hortons. There are now more than 3000 Tim Hortons outlets around Canada.

'Do you like Indonesian?' Jeremy asked as we passed Bhima's restaurant.

'Is it part of a chain?'

'Probably,' he shrugged.

It was Indonesian, but with a Canadian twist. I ordered bison gado gado.

We dropped into the Concordia club, the largest Oktoberfest venue, on the way home, but my heart just wasn't in it. I could feel a cold coming on and, to make things worse, it was Country & Western night. The menfolk were wearing lederhosen and cowboy hats, while Canada's second most popular female country singer (after Shania Twain) was 'yee-haa-ing' and twangin' her gee-tar.

The venue, which was basically a big circus tent, seemed quite busy for a Wednesday night. Or maybe it just looked that way because there were so many security personnel inflating the numbers.

'My mom's here,' the singer announced towards the end of her set. 'But watch out, cause she loves country and she loves to dance like crazy.'

The security goons were immediately on their toes looking into the crowd for a crazy old lady dancing in a cowboy hat.

It was a crisp and perfectly clear morning as I made my way to the train station. As I tramped through a carpet of gold maple leaves past tidy houses, I thought this is a nice town. Quiet, but nice. A well-dressed middle-aged woman stopped with me at the traffic lights. 'Oh, where are you going with that big bag?' she asked politely.

'To the airport,' I said.

'I wish the fuck I was getting out of here,' she muttered as she shuffled away.

ICELAND

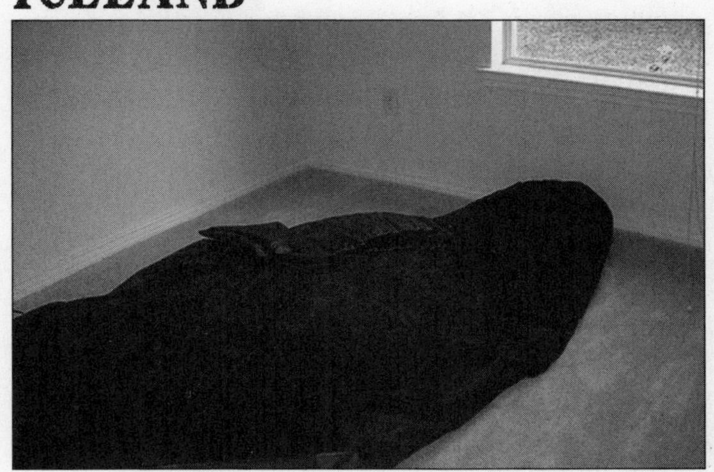

10

'Occupation: Mathematics student, speculative fiction author, professional encyclopedia maintainer, programmer, project leader and beer connoisseur.'
Smári McCarthy, 22, Reykjavík, Iceland
CouchSurfing.com

My head felt like it was about to explode. I don't think I could have chosen a more unsuitable country to go to with an aching head full of snot. The name Iceland doesn't really conjure up images of the sort of place that could lessen the misery of having a cold. If only I'd gone to warm and sunny Cyprus instead. Cyprus was another country on my shortlist as a potential European couch-surfing destination. Applying my criterion of going to places where I hadn't been before—given that I'd already visited 32 other countries in Europe—my choices were quite limited. In the end I chose Iceland because that was where Casey Fenton, the founder of CouchSurfing.com, surfed his first couch.

For such a small country (Iceland's population reached 300 000 in the same month that America's population hit

300 million), there were certainly plenty of couches to choose from. I sent requests to a bunch of people, including Gudmundur Thor Palsson who 'used to be a fat pig, but now I'm a little thinner, but still a pig' and whose interests were 'army, porn and drinking'. I tried Geiri who said: 'If it matters to anyone, I'm gay, but my couch is beige.' I sent a request to Lluks Jón Gunnarsson simply because he lived in a town called Hofudhborgarsvaedhi. I'm not a clown dentist, so I thought I might have a chance with Theodóra Þorsteinsdóttir who said: 'I have two phobias. I'm scared of dentists and I shit my pants whenever I see a clown. So I don't want to host a dentist or a clown . . . or a clown dentist.' I also tried 'programming hippie drummer' Johann Fridriksson who lived with his robot Benjamin. But it was 'half-Icelandic, half-Irish' Smári McCarthy who emailed straight back offering me his couch:

You're welcome to my couch.
I should note, however, that I'm a full-time student these days, and therefore I spend more than my fair share of time studying, so I won't always be available. And when I am, I'll probably be very intent on drinking heavily—I hope you can appreciate my situation. I'm not going to try and over glorify my liver's alcohol processing prowess, but I dare say that when it comes to this it is rather advantageous to have both Icelandic and Irish genes floating about there. So condition one is: You have to keep up with me.

Drinking heavily seemed a good idea when I accepted Smári's couch offer, but now I just felt like snuggling up in bed watching DVDs and eating Mum's homemade chicken soup. There didn't seem much chance of that happening, though. Particularly the DVD part; Smári didn't even own a television.

Aeroplane flights have a wonderful knack of exacerbating the symptoms of a cold, so by the time I shuffled through customs at the small, but incredibly shiny, Keflavík airport, my head was spinning. There was a bus waiting in the car park, but I only got two steps out of the terminal before I scampered whimpering back inside again. 'Bloody hell, it's cold,' I gasped. Over the next few days I would say this, and I'm not exaggerating, at least a hundred times. It was that type of bone-chilling cold that, err, really chills your bones.

I missed the bus. By the time I'd put on every item of clothing in my pack, the bus had gone. Oh well, I thought, there'll be another bus along in a minute. Wrong again, Einstein. Try three hours. All the buses' departures were timed to coincide with the rather infrequent arrivals of international flights.

After finding the bank, tourist office and bus ticket counter all closed, I went for a wander to find something to eat. Feed a cold, starve a fever, they say. Except I didn't think that I'd be able to afford to feed my cold. 'Bloody hell, it's expensive,' I gasped. Over the next few days I would say this, and I'm not exaggerating, at least a hundred times. A basic (as in the cheapest) sandwich was twelve dollars. This was in the upstairs and somewhat up-market cafe. Maybe the small airport shop downstairs would be cheaper. It was. The same sandwich there was only eleven dollars. Well, I think the thing I was looking at was a sandwich. It looked like an egg sandwich, but it was called a *sómasamloka rækjusalat*. When I read the rest of the label I realised why it was so expensive. The sandwich also contained those rare ingredients *smjörliki* and *mjölmeðhöndlunarefni* (try saying that with a mouthful of sandwich).

Iceland itself looked yummy enough to eat. As soon as the bus pulled out of the airport car park, we were driving through a surrealistic lava field that looked like large blobs of melted dark chocolate. There wasn't a tree or blade of grass in sight.

Twenty minutes later we were driving into Legoland. In the middle of this barren landscape was Reykjavík. The world's most northerly capital city is a Lego-like mishmash of ancient wooden houses with bright primary-coloured tin roofs and futuristic buildings made of concrete, steel, glass and lava. The whole scene was as dramatically composed as a theatrical set: The colours of the city buildings looked all the brighter against the dark, jagged backdrop of mountains in the middle distance and their snowy tips created an even stronger contrast with a sky of the deepest blue you can imagine.

The bus station was on the edge of town sandwiched between two busy roads and a windswept field. Just to remind me that it was cold outside the cosy warmth of the bus, large chunks of ice were lying on the ground. There was only one person outside the bus terminal building waiting to greet the bus. It was Smári. The first thing I said to him when I stepped off the bus was 'Aren't you cold?' Smári was wearing a light jacket and long-sleeved T-shirt (and pants of course). 'No, I'm fine,' he said as my teeth began to chatter. Smári had long blonde frizzy hair tied back in a ponytail and he was wearing a black bowler hat. Although Smári had never lived in Ireland, he spoke English with a disconcerting mixture of an Icelandic accent and an Irish lilt. He sounded like the lost love child of Bono and Björk. His Irish father had come to Iceland for a holiday, fallen in love with a local girl and moved here.

On the very bracing ten-minute walk to Smári's apartment, we passed a large modern glass building. 'That's where I work,' Smári enthused. A large sign on the front of the building read 'deCODE Genetics Corporation'.

'I haven't been for a while, though,' he added. Smári hadn't been to work for three weeks. 'I work whenever,' he shrugged. 'They know I've got study.'

'What do they, um, do or make in there?' I asked.

'It's a biopharmaceutical company that applies its discoveries in human genetics to the development of drugs for common diseases using DNA-based diagnostics, bioinformatics, genotyping and structural biology,' Smári explained. Okay, he may have lost me there, but he continued, 'Iceland has become the world leader in gene discovery because of its success in identifying gene stems using the Icelandic Health Sector Database, which contains the medical records and genealogical and genetic data of every single Icelander. Iceland is the ideal testing ground for genetic research because the population gene pool is pretty much pure.' What Smári was trying to say, I think, is that the entire country is virtually one big, somewhat inbred, happy family.

'You won't find more than eight degrees of separation in familial connections between people in Iceland,' Smári proclaimed. 'We have a genealogical website which lists everyone in Iceland. You can pick any two names and the site will find a shared relative.'

As we negotiated our way around a series of frozen puddles, Smári challenged me to name a famous Icelander.

'I know two!' I said proudly. 'Björk and Eidur Gudjohnsen.' [Gudjohnsen is a former Chelsea player and probably Iceland's most famous sportsman.]

'Björk and I share the same great, great, great grandmother,' he said. 'And Eidur Gudjohnsen is my uncle.'

'Wow! Your uncle.'

'Actually no, I haven't checked him yet, but he's probably my cousin or something.'

Smári did however find some relative revelations when the site first went online. His childhood friend's great grandfather was the brother of his great grandfather.

Smári lived in 'student quarters', a series of apartment blocks not far from the university. Outside the entrance was a bike rack full of unlocked bicycles. Smári's front door was also unlocked and he couldn't even remember when he'd last seen his front-door key. I suppose there's not much chance of theft in Iceland when you could very well be stealing from your second cousin.

I winced with revulsion when I walked into Smári's apartment. The entire apartment smelled of a heady mix of mouldy socks and rotten eggs. I actually gagged a few times while he gave me a very short tour of his apartment. It was a very short tour because there were only two rooms. The main room, which was tiny, looked crowded with stuff even though there was hardly anything in it. Squashed into the small space was a double bed, kitchen cupboards and a sink, a fridge, a stove, a small desk with a computer, a bookshelf and a couch that was smaller than José's mini-couch in Santiago. Not that I could really see much of the couch, or the bench, or the desk. Every surface was littered with empty mega-litre plastic Pepsi bottles, jumbo chip packets and empty bowls of pot noodles. On the couch lay a couple of open pizza boxes with half-eaten slices of pizza in them. Basically, it was like most 'student quarters' I'd seen (and lived in).

'Um, is that my bed?' I asked gravely.

'No, I've got this for you,' Smári said as he dragged a blow-up mattress out from under his bed. Well, that was a new one for my slumber collection.

There was something else quite disconcerting about the room. Scrawled on a large whiteboard mounted on the wall and all over the glass door leading to the small balcony were the ravings of a lunatic. Well, that's what it looked like. They were actually complicated mathematical formulas that Smári had been working on as part of his course. 'I've been working on this one formula for over a week and I'm still not close to an answer,' he said, adding another $x^2 = y^2$ to the bottom of the mess of symbols and numbers.

He wouldn't get much help from me. I don't know my pi from a pastie. I couldn't even understand the names of most of the subjects Smári was studying at university, which included Applied Linear Statistical Models, Algorithm Analysis, Numerical Analysis and Life in the Universe.

'One time I had a difficult formula,' Smári said. 'And I'd worked on it for hours without any luck, so I went to the pub and got drunk. When I woke up in the morning I saw that in my drunken state I'd scribbled numbers all over the board.'

'Did it make any sense?' I asked.

'Yeah, it was the right answer.'

We finished our very brief apartment tour in the bathroom where the rancid smell was even more intense. And there they were. The evil-smelling culprits were Smári's socks, which were hanging over the shower rod. Smári must have noticed me wincing, because he said, 'We're so used to the stink that we forget other people aren't used to it.'

'Oh yeah, it is a little smelly,' I said in between gags.

'Get used to it, because everyone's place smells like this.'

Wow, the entire country must be inflicted with foot rot.

'It's the sulphur in the water,' Smári said.

Ahh, so it wasn't the socks. Smári then went on to explain that almost the entire country is one big active volcano that sits on a thin crust of land above a subterranean cauldron of molten rock and the result is an abundance of geothermally heated, and somewhat smelly, sulphur-rich water. This gives

Icelanders an endless supply of hot water, which also heats their homes and even keeps the streets and footpaths free of snow and ice during the winter.

If only they would turn up the heating on the footpaths, because within a few minutes of leaving the apartment to walk downtown I was shivering again (Smári didn't own a car, much to my chilly chagrin). When we strolled past a frozen lake called *Tjörn* (which means pond in Icelandic), I noticed that one end wasn't frozen and was crammed with flapping ducks and swans.

'I wonder why that bit's not frozen,' I said.

Smári then spent the next ten minutes explaining why with a complex mathematical equation. Apparently it's the water density times the volume times the airspeed velocity of an unladen swallow. Or something like that.

The setting sun cast long shadows and a golden glow over the city as we wandered down stone-paved streets past brightly painted peaked-roof buildings. 'The sun sets at around five-thirty this time of year,' Smári said.

'What about in mid-winter?'

'At Christmas the sun doesn't rise until noon, then sets two hours later.'

Gee, that must be depressing, I thought.

'People get depressed in winter,' Smári continued. 'Then, in summer, people get insomnia, and that's just as depressing.' At the height of summer, the sun sets at midnight and is back up again less than three hours later.

When we reached town we stopped at a cafe for a beer. Most of the hip, cool-looking people in the cafe were tapping away on laptops. 'Just about every pub and cafe has free wireless internet connection,' Smári told me as we ordered our beers. 'We also have the world's highest per capita internet access.'

And, I imagine, the world's highest per capita quota of cafes with very little conversation going on. Even groups of friends sitting at tables were stuck in their own little computer worlds.

When I finally dragged my jaw off the ground to drink the beer that cost $12 a glass, it tasted horrible. It was probably very nice, but with my cold it tasted like dishwater. Smári finished his beer before I'd even taken two sips. I certainly wouldn't be keeping up with him unless I was prepared to re-mortgage the house. I didn't really feel like finishing the beer, but for twelve dollars I even drank the very last soppy dregs (or two dollars' worth).

On the short walk from the cafe into the city centre, Smári pointed out Hofdi House, where Ronny Reagan and Mikhail Gorbachev agreed in 1986 that pointing nuclear-armed missiles at each other might not be such a good idea after all. Smári was pointing out all sorts of things, but my cold-induced fuzzy brain was having trouble taking it all in.

The city centre looked more like a small village centre. Even though Laugavegur, the main drag, was full of boutique shops, pubs, discos, theatres and restaurants, it looked positively tiny. We walked past the prime minister's office, which was a modest two-storey building that had no fence around it and no security guards. 'I think Iceland is the only country in the world where the prime minister's name is listed in the phone book,' Smári said.

If I did decide to look him up in the phone book, Smári told me that I would need to look up his first name as Icelanders address each other by their first names. Surnames are just made up of the Christian name of the father with the suffix 'dottir' or 'son'.

'Here is a good example of Icelandic sarcasm,' Smári said as we passed a small bluestone building. 'It used to be a prison and now it's the Ministry of Finance.'

It's amazing that although Reykjavík is the size of a country town, it is a capital city with all that entails, including government buildings, media, arts, museums, headquarters of major companies and all the infrastructure involved in running a country. And, according to Smári, the population is smart, beautiful and a bit smelly. Iceland has the world's highest per capita ratio of Nobel prizewinners and Miss Worlds, and 60 per cent of Iceland's national income still comes from fish.

We met up with Smári's friend Johann in the city centre to grab a bite from 'one of the cheapest places in town'. I liked that idea. And so did my bank balance.

'I offered you my couch,' Johann said when we met. 'But you said that you'd already found one.'

'Oh, you have a robot called Benjamin,' I said.

'Yes.'

'How is he?'

'Good, he was busy tonight, though.'

What a coincidence. Johann was Smari's best friend (and possibly his cousin).

The restaurant did look cheap, but the cheapest thing on the menu was a seventeen-dollar crepe. We all ordered crepes. Like Smári, Johann had a job that had something to do with logarithms and Pythagoras's theorem. And, also like Smári, Johann was only wearing a light jacket and a T-shirt. When I asked if they were both a little bonkers, Johann told me that, although the Arctic Circle was less than 300 kilometres away, the Gulf Stream so moderates temperatures that in winter Reykjavík is never freezing.

'But it's, um, freezing now,' I said with a shudder.

'We're used to it,' Johann said. 'Even in summer the average temperature is only thirteen degrees.'

'It got to twenty-three degrees one summer a few years ago!' Smári said brightly.

'Oh, that's too hot for me,' Johann winced. 'Zero is the perfect temperature for me.'

After we finished our dinner Smári announced, 'Let's go get some dinner.'

Our crepe was just an appetiser.

As we tottered down the road Smári said, 'I'm going to take you to the most famous restaurant in Iceland.'

Oh dear. If a simple crepe was seventeen dollars, how expensive would the most famous restaurant in Iceland be?

'Dignitaries, celebrities and politicians have eaten there,' Smári said. 'President Clinton went there twice.'

Oh dear. The soup is probably 50 dollars.

I was just about to say that I was already full from the rather diminutive crepe when we rounded a corner and Smári announced, 'Here we are!' We had stopped in front of a hot dog stand.

'The most famous restaurant in all of Iceland,' Smári said proudly. The hot dog stand was called *Bæjarins beztu pylsur*, which translates as 'The best hot dogs in town'. And it wasn't just the best hot dogs in town. On the wall was a newspaper clipping from *The Guardian* newspaper in the UK, which selected *Bæjarins beztu pylsur* as the best hot dog stand in all of Europe.

'You can even get a Bill Clinton hot dog,' Smári said.

'Does it come with a free cigar?' I smirked.

We all ordered a *pylsa* with the lot and, best of all, because Smári's friend from university was manning the stand, our hot dogs were free.

Johann had to get home. 'My apartment is disgusting and I've got a couch surfer from Australia arriving at midnight,' he said before scurrying off. It was dark now and the sky dazzled with constellations burning big and so bright they seemed within reach. Some were so bright in fact that I thought they were planes in low approach to the runway.

'Do you think couch-surfing hosts and guests ever, like, get it on?' I asked Smári as we trudged back to his apartment. 'Oh, don't worry,' I hastily added. 'I'm not going to try and make a move on you, I was just thinking about Johann and the Australian girl.'

'Johann has a girlfriend, but I don't think it would happen that often anyway.'

'Yeah, I suppose,' I said. 'If you're a male host, then it's pretty sleazy coming on to a girl you've invited into your house. And the opposite is even worse, when a girl invites you to stay then you try to stay in her bed.'

A few minutes later we passed a bookshop and Smári asked, 'Do you mind if we go in here?'

'No, not at all,' I enthused.

If Smári had asked if I wanted to go into a vacuum cleaner shop, I would have said yes. Anything to get out of the cold for a minute. The bookshop was called Mals & Menningar and it had a huge selection of books in both Icelandic and English.

'Iceland has the highest literacy rate in the world and there are more books published here per capita than any other country,' Smári said, as I flicked through a Harry Potter book in Icelandic (*Harry Potter og eldbikarinn*).

When we got back to Smári's apartment I discovered why he knew so many facts and trivia about Iceland and, well, the world in general. Smári was one of the main contributors to the Icelandic version of Wikipedia and he'd personally added a few thousand articles and pages to the site. It's amazing what you can achieve without a television. Smári was also writing a novel. In English. It was an historical Icelandic fantasy-fiction story. If Smári managed to get his book published, he would join the nation's average of one in ten people who will publish a book of prose or poetry within their lifetime.

Smári told me that he spent a lot of time on the computer either writing, researching, programming or—now and again—downloading a movie or TV show to watch. As this trip unfolded I was witnessing first-hand how the computer is turning the world into one big shared household. Smári showed me a video on YouTube that both Bob in Chicago and Pedro in Rio had also shown me. The internet-connected folk from every corner of the globe are all watching the same YouTube videos, reading each other's blogs, buying each other's junk on eBay, finding info on Wikipedia, chatting to friends on MySpace and Facebook, and all Googling like crazy.

I went to show Smári something on the net and when I Googled for the link, he said, 'Do you know how Google works?'

'Um, you type something in and it finds stuff with that, err, name in it.'

'Google assigns a numeric weighting from zero to ten for each webpage on the net, which denotes the site's importance according to Google,' Smari said as he rubbed out the equation on the glass door and began writing seemingly random letters and numbers in adjoining boxes. 'It's called page-rank and . . . blah blah logarithmic inbound links . . . blah blah analysis algorithm . . . blah blah hyperlinks . . .'

Smári was still explaining and drawing boxes of numbers and letters when I'd set up the air mattress and hopped into bed.

I woke up at four in the morning lying flat on the hard floor. My air mattress had deflated. I tried to blow it back up again, but the hole was too big for my mouth. Then I remembered that there was an electric mattress pump under Smári's bed. I very quietly tiptoed past Smári and carefully plugged in the pump. I even delicately flicked the switch, so there wouldn't be a loud 'clicking' noise to wake Smári. Then . . .

'VRRRRROOOOOOOOOOOOOOMMMMMMMM!'

The pump sounded like a small plane taking off. Smári flew out of bed and landed on the floor with a thud. 'What? Shit! Who's there?' Smári shrieked, with wild eyes and even wilder hair.

When I woke up again later, Smári was already up and sitting at the computer in his baggy underpants watching the sci-fi television series *Babylon 5*. 'Gee, it looks like a beautiful day today,' I said. The bright morning sun was streaming through the window.

'Yeah, a scorcher,' Smári replied without looking up from the screen. 'We're expecting a high of zero today.'

Once you get over the smell of rotten eggs, having a shower in Iceland is heaven. Because there is an endless supply of hot water, you can shower for as long as you like. I only got out after 30 minutes when Smári enquired if I'd fallen through the plughole.

Smári had an Algorithm Analysis class to go to, so I went in search of some Icelandic goddesses. Ever since I'd seen this photo of fifty of the most perfectly gorgeous Icelandic girls posing in the Blue Lagoon, I'd wanted to go there. I was also hoping that the therapeutic and invigorating waters might help get rid of my cold.

When I left Smári for the bus station, he was still in underpants watching *Babylon 5*.

I began my therapeutic program with a sauna. I had no choice. The inside of the bus was so hot and steamy that I soon stripped down to my T-shirt. I was a little worried that by the time we got to Blue Lagoon, I'd be just like Smári in his underpants (except I'd be wearing my own underpants).

On the drive out of town it looked as if someone had plonked a brand new two-lane highway on the surface of the moon. Just as bizarre were the brightly coloured houses, a splash of red here and a drop of yellow there, sitting in the middle of the Sea of Tranquility.

As I caught my first sight of the Blue Lagoon, my attention was caught by the cottonwool balls of smoke drifting up from the geothermal power station alongside. In the midst of this extraordinary vast, monochromatic volcanic landscape was the lagoon itself, which looked more milky than blue.

'The Blue Lagoon holds six million litres of geothermal saltwater (two-thirds saltwater and one-third fresh water), which is piped directly from the source 2000 metres beneath the surface. The water in the lagoon is totally renewed every forty hours.' I was reading this inside the very sleek and modern information-centre-cum-ticket-office-cum-changing-rooms-cum-souvenir-shop.

It felt very odd indeed running barefoot in my bathers across a lava field dotted with frozen puddles. Steam was rising in sheets from the lagoon into a bright blue sky as other bathers loomed up in the mist like ghosts. Most were just floating about, while a few were sipping cocktails at the water's edge.

The water temperature was perfect. I slipped in and wallowed in the biggest bath I'm ever likely to encounter. There is something surreal about bathing in an open-air, steaming hot pool while the lifeguards are wearing ski jackets, gloves and balaclavas—and wouldn't have a hope of seeing anyone who was drowning in the mist anyway. The rising steam often blocked out the bright sun, then it would clear to reveal glimpses of the pipes and large domes of the power station.

There were quite a few people in the lagoon, but no gaggles of gorgeous Icelandic girls. It must have been pension day, because the clientele was mostly drawn from the wrinkly set. Mind you, after 30 minutes in the water I was well and truly wrinkled myself.

I was doing some serious wallowing when, like angels rising up out of the mist, I saw two girls. They were tall and lithe, with eyes as blue as the Arctic sky, hair the colour of sun, skin as creamy as French vanilla and smiles to warm the coldest northern night. I'd found my dream Icelandic girls. Then one girl turned to the other and said, 'This place is fuckin' wicked, innit?' My Icelandic girls were from East London.

After almost three hours in the water, even my original wrinkles were getting wrinkly, so I waddled out and had a fifteen-minute shower just because I could. The Blue Lagoon may have nearly taken my breath away, but the job was completed when I saw the price of a hamburger in the Blue Lagoon cafeteria. Thirty-five dollars, and that was without tomato sauce. I was happy to pay the exorbitant price, though, because I'd had the most marvellous morning. And best of all, my nose and stuffy head had magically cleared.

In my couch request to Smári I told him that I was good at washing dishes and in his reply he had written:

> *I don't do dishes. They happen to end up being done by a grumpy somebody who otherwise resembles me once in a while. You're welcome to them.*

Every single glass and cup in Smári's apartment was dirty. He'd even resorted to drinking out of bottles instead of having to wash a glass. When I'd resolved the dirty dishes dilemma, I started to pick up a few of the empty Pepsi bottles and by the time I'd finished I'd filled two huge black rubbish bags.

'Ah, is that what my apartment looks like?' Smári said when he returned from his Applied Linear Statistical Models class.

We went next door to the small mini-mart to get some dinner. We both got some pot noodles and some savoury-pastry-type-donut-things. I had no idea what they were, but they were the cheapest thing in the mini-mart. 'Right, let's go drink some cheap beer,' Smári said when we'd finished dinner.

The cheap beer was to be found at the Mathematics Club, which was housed in their very own 'clubhouse' near the university. As we stepped outside the apartment, I glanced up into sky and stopped dead in my tracks.

'Oh my God! Wow!' I gasped.

'Oh, that's the aurora borealis,' Smári said casually.

The heavens above were dancing in a light show that glimmered and seemed to swirl as pale curtains of brilliantly shimmering green light were drifting across the night sky. I stood there mesmerised.

'That's just an average one,' Smári said, as he marched ahead. He had more important things to think about. 'If we get there too late, they'll have drunk all the beer,' he groaned.

The Mathematics Club was in one of those building-site workman's huts and was full of seriously intoxicated mathematicians. It took my eyes a while to adjust when I stepped inside because the room was glaringly bright under the industrial-strength fluorescent lights. One entire wall was taken up with a whiteboard that was filled with incomprehensible numbers and symbols. About a dozen students were lounging on couches around a large coffee table covered in empty beer bottles watching two spotty students playing chess. The boys were either tubby and spotty or stick-thin and spotty. There were also three girls in the room and they were all drop-dead gorgeous. Some 'stadium rock band' music was blasting out from an iPod plugged into a computer, while a student with long greasy hair jumped around playing air guitar.

Smári introduced me to a few people, but I didn't stand a chance of remembering their names. I couldn't even pronounce them. There was a Gunnlaugur, a Örlygur, a Þóroddur and a Loðmundarfir. Or maybe they had simple names, but because they were so drunk that's what their scribbles looked like when I asked them to write their names down. One fellow was so inebriated that he was barely able to stay upright as he scrawled some complicated formula on the whiteboard. He kept swaying back and forth so he could focus on his chaotic computation.

We stayed for a couple of hours and everyone was really nice. Oh, except when the swaying student cornered me for twenty minutes to argue that mathematics is better than physics. 'Do you agree?' he slurred, poking me in the chest.

The air mattress did its deflation routine in the middle of the night again, so Smári earned the ignominy of having the lowest couch rating so far:

Couch rating: 4/10
Pro: The bed was soft and flat
Con: The bed went *very* soft and *very* flat

Smári had an Acute Angle lecture (or something similar) to go to, so he suggested that I should go on a tour and see some of the natural wonders of Iceland. I did a quick search on the net and contemplated booking on an Elf Spotting Tour in the lava caves of Hafnarfjodur (many Icelanders apparently believe in elves, fairies, gnomes and trolls), but decided instead to book on a Golden Circle Tour (and for you Australians, it had nothing to do with pineapple pieces).

I only just made the coach departure from the bus terminal and by the time I got my breath back we'd already driven out of town. After 40 minutes of travelling through moonscape, the landscape changed to the plains of Mongolia, with faded-brown rounded hills dotted with Iceland's famous little horses. I find that the more I travel, the more new places remind me of somewhere else.

As we drove past a small group of trees, our guide announced that it was the largest forest in Iceland. The entire 'forest' was no bigger than a football field.

'If you are lost in an Icelandic forest, how do you get out?' the guide asked us. 'Stand up!'

There was a howling wind outside and the trees in the 'forest' were being blown horizontal. The wind was also throwing the bus around as if it was a toy, but this semi-cyclone was 'just a slight breeze' according to our guide.

Our first stop was the small village of Hverager∂i. 'The houses in the village are a fine example of baroque architecture,' our guide told us with a wry smile. The Japanese tourist behind me snapped away with his camera. 'Ahh, baroque style!' he gushed excitedly. All the buildings in the village were very simple wooden houses.

We were stopping in Hverager∂i to visit one of the town's many greenhouses, which are heated by volcanic hot springs and grow most of the island's fruit and vegetables. The largest was called Eden, but we had to walk through the huge souvenir shop, and past the Adam and Eve toilets, to get to the actual greenhouse. Inside was a lush tropical garden with meandering paths, park benches and a few tweeting budgerigars in cages. Locals come to Eden when the country is under the winter's gloomy embrace and wander around and have picnics under bright lights pretending they're in a park on a summer's day (but not an Icelandic one, because then it would only reach 13 degrees).

Back on the bus I sat next to a Canadian fellow. I was quite surprised to discover that Nick was also a member of the couch-surfing collective, but he'd bypassed the couch on this particular leg of his journey. He was only in Iceland for a few days, so he'd opted for a comfortable hotel instead (where he probably didn't have to pump up his bed in the middle of the night). Nick had booked himself on a different tour for each day of his stay. As well as the Golden Circle Tour, he was going on a whale-watching boat trip, a horse-riding tour and a flight to the north of the island to go snowmobiling on a glacier.

'I have done quite a bit of couch surfing in other places, though,' Nick said.

'Do you have any good stories?' I asked.

'Yeah, most people I've stayed with have been really nice.'

'No,' I said. 'I mean have you like stayed with any nutters or had any weird shit happen?'

'Um, yeah, I couch-surfed with this guy in St Petersburg who lived in an empty apartment. He had a couch and cupboards and stuff, but there were no pictures on the wall or books in the bookshelf or *anything* lying about. I arrived late at night and he was just sitting there in this gloomy empty room. The next day I went to check out the city and I dropped into an internet cafe to update my blog. When I got back to his apartment, he said "So you think I'm creepy and you're worried I might axe you in your sleep?" I'd forgotten I'd told him that I had a blog and he'd read it.'

'Shit, what did he do?'

'He actually turned out to be quite nice and he didn't try to axe me once.'

'No one has tried to axe me either,' I said. 'Actually, everyone I've stayed with so far has been lovely, too. I can't believe how nice people are and how much they go out of their way to help you.'

'I did stay with one couple in San Diego who weren't very nice,' Nick said, 'to each other. They had just split up before I arrived and had moved into separate bedrooms. Over breakfast on my first morning they had this huge fight. When I asked the guy if I could have some milk for my tea, he said "Ask the fuckin' bitch!" Then she threw her bowl of cereal at him.'

Gullfoss is a huge and majestic waterfall that roars into a sheer boulder-strewn canyon. Well, that's what I had been told. I couldn't see much of it because I couldn't really see much through my tear-filled eyes. The force-twelve wind was unrelenting and icy drops from the waterfall kept pricking my cheeks, making me gasp. It was the most ferocious wind I'd ever experienced. I fought my way, leaning heavily into the wind, towards the viewpoint, but gave up halfway when a petite Japanese tourist went sailing past me.

Our next stop was Geysir, after which all other geysers are named. In the middle of yet another vast and desolate expanse was a bubbling hole in the ground next to a colossal souvenir shop and cafe. Like everyone else, I stood with camera pressed to face and finger poised on the shutter waiting for Geysir to erupt. And just like everyone else, I had just put my camera down when it belched spectacularly in front of me. And, yet again just like everyone else, I quickly swung my camera back up and took a photo of the tiny puff of steam that was left drifting from the hole.

Our last Golden Circle attraction was Þingvellir, where Iceland's first parliament met in 930. Getting there involved traipsing from the bus across a boardwalk over streams that trickled between undulating, moss-covered lava flows, then climbing up past rocky fissures that reared up like old Viking warriors. The site itself was just a pile of old rocks, but the views over Þingvallavatn, Iceland's largest lake, were lovely (although that loveliness had a lot to do with my relief that there was no buffeting wind blowing me away).

After all the other passengers had been dropped off at their hotels, the tour guide asked me where I wanted to be dropped. That was a good question. Where could he drop me? I didn't know Smári's address.

I thought about it for a minute. 'Um, the deCode Genetics Corporation,' I said.

Both the driver and guide gave me very odd looks when they dropped me off at the entrance.

I got quite excited when I walked into Smári's apartment. There was a proper-non-collapsing foam mattress on the floor. 'Johann dropped it off because the Australian girl is staying here tonight,' Smári said, when he saw me eyeing it off with a longing gleam in my eye. 'Johann's girlfriend is coming from the country for the weekend and he wants the apartment to himself.'

'Oh,' I said glumly.

'Don't worry,' Smári said. 'We'll give her the air mattress.'

Johann invited us around for an interesting dinner. It was interesting because it's not often you get served a plate piled high with boiled horse meat and potatoes. Sadly, Benjamin couldn't join us for dinner. His battery was flat. We were also there to pick up fellow couch surfer Anna, a 21-year-old tall, bubbly girl from Perth. Anna was taking a year off from university, where she was studying literature and history, to travel around the world.

Johann drove us into town after dinner and dropped us off in the middle of *rúntur*. *Rúntur* means 'round tour', but Smári more aptly described it as 'a pub crawl where the entire population gets absolutely wasted'. Every single Friday and Saturday night, the young folk of Reykjavík stroll into and stumble out of bars, dance clubs and beer-soaked coffee houses until dawn.

It was after ten by the time we got to Laugavegur, where most of the action takes place, and we had to navigate our way through the crowded footpaths, where a sea of Icelanders and tourists, many already in moderate to advanced stages of inebriation, was already partaking in some serious rúnturing.

We had our first drink and I had my first heart attack at the Pravda Club. A glass of beer was sixteen dollars. You know the drinks are expensive when you buy just one beer and put it on your credit card. In fact, most of the locals were using their credit cards to buy drinks. I imagine there would be quite a few shocked faces when monthly credit-card statements arrive. Cards were simply swiped through a machine and you didn't have to sign anything or get a receipt.

After one drink we moved on to a funky, tiny wood-panelled pub (or a pub-ette if you like) where we met up with Smári's friend Alli, a jolly, huge (in the girth department) fellow. As soon as we walked in, Alli insisted that he buy us all a drink nicknamed, rather ominously, 'Black Death'. This local concoction, called *Brennivin* in Icelandic, is made from fermented potato pulp and caraway seeds, and its name literally translates into English as 'burning wine'.

'Because it burns the shit out of your throat and stomach,' Alli explained just after we'd burnt the shit out of our throats and stomachs.

The Celtic Cross was next and it looked identical to every other Irish pub in every city around the world. Smári celebrated his Irish heritage by having a Guinness. Smári really was quite the beer connoisseur and he even had a website listing, and ranking, all the different beers he'd tried. So far he had tried 317 beers. And he was only 22. By that age I would have been lucky to have tried three different beers (and one of those was only because there was a beer strike one summer, so you could only buy Swan Lager from Western Australia). The fact that Smári could get hold of so many beers is impressive considering selling beer in Iceland has only been legal since 1989.

I got the next round and I was a bit worried the barman would say, 'I'm sorry, but you don't have enough money on your card. Your credit limit is only five thousand dollars.'

We sat in a small room where the central table was a large black coffin. Not long after we arrived, we were all standing on the coffin singing Icelandic songs. After the beers and Black Death I was probably singing in fluent Icelandic as well. We met more of Smári's friends, but it was hard to tell if they were friends he'd only just met. Everyone was hugging each other.

After the Celtic Cross, I was whisked through dance clubs and bars so quickly I couldn't keep track. Live rock and dance music boomed out from venues up and down the street, while slim blondes in slinky cocktail dresses waited with their dates behind long rope lines to get into the town's hippest clubs. To be honest, I couldn't really remember which clubs and pubs we went to. I seem to remember dancing a lot and handing my credit card over the bar as freely as if I was Eidur Gudjohnsen.

At some point I lost everyone and wandered aimlessly around the streets because I couldn't remember the way back to Smári's place. I must have been a little drunk, because I gave up my child's inheritance and caught a taxi. 'Whatever you do, don't catch a taxi,' Smári had warned me.

'Where to?' the taxi driver said, rubbing his hands.

'I live at the deCode Genetics Corporation.'

I had trouble focusing on the taxi meter. It wasn't because I was that drunk, but because it was spinning so fast.

I also got quite a shock when I stepped into Smári's apartment and caught an eyeful of four legs entwined on the bed and Smári's little white bottom bouncing up and down. We were both wrong. It seems couch-surfing hosts do get it on with their couch-surfing guests. I excused myself and stumbled outside and sat on the freezing grass.

I thought I gave them plenty of time to, ahem, finish, but when I got back inside they were still grunting and groaning and grinding. I grabbed the foam mattress and squeezed it into the storage cupboard. It didn't quite fit, and neither did I, but I managed to curl up the mattress, and myself, into the corner. At least I didn't feel guilty. Anna wouldn't have to sleep on the sagging air mattress.

I awoke at eleven-thirty with a volcanic hangover. There was one good thing about the biting arctic cold. It's amazing how quickly you can forget your hangover when your face has gone completely numb. Anna had already left and Smári was still in bed, so I went for a bracing stroll into town. It was my last day in Iceland and I still hadn't been to the imposing snow-white Hallgrimskirkja Cathedral, which soars above Reykjavík like a Gothic cathedral crossed with a futuristic rocket ship.

I caught the elevator up (I don't think I could have faced the steps) to the top where, from behind the hands of the tower clock, you could look out over the cluster of marzipan-coloured buildings below and at the hinterland beyond—a threatening landscape, featuring icy mountains and a hungry sea that, if anything, looked higher than the land it was lapping against. I was enjoying this peaceful vista when . . . 'DONG! DONG! DONG!'

The church bells began clanging right next to my still somewhat sozzled head. I screamed 'The bells, the bells!' then, clutching my ears in pain, hastily stumbled down the stairs. I spent most of the afternoon on a hangover-induced aimless stroll around town where I'd do things like walk into a souvenir shop, pick up a troll magnet, stare at it for five minutes, then walk out.

Smári had planned a puffin dinner party, but the puffins missed their flight. He was going to roast us up some puffins—and yes I'm talking about those cute little diving birds with rainbow-striped beaks—while Alli was going to make his special puffin sauce. Smári's brother-in-law had tried to send a couple of fresh puffins over from Vestmannaeyjar (the Westman Islands), a small group of islands off the south coast, but he missed the post.

'That's okay,' I said to Smári. 'I'll take you out for dinner instead.'

I had taken all of my other couch-surfing hosts I'd stayed with out for a meal as a thank you. It's just that I was worried a restaurant here might break the bank.

We headed into town and strolled up and down the streets checking out menus in restaurant windows, but there wasn't a single main course less than 55 dollars. We finally settled on *Þrír Frakkar* because they served puffin.

The restaurant was small and cosy with a couple of cute-looking stuffed puffins perched on the bar and National Geographic posters of whales on the wall. They also served up the not-quite-politically-correct minke whale steaks. Other local specialties on the menu included fried fish chins and Cuban-spiced reindeer. What they didn't have, though, according to Smári, were other local delicacies like sour ram's testicles, burned sheep's head, lamb's colon and rancid shark meat.

Smári then did his very best to turn me off my food by describing these delectable-sounding treats. *Hrutspungar,* or sour ram's testicles, is exactly that. The ram's testicles are pickled then pressed either into a kind of pâté or turned into a jam (perfect for your toast in the morning). *Lundabaggar,* or sour lamb, is made from lamb's colons, which are rolled up, boiled, pickled then sliced into tasty bite-sized pieces. My favourite, as in the most disgusting, is *hakarl,* or rancid shark, which is traditionally prepared by digging a hole, placing the shark in the hole, pissing on it, then burying it for about six months until it rots. It's then served cold ala sashimi style. 'They don't piss on the sharks anymore,' Smári said. Oh, then if that's the case, give me two serves.

For entrée I had the very plain, in comparison, smoked puffin. The dark brown meat was cut into long strips and came with a mustard dipping sauce. The texture of the meat was something akin to snot and it tasted nothing like chicken and more like snot.

Puffins are very easy to catch. Smári had gone puffin hunting for the first time the previous summer on an uninhabited island just off the Westman Islands. Well, when I say 'easy', the actual catching sounded easy: The island is less than a square kilometre and there are more than 2 million puffins on it. But the getting-to-the-island part sounded like an absolute nightmare. 'The only way on to the island is to get dropped off at the bottom of an eighty-metre high cliff in rough seas,' Smári explained. 'We had to leap from the boat onto slippery rocks, then scramble up a steep slope using a chain of puffin holes as a ladder.' Joining Smári on the puffin-hunting expedition were two of his friends, including Örn who—Smári was fairly confident in claiming—was 'the only one-armed puffin hunter in the world'. They camped for two nights in the island's one and only log cabin.

Smári went into detail about how to catch a puffin, but it's all rather simple. You lie on the grass with something that resembles a large butterfly net and when a puffin flies past, you take a swing at it and drag it in. I don't think I could do the next part, though. 'You have to snap its neck,' Smári said, 'before it starts asking uncomfortable questions.'

'I didn't catch any on my first attempt,' Smári continued. 'Apparently it was too windy for puffins. Örn caught two and that was it. The next day the wind really picked up and turned into a full-blown gale. A thick fog rolled in as well, so then we couldn't even get off the island. We ended up getting stuck there for four nights. On our last morning when the weather cleared, the other two caught forty puffins each, but all I managed to do was to knock a puffin out when I hit it with the pole instead of the net.'

'Forty puffins! Is that a big catch?' I asked.

'Not really,' Smári shrugged. 'Most puffin hunters can catch up to three hundred birds a day.'

I was just about to eat something else that the Icelanders are fond of hunting, but get in trouble over killing twenty a year. And there goes my Greenpeace membership. For main course I had whale. Yes, I know, save the whale and all that. After tasting it, though, I'm almost tempted to say, 'Catch Willy and chop him up into steaks'. The whale meat was wonderfully succulent, slightly salty and as utterly lean and tender as the best beef tenderloin. Incidentally, Keiko the movie-star killer whale who played Willy was lucky he wasn't turned into whale steaks. The Icelanders put their hands up to look after him when his film career finished and he was kept in a large pen just off the Westland Islands from 1998 to 2003.

'After over twenty years Iceland began officially whaling again only four days ago,' Smári said, chewing away on his whale steak. 'Most of the world doesn't want us to kill whales, but we will only kill around twenty minke whales a year, which is point-zero-zero-two per cent of the population.'

Smári had penned an article on a 'greenie' blog site a few days before and had written 'So what?'.

'I've received tons of hate mail,' he shrugged.

Alli picked us up from the restaurant in a mini-bus. On the weekends he did volunteer work driving the Icelandic Women's Handball team around. Smart man. Alli hadn't eaten dinner and when I told him what I'd just eaten he said, 'I'll take you somewhere special'.

He took us to the cafeteria at the bus terminal.

'Now you must try burned sheep's head,' he said, returning from the self-serve counter with half a sheep's face staring up at me from the plate. If you'd like to prepare this at home, it's very easy. Get a sheep's head, burn it to remove the wool, cut it in two in order to remove the brain, boil it, then serve with mashed turnip.

'I love it,' Alli said with a mouthful of sheep's lip. 'And this place makes the best sheep's head in town.'

Alli very kindly, or I should say very cruelly, gave me half a tongue, a bit of an ear and an eyeball to eat.

'You should see your face,' Alli said as I ate the eyeball.

'That's because I'm eating *a* face,' I winced.

After our progressive (and progressively worse) dinner, we dropped into Johann's place for a drink. I didn't notice Alli leaving (which is quite difficult because he's a big man) and when he returned fifteen minutes later he said that he had a surprise for me. 'Brian has tried nearly all our local specialties tonight,' Alli said to Johann. 'He's had puffin, whale and sheep's head. He just needs to have ram's testicles and . . . um . . . um . . .'

'Rancid shark meat!' I cried, squirming in my seat.

'Here you go then,' Alli said, as he threw me a small ball of something wrapped tightly in plastic wrap.

It was rancid shark's meat.

'Where did you get it?' I asked.

'From my fridge at home.'

It was true. Alli kept some in his fridge to have as a snack with a beer.

Even though it was tightly wrapped, I could smell the distinct aroma of rancidness.

'This hasn't been pissed on, has it?' I asked with a shudder.

'Why do you think I've been so long,' Alli smirked.

I put it aside, but a few minutes later Alli announced, 'It's time to go outside'.

'What for?' I asked.

'The shark feeding!'

Apparently the smell is so bad that you have to eat it outside or it stinks out the entire house.

'Block your nose,' Alli said as he unwrapped the shark. 'Don't smell it, just eat it.'

I picked out a small cube of meat and tentatively popped it into my mouth. It tasted like a combination of sushi that's a bit past its use-by date and strong French cheese with a hint of urine. As I was chewing it, Alli said that I shouldn't eat too much because it gives you diarrhoea.

'Now smell it,' he said musingly.

'Oh, Jesus!' I spat.

The smell was so vile that for a minute I thought I was going to bring up the sheep's eyeballs and my Willy steak.

I scrubbed my hands with soap six times, but I still couldn't get the smell off my fingers. 'You'll have trouble picking up a girl tonight,' Alli said. 'Your breath smells like rancid shark, too.'

It was nearly midnight when Smári and I left to do some more rúnturing. It was a bit quieter this time round. Not the rest of the rúnturers, mind, but me and Smári. We were both a little tired and I had to get up early to catch a plane.

Over a beer at the Celtic Club we talked about living in Iceland. 'The weather sucks and the politics sucks,' Smári said. 'I love this country, but I'd leave in a moment if I could.'

It's interesting in comparison to what Bob from Chicago had said about America: 'I hate this country a lot of the time, but I'm an American and I'm proud to be an American, so this will always be my home.'

We left at 1.30 (an early night for Smári) and, being sober, I not only noticed how drunk everyone else was, but all the broken glass and vomit on the ground. We took a shortcut down a side street and there she was. My perfect angelic Icelandic girl. She had snow-white hair, snow-white skin and a snow-white bottom that was up in the air as she squatted to do a wee in the middle of the road.

BELGIUM & LUXEMBOURG

11

'Give a Belgian a beer and he's happy.'
Joris Willem, 29, Antwerp, Belgium
CouchSurfing.com

I've been to Belgium nineteen times, but I haven't seen any of it. Well, I've seen lots of motorways and chip shops down at the docks, and made one flying visit to Bruges, but that's about it. When I worked as a tour leader in Europe, we would either drive straight through Belgium on our way to Holland or end a trip at Oostende with just enough time to grab some frites before we jumped on the ferry back to England. The one and only time that I went to Bruges was a disaster. As well as getting myself (and my passengers) hopelessly lost, I re-christened the town's most famous buildings—I muddled up all their names and histories during my befuddled and very flustered walking tour.

So I had decided that I would finally see more of Belgium than a chip shop. But where in Belgium should I go? Brussels, Ghent, Liège? I knew where. A city, which I had been on my way to but never reached on my first trip to Europe. I was on my way to Antwerp when I got picked up hitchhiking in Holland and ended up going all the way to the driver's place in Versailles instead. Almost twenty years later, I would finally make it there.

I contemplated sending a request to Indra, whose interests included travel dimensions, natural time, positive vibes and trance dancing; or to Jurriaan, who lived in a squat with 50 other people; or Tom, who was the lead singer of an 'alternative Goth Industrial band' called Foetal Void. But then I stumbled upon the profile of someone I actually knew. You may recall from my previous book *Where's Wallis?* (which I'm sure you've all read), a Belgian fellow I met in Togo called Joris. He had got up one morning in Antwerp, hopped on his bicycle and ridden 6000 kilometres down through France, Spain, Morocco, Mauritania, Mali, Burkina Faso, Senegal and Ghana to Togo. The last time I'd heard from him, he'd been lying low in Ghana after narrowly avoiding a civil war in Togo. I wasn't even sure whether he was still in Africa, but when I sent him an email asking where he was, he emailed me straight back:

Hi Brian.
Nice to hear from you.
After my mysterious disappearance from the Togolese civil war I found myself on a slave ship full of chained white people with black seamen going to the port of Antwerp to fill the local slave market. An old friend bought me for a ridiculously small price (what an insult) and after I helped him build his

house for over a year, fed with Belgian fries and cheap beer, he liberated me (he was a friend after all). So now, yes I'm back recovering from my adventure, and enjoying my liberation.

Joris was now an unemployed slave living in Hove, a suburb of Antwerp. Getting there was easy—a direct train from Brussels and a fifteen-minute walk from the station—as long as I didn't have to stop and ask someone for directions to his street. I didn't stand a chance of pronouncing Wolschaerderveldenstraat correctly. Antwerp is in the part of Belgium where most people speak Flemish, which sounds a bit like someone speaking with a mouthful of frites and a serious case of whooping cough.

Hove was very posh indeed, with grand houses and large gardens dominated by towering ancient trees. Unemployment benefits must be good in Belgium. Joris's street was just as swanky with a long row of tall red-brick houses.

Joris greeted me at the front door with a huge hug. Although we had only spent a couple of days together in Togo, it was like seeing a dear friend. The last time I had seen Joris he looked like John Lennon—albeit an incredibly tall and gangly version—with his little round glasses and long unkempt hair and goatee. His hair and goatee were now a little shorter and a little less unkempt and his clothes were not quite as dusty.

Joris lived on the top floor of his father's four-storey house, which had been converted into a little self-contained flat. There was a little kitchenette, a little bathroom and a little lounge room-cum-bedroom-cum-office. Joris was a full-time couch surfer. His bed was one half of a built-in L-shaped lounge. My bed would be the other half.

Joris had been living in the house since his parents divorced when he was two (although he didn't have his own flat then). He had been with his dad most of his life except for three years he spent with his mum in his teens. Before pedalling across the Sahara, Joris had studied philosophy at university then worked as a teacher. He received 800 Euros a month in unemployment benefits, but he wasn't sitting on his bottom doing nothing. Joris wanted to get into radio journalism, so he was doing unpaid work at a local independent radio station preparing and presenting interviews for various programs. He'd recently sold a five-hour special to Radio France, which he'd compiled from recordings he made throughout his trip to Africa (he took recording equipment with him to Africa, and recorded interviews and commentary in Flemish, French and English!). Now Joris was trying to organise a radio station to sponsor him, so he could complete the second leg of his African cycling expedition (Togo to South Africa).

'You can borrow Dad's bike,' Joris said when he suggested we go for a ride into town. The bike was an old, clunky-looking thing which Joris's 62-year-old father still rode into the city, where he worked as a town planner. Joris said that it was 'a short ride into town', but I was bit dubious about his interpretation of 'short'. This was coming from a man who thought nothing of riding more than 100 kilometres a day through a desert in searing heat.

Joris didn't own a car. 'I ride everywhere,' he said. And with everything it seemed. Joris told me that he had carried a TV, an office chair, a dozen planks of wood and several bags of hash on his bike. Not all at the same time I should add. 'I used to ride to Holland with my brother all the time,' Joris said. 'It's only thirty kilometres to the border, so we used to ride there to get hashish. We'd smoke a little of it then we'd just float home.'

Antwerp has dedicated bike tracks away from the road, but the bike track was busier than the road itself. After twenty minutes on the saddle, we were on the outskirts of the city centre. 'This is called *Joods Antwerpen*,' Joris bellowed over the traffic. We were in the middle of the Jewish area, which was full of diamond shops. 'Antwerp is the centre of the world's diamond trade and four in five of the world's rough diamonds pass through here,' Joris said as we trundled past an ultra Orthodox Jewish family complete with ringlets, hats and ten kids in tow.

As we entered Antwerp's *Oude Stad* (Old City), we had to negotiate narrow cobbled lanes that were lined with gabled townhouses with leaded windows. What made it even more difficult was that I was having trouble concentrating on riding given the delicious smells coming from the chocolate shops and waffle houses. We also had to dodge whooshing blue-and-red trams that were like caterpillars imagined by a Japanese toy maker.

'First we will stop at my favourite place in all of Antwerp,' Joris said as we pulled up on the side of the road. We had stopped in front of a chip shop, or a *frituur*. There was a *frituur* on just about every corner, but this shop had the distinction of being called Frituur No. 1.

'French fries are in fact Belgian,' Joris told me while we waited for our order. 'In Holland they call them the right name. They call them *Vlaamse frieten* or Flemish fries.'

I had my mammoth serving of Flemish fries with mayonnaise and ketchup, but I was tempted to try the 'mammal sauce' which was one of ten sauces on offer, including chilli, BBQ, meatball, garlic and gypsy sauce.

Our bumpy teeth-chattering bicycle tour continued through the stony expanse of the *Grote Markt*, which was surrounded by stately seventeenth-century buildings that once housed Antwerp's powerful merchant guilds—and now contain touristy restaurants serving pots of steamed mussels. We stopped in the *handschoenmarkt* (the glove market) in front of the sixteenth-century *Onze-Lieve-Vrouwekathedraal* (Cathedral of Our Lady) whose tapering tower rises over the Antwerp skyline like an intricately carved Gothic stalactite. 'The church is famous for its impressive collection of Rubens paintings,' Joris said, as we hopped off our bikes. 'Would you like to see them?' I do like Rubens' exuberant Baroque style, which emphasises movement, colour and sensuality.

'Or shall we have a beer?' Joris said, gesturing to the Paters Vaetje pub next to the church.

I opted for the impressive collection of beautifully crafted beers.

This tiny pub had 280 different beers on the menu. We'd grabbed an outside table in the warm sun right up against the church wall. The traffic-free square was full of dining and drinking folk spilling out of the busy terraced cafes and bars.

Some of the high-octane beers on the menu had 12 per cent alcohol, so I'm guessing that after downing a couple of them you wouldn't be able to get your tongue around half of the names. There was a Corsendonck Pater, Dikke Matile, Flierefluiter, Gouden Carolustripel, Couckelaerschen Doedel, Tronbadous Obsura and a Witkap Pater Stimulo.

'At Bierhuis Kulminator across town, they have seven hundred different beers,' Joris said as we perused the beer menu. I was having trouble picking one from the mere 280.

'You choose one for me,' I said.

Joris ordered me a Kwak. 'It's called a Kwak because that's the sound it makes when you take your last mouthful,' Joris said as I was presented with a mini-yard glass that came perched on a wooden stand and looked like something from a mad scientist's lab. Most of the 280 beers came with their own distinctive glass, which is uniquely embossed and specially shaped to enhance the taste and aroma. The Kwak was a dark, or *dubbel*, beer, and was a relatively weak drop with only 8 per cent alcohol. When I got to the bulb-like bottom of the glass, the beer gushed out, mostly over my shirt, and made a distinctive 'kwak' noise.

'Another one?' Joris asked, polishing off his Tripel Karmeliet. 'This is part of our lunch you know, because in Belgium, beer is called a "sandwich in a glass".'

I tried a Couckelaerschen Doedel next simply because it had the longest name.

I asked Joris what the Flemish thought of the Walloons, their neighbours and fellow countrymen and he said, 'It's like a bad marriage. We are two different nations living together and we can't stand each other. There is a lot of resentment from the Flemish people because our stronger economy supports Walonia, which has double the unemployment of Flanders. Also, we have to learn French at school, but the Walloons don't learn Flemish at all.'

Joris was very passionate about politics and he talked about Antwerp's recent elections. 'The extreme right is very popular in Antwerp,' Joris said. 'And one-third of the people in Antwerp want Flanders and Walonia to be divided up into two separate countries.'

After our Belgian beer fix we stopped for a Belgian chocolate fix. This will probably get me thrown out of the CouchSurfing Chocolate Lover's Group, but I have to admit that I'm not a huge fan of the famed Belgian chocolates. I'm a simple man and I don't like those fancy-schmancy 'praline' fillings. Still, just for research purposes, I forced myself to eat a good handful.

No wonder people in Belgium ride everywhere. They have to burn off all the chips, beer and chocolate. We rode down to the River Scheldt—which is home to the second largest port in Europe after Rotterdam—and headed south along the riverfront. We were heading to a restaurant that Joris had suggested for dinner. 'It doesn't really have a name,' he said. That sounded promising. 'It's a bit of a ride, but it's worth it.' Bit of a ride all right. By the time we got there, it was dark. Our monumental trek took us through an industrial wasteland, which seemed eerily bereft of traffic and people. Well, I don't think there were many people. It was hard to tell because there was also a distinct lack of streetlights.

The bar of 'No-name Restaurant' was a crumbling brick building that was lit up with Christmas lights in the middle of decrepit and seemingly abandoned warehouses. The actual restaurant was out the back in a huge open-sided army tent, which was fitted out with long trestle tables and old cinema seats as chairs.

The place was popular, though. As well as people in the army tent eating dinner, behind it there were small groups gathered around fires blazing in huge metal drums.

When we joined the long queue for food, I noticed that most of the people around us were smoking joints. This was very much a dreadlocks and cheesecloth-shirt-wearing crowd. 'You pay as much or as little as you like for a plate of food,' Joris said as we neared the front of the queue. 'Most people pay about three Euros.'

'You wouldn't even get a slice of bread for that in Iceland,' I said.

My plate was piled high with food and, with all the joints and dreadlocks, I wasn't surprised that it was vegetarian fare. We grabbed a cinema row next to a group of friendly happy locals—although the joints may have had something to do with that. The food was delicious. And this is coming from a man who usually says that 'It's not a proper meal unless it comes with meat'. Mind you, I couldn't actually see what I was eating because it was so dark in the tent.

As we were leaving I noticed a poster on the wall of the bar. The bar was having a SLUTFEST. A party for loose women. That could be interesting.

'*Slut* means like final,' Joris said. 'Because the place is closing down in two weeks.'

As part of Joris's job at the radio station, he was involved with the KLAP!DORP! Film Festival (I suggested that the PR department might want to re-look the name). It was the opening night and Joris had procured us two VIP passes.

'Will I be alright dressed like this?' I asked. I was wearing cargo pants and my well-travelled and somewhat shabby fleece. Joris said I would be fine, but I just hoped I didn't look too scruffy walking down the red carpet.

We rode for three hours (well, it seemed like three hours, particularly as my hands had gone numb from the icy wind that was blowing off the water) to the main docks. After we'd passed several hulking cargo ships and more warehouses, we stopped at a small open tent at the entrance to a cluster of small buildings. I was thinking that this couldn't possibly be it, but on the side of the tent was a large 'KLAP!DORP! Film Festival' banner. There was no red carpet, just a hand-drawn arrow on a piece of cardboard pointing the way to the bar.

It wasn't quite champagne and dinner suits. More like beer in plastic cups and tatty grunge wear. The crowd was mostly that grungy, cool crowd that wears sunglasses inside even though they're not famous. There were lots of dreadlocks, shaved heads and novelty glasses. 'It's an alternative film festival,' Joris said.

'They could still have canapés, though,' I said sulkily.

We grabbed a beer and strolled out to the car park behind the bar, which was serving as the drive-in cinema. There were all of nine cars, plus a crowd of hearty folk sitting in a small grandstand. It wouldn't have been more than 5 degrees. The screen was on the wall of an old warehouse and the projector was set up in the back of a truck.

We did get VIP seats, though. We sat in the festival organiser's car in the front row. 'He's too busy running around,' Joris said. As soon as we'd climbed in, Joris opened the sunroof and lit up a joint. The movie was a *film noir* horror flick called *Cat People,* a 1942 black and white film that was in English with French and Dutch subtitles. It may as well have been in Dutch, though, because I had no idea what was going on. The story, I think, was about a woman who married Oliver Reed, but was afraid that when she got sexually aroused she would transform into a panther and kill somebody. Throughout the film, Joris's friends would briefly jump in the back seat, pass a joint around and chat to Joris in Flemish. I don't speak Flemish, but I'm guessing the conversation went something like:

Friend: 'What the fuck is happening in this film?'

Joris: 'I've got no idea.'

Friend: 'Right, see you then. I'm off to find another joint.'

The film ended when the *femme fatale* turned into a panther and chased Oliver Reed's secretary around the swimming pool.

There were two other film venues set up in the surrounding and somewhat shabby buildings and the first 'cinema' we checked out was playing a Flemish film. Mind you, we couldn't actually see the screen through the thick haze produced by the smokers in the audience. An equally thick haze had also enveloped the docks as fog drifted in and transformed it into the set of a classic *film noir*.

We ducked into the largest venue, which was full, and stood at back of the room. The film was a documentary, in English, about a death metal band from South Africa. They were showing one of the band's film clips, which featured the band members jumping about in a forest playing along to possibly the worst song I've ever heard. Suddenly the band stopped playing and began throwing blood all over each other. When they forcibly stripped a girl and covered her breasts with blood, I almost fell over. 'Jesus, what is this?' I blurted out—perhaps a little too loudly.

When Joris burst out laughing in response to my shocked outburst, he spat out a mouthful of burger all over the guy in front of him.

We sheepishly moved away and found a seat. It wasn't the gratuitous violence that worried me so much as the audience's blasé attitude even when the band members started whipping the girl. The fellow sitting next to me was fast asleep, but snapped awake when the girl let loose a blood-curdling scream (as you do when you're getting a serious whipping).

When the band broke into a song that sounded like Satan himself singing, I said 'I think I've had enough'. Besides, I couldn't put off the long ride back through the fog to Joris's any longer.

'We've probably ridden just over thirty kilometres today,' Joris said, when I commented that I was sure we'd done more than a hundred. On the way back, however, we did ride an extra one or two more. We went via an all-night *frituur* because, as Joris said, 'It's important to have some chips before you go to bed'.

I gave Joris's couch a good rating, but I think Joris might have dropped his own couch rating substantially after my performance during the night. Mine was:

Couch rating: 8/10
Pro: A comfortable sleep
Con: An uncomfortable cramp in my leg during the night woke me up

Joris's would probably have been more like:

Couch rating: 4/10
Pro: A comfortable sleep
Con: A kick in the head from Brian (supposedly caused by a cramp) woke me up.

While we were having breakfast, Joris was telling me about the time he and his friends had breakfast in Belgium, lunch in Holland, then dinner in France.

'That sounds like fun,' I said. 'And you could throw in dessert in Luxembourg.'

Joris pondered for a minute. 'You know, I could probably borrow Dad's car.'

Joris dragged out a map and by the time we'd finished our cup of tea we'd planned a whirlwind European culinary tour. We even added another country. We would get up early the next day and have breakfast in Belgium, lunch in Holland, afternoon tea in Germany, dinner in Luxembourg and dessert in France. The only hitch was that we'd be left with a long drive to Antwerp, so I had an idea. 'We'll find a couch to surf in Luxembourg,' I said excitedly. Luxembourg was another country on my shortlist of places in Europe that I hadn't visited before.

There weren't many Luxembourgers offering couches in Luxembourg. Most of the potential hosts were either expats or locals who were out of the country. On the couch-surfing profiles there is a 'last log-in' column which showed there were Luxembourgers currently in Seoul, Berlin, Paris, London, Helsinki, Malta, Madrid, Auckland, Osaka, Mumbai and Idaho.

Among those who were actually in Luxembourg there were worrying signs that they were in the country, but off the planet. Under occupation, Patrick had:

> Play with my toes—does make it hard to pay the rent, though.

A fellow called Spock had:

> None. Time occupies me.

André, on the other hand, had written under 'Types of People I Enjoy':

> If by the people you understand the multitude, the hoi polloi, it is no matter what they think; they are sometimes in the right, sometimes in the wrong; their judgments is a mere lottery.

The rest of the folk that were left in Luxembourg seemed to work in banks.

I sent out a bunch of requests, then spent most of the day pottering about in Joris's flat. It was nice to do some serious pottering about. I'd been on the go practically non-stop since the start of my couch-surfing adventure and some slothfulness was just what I needed. I also felt really comfortable being a sloth in Joris's company because it was like hanging out with an old friend.

On the way into town to get some dinner, we dropped into Radio Centraal. The station was in a tall, rundown, old, gable-roofed house overlooking the river. 'The radio station purchased the building almost thirty years ago,' Joris said as we climbed the incredibly creaky stairs. 'It's now worth absolutely heaps.'

The station was funded by radio subscribers and the income from the ground floor, which they rented out. We waltzed straight into the main studio even though the 'ON AIR' sign was lit up. The two announcers were lounging back in their chairs behind the console with huge joints in their hands. I could barely make out their faces through the haze.

They were in the middle of playing a music track, although calling it music was perhaps a little kind. It sounded like something someone would create (and listen to) after too many huge joints. I could make out a bass guitar, but the rest sounded like stoned people banging pots and pans.

'It's an "experimental" radio station,' Joris told me after we'd grabbed a beer from the fridge.

I don't know if experimental is the right word. I'd be leaning more towards totally weird. Joris told me about a few of the radio shows, including a weekly program called 'Drunken DJs'. As the name might suggest, the DJs get progressively more pissed during the show until they can barely speak. 'After the show the mixing desk is covered with empty bottles of tequila and potato chips,' Joris said.

'We also have another show called The Essence of Bullshit, which is um . . . people just talking bullshit,' Joris said as we made our way back downstairs. 'And we once had a weekly show that had "live sex" on air.'

I scoffed. 'If that was an Australian show, it would only go for three minutes.'

Apparently the show wasn't that popular, so it was pulled (so to speak).

For dinner we went in search of Belgian mussels. Finding mussels is easy because just about every restaurant in the city centre has them on their menu. But I was on a mission. I wanted to find a restaurant *without* an English menu. That wasn't anywhere near as easy. I once spent more than two hours wandering the streets of Rome looking for an 'authentic' Italian restaurant that didn't have an English menu and I ended up finding a delightful little place down a back alley which had waiters who could only be rude to me in Italian.

I think we tried just about every restaurant in central Antwerp, but we couldn't find a single menu that wasn't in at least four different languages. We eventually settled on Corsendonk Stadscafe only ten doors up from the radio station. It was a lovely candlelit place full of couples holding hands. And Joris and me.

The restaurant had twelve different types of mussels on the menu.

'Sorry, there are no more mussels left,' our waiter shrugged.

'What?' I gasped. 'But . . . this is Belgium.'

'Okay, I'll check,' he grunted, before scampering back to the kitchen.

'We have found three bowls of mussels,' he said on his return.

I'm not sure exactly how and where you *find* three bowls of mussels at such short notice, but we ordered two bowls anyway.

As we were devouring our huge steaming cauldrons of delicious mussels and frites, I said, 'Hmm, I do like Belgian mussels.'

'Yes, except most of Belgium's mussels come from Holland,' Joris shrugged. 'The Belgian coast is only sixty kilometres long.'

After dinner we adjourned for an après-mussels aperitif at De Vagant, a gin joint with 200 types of gin or *jenever* on the menu. The convivial little wood-panelled bar, with posters of aristocrats enjoying the fiery liquor on the walls, was full of locals downing tiny glasses of gin.

We sat at one of the long tables shared with other patrons and Joris ordered us a mandarin-flavoured gin. The drink was strong and sweet, but quite tasty. I couldn't say the same for the cactus-flavoured one we had next, though. Slumped next to us were two ruddy-faced fellows who looked as if they'd been there a while. They were onto their second, or possibly third, bottle of gin and were having quite a bit of trouble pouring it into their tiny glasses. Most of it was spilling across the table. When they staggered out of the bar and jumped on their bikes, I said, 'That should be an interesting ride home'.

'The gin makes you ride better,' Joris said. 'And you get home quicker because you don't remember riding home.'

We only had two drinks, because we wanted to make an early start on our grand culinary tour. On the ride back, Joris got a call on his mobile. 'That was my best friend,' Joris said. 'He's in a local bar near my house and I said that we would drop in for one drink. Is that okay?'

It would have been okay if my one drink, which Joris's friend bought for me, hadn't been a *Duvel Tripel* or a 'Triple Devil'. The beer was triply strong and the glass was triply large. The inevitable consequence was that our one drink turned into a couple, and a couple turned into a few.

So it was that I found myself sitting in a dank cave under one of the city's old forts with Satan and Lucifer (as well as *Duvel* there are also brands of beer called Satan and Lucifer) at two o'clock in the morning. We had been invited, or we'd just tagged along (I can't quite remember), to a party in a crumbling brick fort that was once part of the ancient fortifications that ringed the city. Although there are a number of old forts surrounding Antwerp, we knew we had arrived at the right place—there was a long line of parked bicycles out the front. Why drink and drive when you can drink and ride? To get to the party we had to follow a line of candles through a labyrinth of long dark tunnels that belonged in a gothic horror movie. This led us to a series of adjoining small, hot, sweaty and smoky rooms (the Belgians seem to have chain-smoking down to a fine art). One room housed the dance floor, but it was difficult to tell if people were dancing or just staggering about. We found a room with tables and chairs and I spent a couple of hours shouting to people over the loud music and pretending to hear what they said in return.

We finally escaped at 4 a.m. and as we rode up the road leading from the fort we passed a seriously intoxicated fellow lying on the road. One side of his face was totally covered in blood. He'd fallen off his bike. Joris asked if he was okay and he said, 'I'm fine, but would you mind calling me a taxi?'

Maybe drinking and riding wasn't such a good alternative after all.

12

'I like to receive and be received.'

Cecile Perrin, 27, Luxembourg City, Luxembourg

CouchSurfing.com

I wanted to begin our culinary road trip with Belgian waffles for breakfast, but after our night with the devil I desperately needed a greasy bacon sandwich. Mind you, it was more like brunch anyway by the time we'd crawled out of bed and hit the road.

When Joris told me that he was going to take me to see some 'non-tourist sites' on the way to the Dutch border, I think perhaps he meant 'no-tourist' sites. In the sense that no tourists had ever been there before. Joris bypassed the motorway and took us down an empty road past endless docks filled with cranes and petro-chemical plants. The highlight of our tour was a monstrously menacing, and menacingly monstrous, nuclear power plant. 'They put it right on the border,' Joris said, 'so if anything goes wrong, half the problem is another country's.'

It wasn't until we spotted a small sign on the motorway saying 'Nederland' that we even realised we'd crossed the border into Holland. Oh, except for the tall folk in wooden clogs growing tulips next to windmills in the neighbouring fields—only joking. We passed a turn-off to the town of Bergen-op-Zoom, which sounded like a whole lot of fun, but we were heading to the fisherman's hamlet of Vlissingen (Flushing in English) at the mouth of the River Scheldt.

'Holland is neater and better organised than Belgium,' Joris said when I asked him what the main difference was between Belgium and Holland. 'Oh, and Belgium has more holes in the road.'

It was only a 30-minute drive to Vlissingen and about a 3-minute drive into the centre of town, where a handsome little cobblestone square overlooked a quay packed with fishing boats. The square was home to several inviting cafes and restaurants, but we decided to go for an exploratory amble around town first. We walked to the end of the quay, where a stiff breeze was blowing off the North Sea and a towering cargo ship glided by within touching distance.

'Over fifty thousand ships from every corner of the globe pass by here each year on the way to Antwerp,' Joris said. 'And nowhere else in the world do ships pass this closely to the shore.'

'You know your stuff, don't you?' I said.

'No, I just read it on this plaque,' said Joris with a cheeky grin.

Before we found somewhere for lunch, Joris wanted to go to a 'coffee shop' to buy something a tad stronger than coffee. When Joris asked a local man for directions, he rolled his eyes as if to say 'another bloody Belgian buying dope'. The 'coffee shop' was easy to spot. It had a large green marijuana leaf painted on the front window.

'I suppose it's quite easy taking stuff across EC borders nowadays,' I said after Joris purchased a large block of hash (for 25 Euros).

'I did get caught a few years ago, though,' Joris said. 'On the day I got my licence I took my dad's car and, with four of my mates, we drove to Holland to buy bags of grass. We were stopped at the border on the way back to Belgium and the border police asked us if we had any grass. We said no, but they found the bags. "No more lies or you will be in big trouble," he told us. "Are you going to come back and buy some more?" he asked as he took our bags of hash. "Yes," I said. "Why would you say yes?" he asked. "Because you told me not to lie," I said. He ended up letting us go with our grass when he found out that were philosophy students. "You guys probably need it," he said.'

On the way back to the square we walked past a restaurant that was full of men wearing black-and-white striped shirts, black waistcoats, red cravats and fisherman's caps. Most of them were waving large jugs of frothy beer, smoking fat cigars and singing sea shanties while a rosy-cheeked accordion player danced precariously on the bar. 'This is perfect,' I said. It looked just like a film set—although admittedly I can't recall a film about drunk Dutch fishermen dancing the polka. The Brasserie Sans Étoile completed the film-set picture with its rough wooden floors and low ceilings where fishing nets were strung up on dark wooden beams.

We grabbed a table and Joris spoke to a red-nosed fellow, one of the few who wasn't singing, who told us that they were seamen from a neighbouring region. They had been singing in the town square all morning and were having a 'quick' drink to celebrate. The somewhat sozzled sailors were supposed to be heading back to their village, but they didn't want to leave. Some of them would have had trouble standing up, let alone walking out the door.

The meal servings looked huge, so we ordered a fish dish to share. The cook wasn't happy, though, and he came out of the kitchen to tell us that we couldn't share a meal. Joris argued with him and the cook stormed off back to the kitchen—where there was a good chance he would add something horrible and possibly quite gross to our food.

'It's only because the Dutch don't like Belgians,' Joris sniffed.

When the seamen left the bar arm-in-arm, singing 'Goodbye my love, goodbye', there were only four of us left in the restaurant. Five if you include the grumpy chef, who was smoking a cigarette at the bar and glancing over at us to see if we'd noticed the bits of snot in our fish sauce. Still, if it was snot sauce it was very tasty.

We left Vlissingen and headed north on a motorway that could have been anywhere in Europe. We knew we were getting closer to the German border, though. Signs for the towns of Vroenhoven, Smeermaas and Voerendaal were suddenly replaced by signs for Burgholzer, Schmithof and Gross Hürtgenwald.

It was almost four o'clock by the time we crossed the border, so we took the first turn off the motorway towards the city of Aachen. I had it in my mind that we'd have a quick look around the city (Aachen was once one of the most important cities in Europe when it was the capital of Charlemagne's Holy Roman Empire) then stop at a beer garden, but we were running behind schedule and didn't want to get into Luxembourg too late. We stopped at the first pub we came to in the rather nondescript suburb of Laurensberg. By a stroke of luck the Gaststätte Zur Post was a charming little corner pub and we grabbed a table outside in the sun.

I ordered a couple of Dom Kölsch beers from the extensive beer menu, but the food menu consisted mostly of pizza and a rather unappetising sounding *krapfen*. We were in luck again, though, because they also had an Aachen local specialty called *printen* on the menu. The *printen* was a bit like gingerbread, but with one special added ingredient. Concrete. I suggested to Joris that perhaps they should supply a jackhammer with each serving. When the old fellow sitting next to us heard my accent, he asked, 'Vhere are you from?'

'Australia.'

'Ah, that is much far away. So for how long are you staying in Germany?'

I looked at my watch. 'Oh, about fifteen minutes.'

That wasn't true. By the time we crossed the border back into Belgium we'd been in Germany for all of 42 minutes.

'Have you been to Luxembourg before?' I asked Joris as we crossed the grand duchy's border almost two hours later.

'Yes, a few times.'

'What's it like?'

'Well, I actually didn't see much,' Joris declared. 'We only drove through Luxembourg so we could stop at one of the services to buy cheap petrol, cigarettes and whisky.'

In a blink of an eye we were driving into the capital of Luxembourg, the imaginatively named Luxembourg. No wonder a lot of Luxembourgers on CouchSurfing.com said that they worked for a bank. The wide boulevard that led into the city centre was lined with shiny offices of every major bank you've ever heard of. And a few that only money launderers know. The bank clerks must get hefty pay packets as well, because the roads were full of brand new Beamers, Jags, Mercedes and Ferraris.

We parked the car and strolled into the charming Place d'Armes just as the sun was setting and a rich golden light struck the surrounding buildings' seventeenth-century facades—and the tacky red facades of McDonalds and Pizza Hut. Suddenly this charming square wasn't so charming anymore. Joris was very impressed with the square, though. 'Look at that!' he exclaimed. 'They've got public toilets.'

We eventually found Cecile's apartment block by accident. We managed to get ourselves hopelessly lost, but when we turned off the busy road so we could stop and look at the map, I glanced up at the street sign and said, 'Hey, this is the street!'

Cecile was petite with dark, bobbed hair and wore glasses almost identical to Joris's. Cecile wasn't Luxembourgish, though. She was French and lived with her French boyfriend Francois. Francois worked in a bank. Their three-room apartment was small and in the lounge/bedroom there was only a thin see-through curtain dividing the bedroom from the lounge room. Joris and I would be sharing the fold-out sofa bed.

We chatted over a bottle of red and Cecile told us that she had been living in Luxembourg for two years where she worked 'organising cultural events'. Cecile had gone to university in Metz in northeastern France and when she finished her course she went to a recruitment agency and asked them to find her a job in a foreign country. They sent her 30 minutes' drive north to Luxembourg.

'We have no Luxembourgish friends,' Cecile said when I asked if she knew many Luxembourgers. 'We have French, English, German and Irish friends.' Francois told us that fewer than half of the 300 000 residents of the capital are native Luxembourgers, while another 140 000 'guest workers' commute in from France, Germany and Belgium. There were also no Luxembourgers in their apartment building. 'There are Spanish, Portuguese and French living here,' Cecile shrugged. 'I don't think I even know a Luxembourger,' she added.

'I think our landlord is Luxembourgish,' Francois said.

Finding Luxembourgish cuisine proved just as challenging as finding a Luxembourger.

'Are there any Luxembourgish restaurants we can go to?' I asked.

They both shrugged. Francois checked the net while Cecile called her Portuguese and Irish friends. Francois found two, but one was closed and the other was obscenely expensive.

'I know a good Alsatian restaurant,' Cecile enthused.

It was easy to find a car park in town. On the way in we passed a huge and hugely empty car park that Cecile told us was packed during the day with the cars of the commuters from the surrounding countries. Although we scored a good car park, we still had to traipse up a series of steep and narrow cobbled streets that were so perfectly clean and orderly it was like a Disneyland version of a medieval city. A cast-iron staircase led us up to our Alsatian restaurant, which was called Goethe Stuff. 'Do you get it? *Good* Stuff?' Cecile said. The restaurant did have some Luxembourgish cuisine on the menu but there were no Luxembourgish people working there. The waiters were Portuguese and the chef was French. 'It would be nice to meet at least one Luxembourger while we're here,' I said.

I had *bibeleskas* for dinner, which was a simple but tasty dish made with boiled potatoes cooked with cheese, bacon and sour cream. I wanted to try some Luxembourgish white wine as well, but Francois said it was pretty horrible, so we had French wine instead.

Cecile had hosted a few couch surfers and she'd also couch-surfed herself in India. 'I stayed in Mumbai with a family of four who only had one room and they shared one bed,' she said. 'They gave me the bed and slept on the hard floor. I tried to say no, but they insisted I take the bed.'

After dinner Cecile and Francois took us on a short guided tour of the city. We began by taking a lift that was built into the cliff face just like they have in Monaco. And just as in Monaco, the lift was spotlessly clean. According to Francois some of the local banks weren't very clean, though. 'The banks are very busy at the moment handling money from Russia and Iran,' Francois told us. Whether clean or un-clean, there certainly was a lot of money about. Francois also told us that that there are more than 250 different banks in Luxembourg and their combined balance sheets total more than EUR 700 billion, which is how Luxembourg manages to (just) beat Switzerland for the title of Europe's number-one country for private banking. The locals also had plenty of cash to deposit in their banks because, at US$48 000 a year, Luxembourg has the highest average income in the world.

For a city full of people with lots of money, no one seemed to be out and about spending any of it. The streets were deserted. 'The locals must be at home counting their money,' Joris said. Either that or holidaying in five-star resorts everywhere else in the world.

When we walked past a restaurant that Francois frequented, the owner, who was having a cigarette on the street, invited us in for a drink. Francois asked him what the most famous Luxembourgish dish was and he thought about it for a minute. 'Boiled tripe,' he said.

'Are you Luxembourgish?' I asked him.

He gave me that unmistakable Gallic shrug. 'No. French.'

The staff were all Portuguese and Spanish.

We continued our tour through the enchanting Old Town, which was flanked by mighty fortifications that were dug into sheer stone cliffs. The view from the cobblestoned corniche at the top was an imposing array of turrets and gates above the walls of the rocky promontory known as the Bock.

When we got to the Alzette River, after negotiating a series of winding steps, I finally met my first Luxembourger. He was a scruffy-looking, and somewhat smelly, homeless fellow who was camping down by the river.

It was getting late and we still had to get to France for the final leg of our grand culinary tour, so we hurried back to the car. We were heading for the town of Volerange-les-Mines, which was the first town over the border.

We almost didn't make it. Not only was it one of the very rare occasions on which the border was even manned, but the border police on duty went the whole hog and stopped us.

'Where are you going?' the border guard asked Joris.

'Volerange.'

The guard stuck his head in the window to check us out. 'What for?'

'To have some cake.'

He gave Joris a puzzled look. 'What else?'

'Um, that's it. Then we're coming back.'

The guard grunted at us, then turned around and called out for a senior officer. Joris explained that I was an Australian (as proof he pointed out that I was wearing shorts) and that we were on a grand one-day culinary tour. The officer said something to Joris in French and waved us through without even looking at our passports.

'What did he say?' I asked.

'He said, "What a fantastic idea"'.

'You can tell we are in France,' Joris said after we'd left the autoroute. 'The French love roundabouts.'

By this time it was close to midnight and there were no restaurants open in town, only a bakery and a bar. 'That doesn't matter,' Joris said. We bought some lemon tarts from the bakery and ate them in the bar. Joris also bought a large baguette because 'Belgians don't know how to make baguettes. Four hours after you buy one, you could use it to kill someone.'

The bar was quiet but it was perfect. It felt very French. Particularly when Joris asked the barman a question and he shrugged as if to say 'It's not that I don't know, it's just that I don't care'.

Couch rating: 7/10

Pro: The bed was cosy and warm . . .

Con: . . . until Joris stole all the blankets

'That's the last time I'm sleeping with you,' I said to Joris over breakfast. It actually took us a while to sit down for breakfast. The kitchen was so tiny that getting to your seat was like the closing stages of a game of Twister. For me to get to my chair, Cecile had to get up from the table and slide her chair to the left. I then took two steps forward and moved the bin while Joris moved the entire table to the right before moving my chair back. Or was it Cecile's chair? It took us almost fifteen minutes to get back out of the kitchen when we'd finished.

On our drive out of Luxembourg, Joris announced, 'I'm going to take you to Luxembourg's most famous site.'

The 'famous site' was the largest petrol station in Europe, which had more than a hundred petrol pumps. 'Isn't this great?' Joris exclaimed as we walked past a cigarette machine that was the size of a small house. The machine dispensed *cartons* of cigarettes. Joris brought a giant pack of rolling paper to go with his giant block of hash.

Joris was dropping me off at Brussels airport, but halfway through Belgium he suddenly said, 'You can't leave Belgium without having a Trappist beer!' The fact that I had a plane to catch and it was 9.30 in the morning didn't seem to faze him and he turned off the motorway towards the town of Rochefort.

I knew that Trappist beer is a beer brewed by Trappist monks, but I didn't know that only seven Trappist monasteries in the world produce beer. There are six in Belgium and one in Holland. The road to the Abbaye Notre-Dame de Saint-Rémy wound its way through a forest of huge oak trees, while the abbey itself—which was founded in 1230—is a magnificent cluster of showpiece buildings from different eras where medieval stonework stands alongside antique brick buildings covered in ivy. Crates of freshly brewed beer were stacked up next to a wall of the ancient church, although there was no beer for sale in the abbey complex. We found that out when Joris asked a brown-robed monk who was solemnly wandering past us before he jumped into a sporty new VW and zoomed off, spinning the wheels and spitting gravel all over us.

We drove into the village of Rochefort and grabbed a table at Brasserie de Rochefort, where a few of the patrons were already downing beers. I was glad to see that we weren't the only drunkards drinking beer at ten in the morning. There were three Rochefort Trappist beers on the menu. The beers didn't have names, they were simply numbered: Rochefort 6 (7.5 per cent), Rochefort 8 (9.2 per cent) and the daddy of them all, Rochefort 10 (which was a whopping 11.3 per cent). 'If we're going to have a Trappist beer, we may as well do it properly,' Joris said when he came back with two tall glasses of Rochefort 10. The beer was a dark reddish-brown colour with a creamy white head that was so thick it was like drinking beer-flavoured soup.

When Joris dropped me off at Brussels airport, our parting was quite emotional. We had slept together after all. We gave each other a hug knowing that there was a good chance we might never see each other again. Then again, I'll probably bump into him while he's riding his bike across the Gobi desert or some other dusty place that he likes to frequent.

TURKEY

JAN 20
USPS

13

'I can take you around the most unknown and interesting parts of the city. Which, I imagine, will be a lot of fun.'

James Hakan Dedeoğlu, 30, Istanbul, Turkey
CouchSurfing.com

'Ey oop, lad. Let's gaw t' poob!' my Turkish host said when he greeted me in the middle of the incredibly crowded Kadıköy wharf and bus station.

Okay, I may be exaggerating a little, but I was taken quite aback when my Turkish host had a broad Yorkshire accent.

'Me moom's from Bradford,' James told me when I commented on his accent.

Although James's moom was born and bred in Bradford, Yorkshire, James was born and bred in Istanbul. James didn't look very Turkish (well, apart from the fez he was wearing). He was slightly built, with brown hair, a ginger beard and blue eyes.

On the short walk to his apartment, he told me that his parents met at university in Birmingham in 1972 where his dad was studying economics and his mum was studying to be a teacher. A year later they married and moved to Istanbul, which was then a relatively small city with less than 2 million people (there are now more than 15 million residents). Just to confirm that they were trailblazers, they settled on the Asian side of the city. The two halves of Istanbul, separated by the Bosphorus River, are in different continents. In those days the Asian part was mostly made up of holiday houses for people from the European side. 'After a few months,' James said, 'me dad asked me moom if she wanted to go back to England and she said "No, sod that, I want to stay here". She's never been back to England since. Me dad passed away four years ago, but me moom won't go back to England because Istanbul is her home.'

James had two names—an English one and a Turkish one. His mum and English relatives call him James while his Turkish friends call him Hakan. James also had a split-personality brother: John and Batu.

James was one of a number of people in Istanbul who I'd emailed to ask for a couch. There were certainly lots of couches to choose from. Istanbul is the sixth-ranked city for couch-surfing membership. The number one city is Paris—and who said Parisians were rude and inhospitable. The top ten couch-surfing cities from the 20 000 cities represented are in order: Paris, London, Montreal, Berlin, Vienna, New York, Istanbul, San Francisco, Melbourne and Toronto.

As usual in my search for a host, I was looking for someone who sounded 'interesting'. This turned out to be quite easy, because some people hadn't waited to be asked. They knew just what people like me are looking for in a host:

> I am a very interesting person, but please do not disturb me with stupid ideas.
> Okan, 29

> My visitors should be interesting like me, honest and respect the ordinary home regulations such as throwing out the bins.
> Anil, 32

> I'm a interesting man. u can learn all mafia history from me. give me a hug
> Can, 23

I did find one host who was very interesting without feeling any compulsion to tell me that he was. Serhat Bilgiç must be the King of Couch Surfing (or the King of HospitalityClub to be more specific). A 36-year-old retired banker, he has had waves of surfers through his door. I don't know who holds the record for the most couch-surfing guests, but Serhat must be right up there. In a space of less than two years Serhat had hosted 327 travellers from 38 different countries. As I write, his record for the number of guests staying at the one time is thirteen, while Jasmina from Macedonia holds the record for the longest stay of 42 nights. His oldest guest (so far) is 61-year-old Wolfgang from Austria and the youngest is Eric from Estonia at only nine months.

In the glowing online references for Serhat, he is dubbed the Sultan of Istanbul. He certainly loves his city: 'Istanbul is Queen of all the cities because Istanbul is a dancing lady of the Bosphorus. She is a salsa dancer during the day and a belly dancer during the night; always ready to hug you and kiss you.'

Serhat was away when I was in Istanbul, which was a pity. With 327 people giving him such good references, I imagine he must have a pretty fancy couch.

At the other end of the hosting numbers scale was James Hakan Dedeoğlu. I was to be his first couch-surfing guest. The reason he'd not had a guest before was the very reason I thought he would be an interesting host. James was often too busy to host because he was the founder and Editor-in-Chief of *bant*, a hip monthly magazine which featured music, cinema, art and general arty stuff. 'I can take you around the most unknown and interesting parts of the city,' he told me in an email.

I was actually looking forward to seeing even the known parts of the city. I'd been to the Turkish coast before, but not to the city that was once capital of the Byzantine empire, the Roman empire (they even changed its name to New Rome for a few years to silence the critics) and the Ottoman empire. The history of the city reflects the whole amazing story of Western civilisation, religious conflict and kebabs.

Mind you, I saw most of the city on the way to meet James. I had to go all the way from Europe to Asia—on a bus ride that cost less than 2 dollars. The airport bus whisked me through a modern if somewhat grubby city, across the huge span of the Bosphorus Bridge where rust-streaked cargo hulks loomed up out of the Golden Horn, and on to the expansive Taksim Square in Europe. The square was teeming with locals wandering around with kebabs in one hand and Cokes in the other. I had to fight my way through hordes of people just to get across the road to catch the Kadıköy bus.

Even on the walk through the suburban streets of Moda on the way to James's apartment, we occasionally had to step onto the road as the crowd squeezed us off the footpath.

'Today is a holiday,' James explained when I asked why the entire city's population was out and about. 'It is *Eid ul-Fitr*, or the Festival of Breaking, which is the first day after the end of Ramadan. The next three days are also holidays, called *Şeker Bayramı*. Everyone puts on their best clothes and visits relatives and friends and eats lots of food. Today is also the most important day to go to the mosque and pray.'

'So you are Muslim?' I asked.

'Yes. Ninety-five per cent of Turkish people are Muslim.'

'Did you go to the mosque this morning?'

'Um, no. I am a Muslim, but I don't really do the Muslim things,' James said irreverently. 'I only go to the mosque for funerals. We do the family thing at end of Ramadan because we get lots of good food and when we were young we used to get presents.'

'I'm exactly the same,' I nodded. 'I'm a Catholic and I only go to church for funerals and I celebrate Christmas so I can get presents and have an excuse to drink a lot.'

'Most of my friends are like me,' James shrugged. 'I have a Canadian friend who is living here and he is more of a Muslim than all of my friends.'

That reminded me of something that puzzled me at the time.

'Do the Turkish have something against Canadians?'

'Um, no. Why?'

'At the visa payment counter at Istanbul airport, there's a large sign on the wall which lists all the countries and their relevant visa fees. Most of them were around twenty dollars, but the Canadian one was sixty dollars.'

'That's strange.'

'Yeah. Why the Canadians? They're nice enough.'

'You'd think the American one would be most expensive,' James said. 'No one likes them.'

It was almost as strange that there were only three countries whose citizens were exempt from having to pay for a visa: Kyrgyzstan, Bolivia and Macedonia. They must have just pulled their names out of a hat.

'It's a pity that you won't be here in ten days' time,' James said as we traipsed up the stairs to the fourth-floor apartment. 'I'm getting married and you could have come to the wedding.'

I'd spent less than an hour with James and he was inviting me to his wedding. The hospitality and generosity of the couch-surfing folk I'd met so far was quite astonishing. So much so, in fact, I wouldn't have been surprised if James asked me to be his best man.

James and his fiancée Aylin had only just moved into the apartment and were still in the process of unpacking boxes. James had been living with Aylin in her small rented apartment in a nearby suburb. James and Aylin's new apartment was huge. Well, it seemed huge after Smári, Joris and Cecile's tiny abodes. Although the apartment building looked rundown, the apartment itself had recently been renovated. There was parquetry floor throughout and a new kitchen and bathroom. Their rent was US$1200 a month (as a comparison, Smári paid $2000 a month while Bob's three-bedroom flat was $780 a month).

The lounge room alone was bigger than Smári's entire flat. Besides a few unpacked boxes, the room was almost empty. The only furniture in it was a new leather lounge suite, a new coffee table and a new LCD TV. James told me that they also had a new fridge, new dishwasher and, of course, a new toaster. 'We are already getting wedding presents,' James smiled. 'That's why we had to move to a big apartment.'

Sitting on the couch busily typing away on a laptop was James's fiancée Aylin. 'It's my day off and I'm still working,' she said, flashing me a gorgeous smile. There were also two other laptops on the coffee table and a clutter of mobile phones. James and Aylin set up *bant* magazine together after they'd met working for a computer games magazine. They were up to their 25th issue and were just about to launch a *bant* television show.

James gave me the apartment tour, which took in what I instantly imagined would become the highest-ranking 'couch' so far. I had my very own bedroom with a huge double bed and my own bathroom. Aylin's mum and sister (who were both in town from Izmir for the two weeks leading up to the wedding) were busily baking, blanching, braising and boiling away in the kitchen. 'Mum has been cooking for three days,' Aylin said.

Aylin's mum told me that I had to eat. 'Just a little bit,' I groaned, patting my ever-expanding stomach. 'I've eaten so much food on this trip.' (Although my bulging waistline was probably more of a consequence of beer rather than food.) My 'little bit' was a plate piled high with spicy meatballs in tomato sauce, baked stuffed eggplant, pasta and rice.

'So, are you nervous about the wedding?' I asked Aylin with a mouthful of stuffed eggplant.

'A little bit,' she said musingly. She then showed me a red rash and splotches all up her arm. 'This is from the stress,' she sighed wearily. 'We really have made it hard on ourselves. As well as the wedding to organise, we're moving into the new flat and, to top it off, the deadline for the latest magazine is in three days.'

I asked Aylin what happens at a traditional Turkish wedding and she said that theirs wasn't going to be very traditional at all. 'There will be three stages,' Aylin said. 'First there is an official ceremony which is very short. It is so short that I missed a wedding a few weeks ago. The official ceremony started at seven. When I arrived at three minutes past, the ceremony was over. After the ceremony we will eat a meal with the family and then we're having a party with two hundred guests and we'll all get trashed.'

'Then we are having our honeymoon in Iceland,' James said excitedly.

'Oh, I was there a week ago,' I said.

'Do you have any recommendations?' Aylin asked.

'Yeah, double the limit on your credit card.'

After lunch we all squeezed into a taxi to go to James's nanna's place for a family get-together—except for Aylin's mum, who still had a little bit more space in the fridge to fill up with meals.

'We used to love this day when we were kids,' James said. 'When you kiss the hand of a relative, they give you money and we used to make loads.'

James also had an ulterior motive for making sure he caught up with all of his relatives. 'We want to be in the good books,' James said with a cheeky grin. 'So we get good wedding presents.'

It sounds like they do all right in the wedding gift stakes. Aylin said that she would also get gold pinned to her dress on the wedding day. 'It used to be money,' James said. 'But the Turkish Lira devalues too quickly.'

James's mum Julie (or Jool-ay as she pronounced it) met us at Nanna's door and there were hugs and kisses all round. Julie had a broad Yorkshire accent and she jumped effortlessly from rapid-fire Turkish to 'Ey oop'. As each relative greeted us, we were given handfuls of chocolates and sweets.

James introduced me to his brother John who was hanging halfway out of an open window smoking a cigarette.

John's accent was even stronger than James and Julie's. He had been working in Leeds for the past three years as a stonemason for a Turkish company that also had an office and factory in Istanbul.

The only reason he'd moved to Leeds was so he didn't have to do a long stint in the military. 'If you go to university, like James did,' he said, 'then you only have to do five months instead of fifteen months. I didn't want to do fifteen months, so I had to work abroad for three years. Then I only had to do twenty-one days military service.' John hadn't been able to come home to Turkey in that time. He returned to Turkey three years to the day after he'd left.

'I also had to pay for it, though,' he grumbled. 'To only do twenty-one days, I had to pay four thousand pounds.'

When some more relatives arrived, they stared at John in wonder. 'Everyone keeps staring at me,' he said. 'Before I left to do my military service I had long hair and a beard.' John, who had only finished his service the day before, was now clean-shaven and sporting short-cropped hair. 'I also lost a stone in weight,' he said as Nanna handed him a massive slice of cream cake. I think John may have been on a mission to put it all back on, though. When he'd devoured the cake he had a second serve that was bigger than the first.

'Are you going to move back to Turkey?' I asked John.

'No, I'll stay in England,' John said. 'That way I get the best of both worlds.'

I didn't want to be rude, but I wasn't sure how Leeds could be the best of any world.

'So, are you ready to go out?' James asked after I'd finished my third cup of tea.

'Right, let's go out and get fookin' pissed,' John said, rubbing his hands. Yes, I think John had turned English.

'Asia is boring, so we're going to Europe,' John said as we jumped in a taxi to the wharf. We were catching a ferry from Asia back to Europe.

'The city goes a bit crazy tonight,' James said aboard the ferry. 'There will be a million people in the streets that haven't had a drink for a month.'

The view from the ferry as we chugged across the Bosphorus was striking. Under the blanket of night the modern city took on its historic mantle as ancient mosques, including the imposing *Yeni Cami* mosque (which James informed me means New Mosque, even though it was built in 1663), and the old city walls were spectacularly illuminated with not quite so historic coloured lights.

We walked over Galata Bridge, constantly side-stepping the crowds. Scores of men were selling silvery fish displayed in baskets, while hundreds more lined the railings of the bridge fishing between the ferries. At the far end of the bridge, along the water's edge, a long line of charcoal barbecues was cooking the fresh fish that had just been caught. Not sure 'fresh' is the right word, though, and I think the fish themselves are probably thankful for their release from the dank and polluted waters of the Bosphorus. There were also folk cooking kebabs, pretzels, pancakes, mussels and corn on the cob.

We sauntered into 'Old Stamboul' and caught the world's second-oldest subway (after London's). We did the entire system, which is all of one stop. It did save us a walk up a very steep hill, though. When we stepped out of the station, we were immediately swept up among the throngs of revellers roaming up and down the traffic-free main street.

'All the foockin' idiots from the suburbs come into town after Ramadan,' John declared. We headed off the main drag and down a quiet narrow cobblestone lane, which was lined with hip bars with tables spilling out into the street. We grabbed an outside table and ordered large mugs of Efes Pilsen (on this trip alone, I think I'd sampled enough different beers to rival Smári's impressive list).

Over the next hour a whole gang of friends turned up to join us, including John's two new best friends from his short military stint. Neither of them lived in Turkey, though. One was German and the other lived a few kilometres away from me in Melbourne. Buyruk emigrated with his family to Australia when he was eight and he'd come back to live and work in Turkey for twelve months. For that privilege he had to do his military service and pay AU$8500.

'We had an American guy in our regiment who did military service so he could get his father's inheritance,' John told us. 'He didn't speak a word of Turkish, so the guys in our regiment taught him complicated swear words. He couldn't ask where the toilet was in Turkish, but he could say "I'm going to pour concrete into your mother's pussy, so I can't fuck her and neither can your father".'

Clearly, compulsory military service is a character-building experience and bolsters national pride.

'Did they do the fasting thing in the military?' I asked John.

'Nah, we'd be foockin' knackered if we did.'

The danger of becoming knackered seemed to be the main reason why most of James and Aylin's friends didn't fast during Ramadan. 'I did the whole Ramadan thing when I was young,' Aylin said. 'But not anymore. I'm too busy working too hard. You can't work without eating or drinking anything for twelve hours, you have no energy.'

'New Year is really the biggest day in Turkey,' James said. 'People put up Christmas trees with Santa Claus decorations and the devoted Muslims hate it.'

All the bars in the street were now busy with locals boozing up with abandon.

'I thought Muslims didn't drink,' I said to James.

'We are Muslim,' James shrugged. 'But we like to drink.'

'Turkey even has a ban on women wearing a burka,' Aylin said. 'It is forbidden by law for female politicians, lawyers, public servants and tertiary students to wear the veil in their place of work or study.'

The Muslim women of Turkey may not wear traditional veils, but they seemed to follow the Muslim doctrine of staying at home. When we went to another bar I noticed that at least 80 per cent of the people roaming the streets were men.

By the wee hours in the morning, only James, John and I were left as we sipped raki in a lovely rooftop bar looking out across the city. 'Let's get something to eat,' John suggested when we finished our drinks. We were in the right city for the perfect fodder after a few beers. And it wouldn't matter how drunk you were, you wouldn't have any trouble finding a kebab. Every second shop in Taksim Square was selling them. 'I know someone,' John said, tapping his nose. 'So we can get freebies.' I was quite excited as I took in the delicious smell of grilled meats that permeated the square.

'Here ya go,' John said. Much to my disappointment, John had come back with hamburgers.

I didn't get to try out my luxurious 'couch' at James's apartment because his mum's apartment was easier ('and a lot foockin' cheaper' John said) to get to. James gave me his old bedroom and it wasn't until I woke up in the morning that I realised what a lovely gesture that was. James had slept on the floor in John's bedroom on a pile of lumpy cushions.

'This is our office,' James announced as we stepped into the courtyard at the back of a cafe. 'They have wireless connection here and this is also where we do most of our interviews for the magazine.' The cafe was below their old flat and James told me that they spent more time working at the cafe than at their real office.

'This was an expensive area in the seventies,' Aylin said as we grabbed a table. 'Then drug addicts moved in and it became rundown. Now it's cool again.'

Too cool, according to James. 'All the *Sex and the City* wannabes are moving in now.'

I burst out laughing. 'The guy I stayed with in Chicago said *exactly* the same thing about where he lived.'

We had a traditional Turkish breakfast, which James and Aylin had most mornings. I was surprised James and Aylin were so slim when I saw how much food came out. We were served an array of plates that were piled high with cheeses, *sucuk* (spicy Turkish sausage), olives, sun-dried tomatoes, green peppers, *reçel* (a preserve made with whole fruits), cucumbers, tomatoes, *simit* (a circular roll with sesame seeds) and a huge omelette for each of us, served in a sizzling pan with cheese and tomato.

After our morning feast we went to the less-cafe-style offices of *bant*, which they shared with the same computer games magazine they'd been working for when they first met. James and Aylin had five full-time staff: an illustrator, advertising sales rep, designer and two writers. I left James and Aylin frantically typing away to go do the tourist thing. James did have one of piece of advice for me. 'Beware of men wearing fezzes,' he warned. 'If you go to a restaurant or shop and they are wearing fezzes then it's only for tourists.'

Only a short walk from the *bant* office is the most visited site in Istanbul: *Şişli Kültür ve Ticaret Merkezi*—in English, the Cevahir Shopping Centre. It is also the biggest shopping mall in Europe (and third largest in the world after South China Mall in Beijing and West Edmonton Mall in Canada). Yes, it was a mammoth mall of monumental proportions, but it looked like any other mall in the world, with the same mega-global brands. And like malls the world over, the place was teeming with teenagers—guys with an overabundance of hair product and girls with an overabundance of make-up—loitering about eating Macca's and texting each other. Naturally I got lost in there, and in hindsight it probably wasn't such a good idea to come to a shopping centre with hundreds and hundreds of shops when all I wanted to buy was a pack of chewing gum.

I caught the incredibly crowded Metro into the city. Public transport was free throughout the three-day holiday and, as John put it, 'All the foockin' idiots from the suburbs go on public transport just for the hell of it'. The tram was even more crowded. So much so, in fact, that the impatient folk at the tram stops didn't even wait for passengers to get off as they pushed and shoved their way aboard.

At every stop, more and more people somehow squeezed on until my face was rammed up against a fellow who could very easily have been mistaken for a gorilla. I was getting to experience a real Turkish bath as sweat dripped off everyone squished up against me. At one point the tram got so packed that the driver couldn't shut the doors. He tried and tried, and in the process kept slamming them into people's faces. The gorilla next to me began freaking out a little and started screaming and ranting at the driver and shoving people around. When the driver finally closed the doors, he kept on abusing him. The driver soon got his revenge, though. He suddenly slammed on the brakes and sent everyone surging forward. There was more abuse, so he slammed on the brakes again even harder. It was like some sadistic amusement-park ride. I got off one stop after the one I wanted, and even then I only escaped because Mr Gorilla pushed me out.

I devoted the rest of the day to the Istanbul Tourist Trifecta: the Blue Mosque, Hagia Sophia and Topkapi Palace.

The magnificent Blue Mosque (which was grey, but I won't bicker) is a mass of domes and arches topped with six slim minarets pointing heavenwards like defending rockets. James had another name for this famous place of worship: *Kokan Ayaklarin Büyük evi Kokan Ayaklar Konağı*, or The Grand House of the Smelly Feet. I added to the smell somewhat when I took off my sweaty boots, thanks to my time on The Grand Tram of the Sweaty Commuter. Inside the mosque was a huge open space with no pews, no icons, no ornaments, just acres of soft carpet and rows of devout people kneeling and praying. And not-so-devout Turkish teenagers. They were all taking photos of each other with their mobile phones underneath large signs saying NO PHOTOGRAPHS.

When we non-believers were ushered out for the official prayers, I saw the same teenagers slouching on steps under a huge sign which read: SITTING ON STEPS IS ABSOLUTELY FORBIDDEN.

The Hagia Sophia, which was built in the sixth century, was the largest enclosed space for more than a millennium. When I was there it happened to be housing a huge, and world-renowned, sculpture that travels extensively around major historical sites throughout Europe. Amazingly, and almost eerily, I seem to catch it a lot in my travels. I'm not sure of the exact date of the sculpture, which filled up about a quarter of the space inside and reached all the way to the top of the dome roof, but I'm guessing probably late last century. That's when I think most modern scaffolding was built. Admittedly, it was up there with the best when it came to nice scaffolding. It had a rather fetching matching orange staircase and fence around it. The Japanese tourists seemed to be impressed. They were taking lots of photos of it. I wandered past Thai, German, Italian, Spanish and French tour groups who were all undoubtedly talking about the intricate detail in the joinery work of the scaffolding.

Topkapi Palace was the administrative and erotic centre for the rulers of the Ottoman empire. I won't go into too much detail, but it is big, opulent and has lots of old stuff. It also gave me the chance to collect another site whose name has become generic, like Geysir in Iceland. Topkapi Palace was home to the many wives of successive Turkish sultans. The wives slept in a hall called 'Harim', which then began to be used as a generic name for the home of many wives. This famous harem typically housed at times up to a thousand women. That's a lot of nagging about leaving the toilet seat up.

I watched the sun set majestically over the Blue Mosque from the tram stop. I had to wait almost an hour for a tram that wasn't bursting at the seams with 'foockin' idiots from the suburbs'.

Back at the *bant* offices, everyone was still working hard. 'I'm so sorry,' James lamented. 'We're not very good guides.'

'That's okay,' I said. 'It can't be helped.'

'We've just got some dinner, if you want some.' James said.

Dinner was tuna sandwiches, Doritos and bottles of Diet Coke, but it wasn't quite the traditional Turkish cuisine I was hoping for. When I asked where I might find some traditional Turkish fare, James recommended a restaurant around the corner.

Külünçe Sofrası restaurant was a traditional Turkish restaurant (but minus the belly-dancing show). The restaurant didn't serve alcohol, but that was fine by me. I was having an AFD (Alcohol-Free Day) anyway. Not only was it nice (and nicer for my liver) to take a night off from drinking, it was also just nice to have a night out by myself. One of the problems with couch surfing is that, as a guest, you feel obliged to be constantly 'entertaining' your hosts. You can't just sit back at your host's house and say 'pass me the TV remote and keep the noise down will ya'. Although maybe I could cater for that market by starting up my own website: GlobalCouchPotato.com.

Külünçe Sofrası restaurant fitted my 'no English menu' criterion, but there weren't any English-speaking staff either, so ordering was a little more tricky. I had one of those uneasy exchanges you experience whilst travelling where you ask for something with a mix of English and charades (and it's not easy doing 'What's the specialty of the house?'), then the waiter speaks for five minutes in their own language pointing at something on the menu that you can't read anyway.

For all I know this guy was saying that, since you are a stupid tourist who has accidentally wandered into a restaurant where the waiters do not wear fezzes and you can't understand a word of what I am telling you, allow me to recommend the least popular and most expensive dish on the menu.

I just nodded my head and said, 'Yes, that would be lovely!'

I think I may have ordered 'the banquet for ten'. My 'entrée' of bread and dips was a meal in itself. The flat Turkish bread was the size of a placemat. The main course was a platter piled with chicken wings, *köfte* (meatballs), shish kebabs, pizza, various *böreks* (savoury filled pastries), large grilled green chillies, grilled tomatoes and salad. When my waiter served it up, he spent a good ten minutes explaining everything that was on the plate to me in Turkish.

When I waddled back to the *bant* office, James said, 'I rang some friends and they will take you out for a drink if you like.'

'Um . . . I'm actually happy just to hang out here,' I said. 'Plus I'm having an Alcohol-Free Day.'

'I'm so sorry,' James said two hours later. 'You must be so bored.'

'I've been out every night for the past five weeks,' I said. 'I'm so happy to be bored.'

I was so happy to be bored, in fact, that I fell asleep at one of the desks. James and Aylin finally called it a day (or night in this case) at 12.30. 'Shall we go out for a quick drink?' James asked.

'What about my Alcohol-Free Day?'

'It's after twelve, so it's technically the next day,' James said.

'Yeah, okay.'

James had a very romantic morning for two planned: picking up the wedding rings that James and Aylin had helped design at a jewellers in the Grand Bazaar, and then having a massage together. Except it wasn't that romantic, because it was just James and me.

Istanbul is not only the home of Europe's biggest shopping mall, it's also home to Europe's oldest shopping mall. The very grand Grand Bazaar is made up of 60 covered streets with more than 4000 shops housing stalls that have been selling the same wares for centuries—gold and silver jewellery, copperware, pottery, carpets and Viagra. Near the gold jewellery section was the spice market (as in spice-up-your-marriage market). Rows of stalls were selling, amongst other things, Deadly Shark Power Delay Spray (for your premature ejaculation); Super Stay Delay Spray; mega-packs of Viagra; and an impressive collection of porn DVDs. The fellow selling Deadly Shark Power Delay Spray was holding up a box and bellowing out in Turkish, which James translated as something like 'Go like a ram all night'.

Most of the stalls in the Grand Bazaar were closed for the holidays, but there were still more than enough merchants to pester us. Thankfully, having a local with me meant that I was mostly left alone. And when we did get hassled by a couple of persistently insistent shopkeepers, James said something to get rid of them very quickly. I'm not sure what he said, but I guessed it was 'I'm going to pour concrete into your mother's pussy, so I can't fuck her and neither can your father'.

James still had a lot of work to do on the magazine, but he very kindly offered to spend the morning with me and try to squeeze in as many quintessential Turkish experiences as we could into a couple of hours. After we'd sprinted around the market, we ducked through a tiny doorway leading off the street, to a large open courtyard that was decked out with colourful carpets, low tables and glass cabinets filled with water pipes that lined the walls. 'The locals bring their own and leave them here,' James said. 'You can't come to Turkey and not have a water pipe,' he said as we perused the water pipe menu, which came in flavours of banana, strawberry, cappuccino, chocolate and apple.

'We used to come here every day when I was at university,' James said as we sat back, puffing away.

'Did you study journalism?' I asked.

'No. Spanish,' he shrugged. 'And most of my friends from uni are now Spanish tour guides.'

The last stop on our whistle-stop tour was the Çemberlitas Hamamı, a Turkish bath house that was built in 1584. We booked in for the full-service grease and oil change.

'You. Undress. Now,' the locker attendant barked at me. 'Go in locker.'

'In locker?' I asked incredulously.

The locker, which was actually a small cubicle, even had a bed.

'You remember me for tip, okay?' he winked.

After I'd barely covered my naked body with a tiny towel we headed into the steam room (the *hararet*), which had a high-domed ceiling with walls and floor of silver-grey marble. We were instructed to lie on a massive heated marble slab where I promptly dozed off to asleep. I woke with a fright to howling and moaning. It was James being pummelled and pulled apart by a gorilla. My masseur, who I'm guessing was once part of the Turkish wrestling team, approached me with a rough mitt on one hand and a bucket of suds in the other. He then began singing lustily as he exfoliated my skin, or more like tore it off, while he poured boiling water and soap suds all over me.

This was followed by a massage, which involved my large friend mounting me and trying to tear my limbs off. It was my turn to howl and moan. He finished off the 'relaxing' massage by throwing a bucket of ice-cold water over my head.

'You remember me for tip, okay?' he said. That wasn't going to be easy. All the staff looked identical with their dark curly hair, hairy chests, long droopy moustaches and bulbous bellies.

After our greasing, it was time for the oiling. A different, but identical, masseur oiled me up for more stretching, bashing, pummelling and howling.

Admittedly, after a lovely hot shower, I felt incredibly relaxed and refreshed. Then we got on a packed tram and in less than a minute I was hot, bothered and stressed again.

James went back to work while I went to a restaurant that James had suggested for lunch. Hamdi et Lokantasi

Restaurant was on the rooftop of an apartment building that overlooked Galata Bridge and the Golden Horn. The view was outstanding, although I was put in the corner with an outstanding view of the waiter's station. At the top of the menu it had: 'Hamdi—The same taste and address since 1970.' The time-warp effect went further than that. They had also retained the same plates and cutlery and the same waiters wearing the same uniforms.

Thankfully, the fish and kebabs I ordered were more recent additions.

As I left the restaurant, a taxi slowed down out the front and the driver asked if I wanted a 'ride for you'. I said yes and jumped straight in. I had planned to see more of the city, but I was so tired I was more than happy just to head back to the *bant* office and do very little at all.

James and Aylin were initially a bit surprised when, just after eight o'clock, I asked if I could head back to the apartment because I was ready for bed. They were then pleasantly surprised to discover that the reason I was so looking forward to bed was that I had bestowed the highest ranking so far on their 'couch'.

Couch rating: 9/10

Pro: A big comfy double quilt

Con: Not quite as comfy single-quilted toilet paper in the ensuite

James and Aylin didn't get in until 7.30 in the morning. They'd been working all night. Although both of them were utterly exhausted, they very kindly offered to escort me down to the ferry terminal (the ferry's last stop was only a short taxi ride from the airport). We still had a bit of time before the ferry departed, so we wandered down to a delightful little outdoor cafe on the waterfront and ordered black tea and some particularly sticky buns.

After our tea we were sitting back taking in the view when I interrupted our companionable reverie and said, 'Thanks for being such lovely hosts'. This heartfelt if rather trite declaration was greeted with absolute silence.

I turned around and both James and Aylin had dozed off.

KENYA

15

'I am a real Kenyan, I love my country, I love my family and you will go home full of mamories.'
Thadeus Mutinda Mutisya, 34, Nairobi, Kenya
CouchSurfing.com

'Welcome to Nairobbery!' my host Thadeus Mutinda Mutisya beamed as we drove into the centre of Nairobi. 'Some people call it Nairobbery,' he continued, 'because some people get robbed often.'

When Mutisya then told me about a story in the *Daily Nation* newspaper that morning, I contemplated heading straight back to the airport. A man had been robbed in the slums, then his penis was chopped off with a machete and his body was dumped on the rail line. Gee, times must be tough to have to steal a penis—although I'm not exactly sure why you'd need a spare penis.

Maybe it would have been safer if I'd couch-surfed with George Ndungu, who listed his occupation as 'Chief Head of Security'. Then again, I didn't quite fit his criteria for

'Types of people I enjoy'. He said: 'I enjoy young mature woman serving in social services, but who fancy enjoying the inner gift.'

Catherine might have also been a safe bet: 'I live in a peaceful neighbourhood, clean and bully-free. No guns allowed.' In her case, though, I may not have been considered serious enough for her liking because she said 'I don't like jokers'.

Chal, on the other hand, would only take guests who were safe: 'We would like to welcome born again Christian guests who are safe and will not drink beer, smoke or use drugs. They should note that we don't go to the pubs or have drinking sprees.'

My host Mutisya was not quite so confident about his guests' safekeeping. He said: 'Security is ok sometimes when in my place.' He did, however, offer to teach his guests how to kiss a giraffe:

> Enjoy a home far away from home, learn about our culture, visit my village with our family on weekends, help in shopping, learn a bit of Kiswahili language, visit our beautiful places in town and learn how to kiss the giraffe.

I told him that I might pass on kissing a giraffe. Have you seen the size of their tongues?

I rang Mutisya from the airport and he offered to pick me up. He was right when he said that he would be easy to spot—Mutisya waltzed into the arrivals hall wearing an over-sized bright red Coca-Cola T-shirt with smart beige slacks and yellow thongs.

'We are not staying in Nairobi,' Mutisya said when I jumped into his dusty Toyota. 'We will visit my wife and children for a short time, then we will go to my village.' Mutisya's village was Mukuyuni in the Kangundo region, two hours east of the city. 'I have big plans for you,' Mutisya gushed excitedly. 'You will meet all of my family in the village and you will be very tired.'

'How many are in your family?' I asked.

'I have five brothers, three sisters and many, many cousins and you will meet them all. Then we will go meet some animals.'

Mutisya should have had a fair idea where to meet some animals. He ran his own tour and safari company.

Before we went to visit his wife and children for a short time, Mutisya took me on a tour of the city. Which turned out to be a tour of nondescript buildings. Our first stop was the National Conference Centre, a tall modern building in the centre of the business district.

'You must get out and take a photo,' Mutisya urged. 'It is the tallest building in *all* of Nairobi.'

Mutisya must have been very proud of Nairobi's tall buildings because at our next stop Mutisya said, 'Take a photo. This is another nice tall building.' Mind you, we did stop a number of times to take photos of other buildings that weren't blessed with that crowd-pulling height advantage, including the Ministry of Finance building, Ministry of

Foreign Affairs building, Ministry of Police building, Ministry of Education building and the City Morgue.

Besides the 'very nice buildings', Nairobi was just as I imagined it: dusty, smelly, noisy—and that was just the people on every street corner jostling for pole position to sell stuff to passers-by.

'Take a photo of the street,' Mutisya commanded as he pulled up in the middle of Kenyatta Avenue. 'Now take one the other way. And look, there is a signpost, take that too.'

I'd been in the country for less than an hour and I'd already taken almost a hundred photos.

At the end of our tour we did stop somewhere that wasn't a modern building. It was more of a collection of wooden sheds. We had a brief stroll around Nairobi's oldest city market, although the old stalls were mostly selling very modern souvenirs like T-shirts and key rings. Well, the ones that weren't selling wooden giraffes, that is. I did purchase two authentic African souvenirs, though—two very authentic African bananas.

'Nairobi has a small city centre and the rest is mostly slums,' Mutisya said as we drove down a street lined with corrugated-iron shacks and thick with ragged children slinking about in the shadows.

'This is a very dangerous area,' Mutisya said matter-of-factly. 'Make sure your door is locked.'

I'd checked before he'd finished saying 'locked'. 'If someone knocks on the window, ignore them,' he continued. 'And whatever you do, don't open your window.' There was no way I was going to open my window. I'm quite attached to my penis and anxious to stay that way.

When we turned down a potholed dirt road where people in rags and yapping dogs huddled around piles of burning rubbish, Mutisya said, 'This is a nicer part of town'. This nicer part of town was where Mutisya lived. We parked next to a donkey and cart and entered a small doorway set into a whitewashed brick wall that led into a dusty courtyard criss-crossed by crowded clotheslines. Several lodgings that seemed to be mostly full of screaming children overlooked the courtyard.

When Mutisya's five-year-old boy William skipped out to greet me, I gave him a colouring book and a big pack of crayons and I don't think I'd ever seen such delight in a child's eyes.

'That's not my son,' Mutisya said.

I don't think I'd ever seen such sorrow in a child's eyes when I took the presents away from him and gave them to the real William.

The inside of Mutisya's house was quite gloomy, with the only light coming from one small candle. And when I say house, I'm actually talking about a one-room hut. Most of the space in that room was taken up by a double bed. There was a rather fetching brown-velour couch against one wall and an ornate brass glass-topped coffee table was squeezed in between the bed and the couch. There were no wardrobes or cupboards, so all the family's clothes were hanging around the walls. In one corner was the 'kitchen', which amounted to nothing more than a small gas cooker and a sink. In the other corner was a separate 'room' with a flush toilet. Just that alone made Mutisya's house worthy of being in a 'nicer part of town'. I remember reading somewhere that in one area of Nairobi there were only ten pit toilets for 40 000 people.

Mutisya's wife Terry Mwongeli was happy to see me—particularly when I gave her a big box of Belgian chocolates that I'd bought in Turkey. Terry very proudly showed me five-week-old Lorenzo, who was gurgling away in a bassinette on the bed.

'I named him after a couch surfer from Italy who stayed here,' Mutisya said.

Terry prepared us a breakfast of bananas, avocado, fried egg, coconut and bread, while William, like kids the world over, was happily colouring in with his tongue sticking out.

'When is William's birthday?' I asked.

'February the twenty-fifth.'

'Oh!' I said. 'My daughter Jasmine was born the day before.'

'Then they *must* marry each other,' Mutisya said. 'I will come to Australia with some cows.'

'Cows?'

'Yes, to give to you and your wife as a dowry.'

I showed Mutisya a photo of Jasmine and he was suitably impressed. 'She is very beautiful,' he nodded. 'I think she is worth five cows. Maybe six.'

It was a good offer. Mutisya's parents only got one cow from his wife's family.

The minute we finished breakfast, Mutisya stood up and said, 'Now we must go'. Then, without even a glance in farewell to his wife, we were out the door.

On the drive out of the city Mutisya kept pulling over to the side of the road. He seemed to know just about everyone in Nairobi and, like some royal dignitary, he would either stop to shake hands or wave and smile as we drove past. On one of our regal stops we picked up Mutisya's cousin Willy, who jumped into the driver's seat. 'I don't have a licence,' Mutisya shrugged. 'And I don't know how to drive.'

That would certainly help explain the seemingly random careering all over the road.

'You can just buy a licence in Kenya,' Mutisya said. 'Or you can do the test, which is easy anyway. You just have to drive fifty metres and be able to go from first to second gear, then they stop and hand you your licence.'

Mind you, I was soon unsure if Willy knew how to drive either. He had a somewhat unnerving penchant for overtaking into oncoming traffic and then veering uncontrollably onto the shoulder, scattering chickens and the odd startled bystander. Willy hailed from Mutisya's neighbouring village and was working as a driver so he could afford to finish the fourth and last year of his training as a motor mechanic. A driver who is also a mechanic is highly sought after in Kenya. Given the state of the roads and the state of the driving, it wasn't hard to see why.

When we stopped for petrol, Mutisya asked me if I wanted to get out and take a photo of the petrol station.

'I'm fine, thanks.'

I also declined to take a photo of the supermarket where Mutisya stopped to get some rice and oil for his family in the village.

Not long after leaving the supermarket, we were out of the city and speeding through wide-open plains dotted with flat-top trees that looked just like the plains in *The Lion King* (but without the musical accompaniment). Within minutes I spotted my first African animals. Okay, they were only local cows and goats, but African animals nonetheless.

After more than an hour of driving across the unchanging plains, we turned off the main road and drove through the village of Tala, which was the last major town before Mutisya's village. And when I say drove through, I mean we drove right through the middle of the weekly market, scattering people, cows, goats and an entire class of schoolgirls in neat green dresses. Most of the produce in the market, which included maize, coffee beans, millet, sweet potatoes and onions, had been harvested from the surrounding farms.

We stopped for lunch at the Backyard Club Restaurant on the edge of town. A waiter in a crisp white shirt and bow tie greeted us at the entrance, then escorted us to our own private whitewashed mud-walled dining hut with a conical thatched roof. The hut was one of about a dozen clustered around a large central, open-sided bar. Each dining hut housed six to ten built-in, throne-like chairs set around a small central table. These 'traditional' huts were named after 'traditional' European football teams. As soon as we sat down in the Juventus hut (I refused to sit in the Arsenal one), Mutisya immediately summoned the waitress, by grunting at her, and grunted an order for some grilled chicken and Tusker beers.

'The owner's father is a senior police official,' Mutisya whispered as we sat down. 'So that is why he can afford to own this place.'

Mutisya leant over and gave me a sly wink. 'It helps if you have corruption.'

'Does Kenya have a lot of corruption?' I asked.

Mutisya scoffed. 'Kenya is the world capital of corruption.'

Wilson, the owner, joined us for a drink before taking me on a tour of his recently opened, and somewhat empty, corruption-funded restaurant.

'Your lunch is very fresh,' Wilson said as we stopped at the open-sided kitchen. The chef was plucking a chicken, which up until only a few minutes before had been clucking away happily in the cage next to the kitchen.

Back in the Juventus hut a gorgeous waitress appeared with a jug of warm water and soap to wash our hands. 'In Kenya we eat with our hands,' Mutisya said, miming putting food in his mouth with his hands.

'I think we should order some more food,' Mutisya said. 'You must have the famous Kenyan dish *Nyama choma*. Do you want cow or goat?'

'Um . . . I'm not sure,' I stammered.

I couldn't quite get the picture out of my head of a cow or goat sitting out the back just waiting to be plucked.

'Do you like her?' Wilson asked when he saw me smile at the waitress as she poured the water onto my hands. 'Would you like her for your second wife?' Wilson urged. 'I can arrange it if you like.' The waitress gave me a shy smile.

'I'm okay, thanks,' I said as another waitress turned up with the grilled chicken, rice and big slabs of the East Africa staple *ugali,* a maize-based dish similar to polenta. Willy ordered another round of beers even though I'd only taken a few sips from my first beer. 'How much beer can you drink? Willy asked me.

'Um . . . a bit I suppose,' I said.

'We can drink a whole crate!'

'Kenyans drink too much,' Wilson said, shaking his head. 'And they all get very drunk.'

'Everywhere I've been on this trip so far everyone gets very drunk,' I said.

'Why is that?'

Because it's a whole lot of fun.

'I don't really know,' I said musingly.

'In Kenya it is stress,' Wilson sighed. 'And mostly when you are married. The wife stays at home while you have to support her. And if she works you still have to pay for everything and the woman keeps her money to herself.'

'What do they do with their money?'

Wilson shrugged. 'Clothes and hairdressers.'

After we left Tala the brown dirt road turned blazing red as we climbed up into lush hills covered with banana and mango trees and pink, purple and yellow flowering trees. The 'main street' of Mukuyuni village was a haphazard collection of tumbledown shacks with men, who were mostly wearing jeans and T-shirts covered in red dust, slouching lazily against doorways. Willy had to drive at a snail's pace so Mutisya could greet every single person with a handshake and a smile.

Mutisya's family home, which overlooked a verdant valley in which coffee and maize were grown, was a cluster of red mud-brick buildings in amongst chicken coops and a few goats and cows. As well as Mutisya's parents, the farm was home to his brother's family and his 96-year-old grandma, who was sitting up on her matriarchal throne in front of the main house. Grandma didn't look a day over 70—until she smiled at me and revealed her three remaining teeth.

Most of the main house consisted of a large and brightly lit lounge room. The light shone from a solar-powered fluorescent lamp, which was the only light on the entire farm. And one of the very few in the entire village, which had no electricity or running water.

Mutisya showed me to the back of the house, where he was in the process of renovating two bedrooms specifically for couch surfers. 'I want everyone in the world to come to my village,' he said brightly. From the back door he swept his arm in the direction of a pile of cow shit and said, 'I'm going to put a barbecue and a bar here for the couch surfers.' Mutisya had already hosted quite a few couch surfers, including folk from Japan, Poland, New Zealand, America, Canada, England, Germany, Spain, France, Italy and Brazil. 'It is good that many people come, because they spend money in the village,' Mutisya said. 'Which is much good for my community.'

Quite a few of those couch surfers, I later discovered, also happened to spend money booking a safari with Mutisya. Which is much good for Mutisya. Yes, making a buck out of couch surfers is not really in the spirit of couch surfing, but in Mutisya's defence he was also genuinely interested in just getting people to experience an authentic Kenyan village—and an authentic Kenyan safari without the zebra-striped jeep.

After my brief tour we headed back into the village to the local pub, which was less of a pub and more of a tin shack with rough concrete floors and tables and chairs that looked as if they'd been hastily cobbled together using a few old branches. The only light came from a solitary gas lamp sitting on the bar, while an ancient radio, which was plugged into a car battery, was barely audible through the static. What I could make of the chorus of the song playing did seem quite apt, though: 'I want a Tusker, no women for me, I want a Tusker.' The bar was full of men and most of them were totally tanked. I was introduced to everyone as a very famous author known all around the world. I told Mutisya that I wouldn't quite go that far—I'm still having trouble selling my books in Kyrgyzstan.

I grabbed a round of warm beers (no power meant no fridge) and sat down at a table with Mutisya's dad and 80-year-old Moses, who gave me a huge toothless smile. Neither of them spoke English. Mutisya told me that Moses once had three wives and eighteen children, but all three wives and fifteen of his children were dead—more than half of them from AIDs. Also sitting at the table was Norman, a neatly dressed English teacher with bushy white sideburns. He was also one of the very few men in the room who wasn't rolling drunk.

'Our village has many, many problems,' he said, opening the conversation on a high note. Norman then went on to list all of the village's problems. 'The total welfare of the village depends on water,' Norman said. 'There is only one well, which is twenty metres deep, and in the dry season people have to queue for up to twenty-four hours to get a few litres of water.'

There was also not much work in the village. 'Most of the people in the village work in the fields as casual labour,' Norman said. 'The only other work is building roads, but it is very hard work and you do not get paid. You work only for food.'

'The village really needs electricity,' Willy said, adding his two cents' worth to the village's tale of woe. Willy's village, which was only twenty minutes' drive away, had electricity. 'My father was very smart,' Willy said, tapping his nose. 'He organised electricity for our village twenty years ago. Now it is much too expensive for this village to get it.'

The list of problems went on. The village wasn't serviced by any public transport and the roads were so poor that it was difficult to get produce to the market.

All things considered then, I wasn't that surprised when Norman told me that alcoholism was another big problem. Some of the men in the bar were so drunk that it took them a few minutes of extreme concentration just to get their drinks to their mouth. Most of the men had been drinking *chang'a*, which is a lethal methyl alcohol concoction that is often supercharged with the added ingredients of marijuana twigs, cactus mash, battery alkaline and formalin. 'Last year a batch made in Machakos killed more than fifty people,' Willy told me.

'We are always positive that we can make a change,' Norman said with resolute confidence. Each week the menfolk held a meeting to discuss ways to develop and better the village. 'It takes a long time to get anything done, though,' Norman shrugged wearily. To even get their grievances heard, the village administrator has to present to the AC (Assistant Commissioner), who in turn goes to the DO (District Officer), who goes to the DC (District Commissioner), then finally to the PC (Provisional Commissioner). Sadly, it seemed like a lot of BS to get FA.

We all squeezed into Mutisya's Shuttle Service after we left the pub. The car was chock-full of drunken uncles. One uncle couldn't even stand up—he would have had no chance of walking, let alone finding his way home in the total darkness.

By the time we got back to the house and sat down for dinner it was after 10.30. Mutisya's mum, who had been waiting patiently for the men to come home from the pub, served up a tasty dish of large slabs of *ugali* and cabbage mixed with tomatoes and onions.

My bed was in another house, because the newly renovated 'couch surfing' rooms reeked of paint fumes. I couldn't give my new 'couch' a rating just yet, though—I couldn't even see my room or my bed in the dark.

In the middle of the night I needed the toilet and, although there was a squat toilet outside away from the house, Mutisya told me to simply walk to the end of the corridor and just wee on the washroom floor. The 'washroom' was a small, empty room with a concrete floor. Finding the washroom, however, was more easily said than done. When I stepped outside my room it was so dark that I couldn't figure out if I should go left or right. I think I pissed in the right place. Either that or I relieved myself on the lounge-room floor.

Mutisya knocked on my bedroom door at eight o'clock and I stumbled out rubbing my eyes. 'This is a bit too early for me,' I moaned pathetically. I felt even more pathetic when Mutisya told me that 96-year-old Grandma had been up since five o'clock and that she still worked in the fields planting or collecting maize. She even had to walk a few kilometres just to get to the fields. Grandma had already returned from her morning's toil and was standing out the front of the main house pounding a long wooden pestle into a large mortar, transforming dried maize kernels into a fine powder to make the base for *ugali.* Just to absolutely confirm my place in the upper echelon of patheticness, I had a go and only lasted four minutes until my arms got too sore.

Mutisya kindly organised a large bucket of warm water so I could have a wash and set me up in the small, empty washroom—but thankfully not the one in the house that I may or may not have pissed in. Actually, the room *wasn't* empty. The walls were crawling with giant ants. 'Watch it, they bite,' Mutisya warned.

'I left my towel in Istanbul, do you have one I could borrow?' I asked.

'You can use this,' Mutisya said, handing me a dusty and somewhat smelly piece of crumpled-up cloth.

It was raining sheets when we headed out for a guided tour of Mutisya's relatives. Our first stop was Uncle Edwin's 'butchery', which was housed in a wooden shack with no refrigeration and no glass in the shop windows. Uncle Edwin was inside, busily hacking up meat that was covered in flies. Fresh goat meat, with blood dripping onto the floor, was hanging up in a cage behind him while chopped-up delights such as cow brains, livers and pigs' feet were laid out on wooden shelves that were open to the dusty road outside.

Although we'd just eaten breakfast we headed to the back room for a 'morning snack'. I almost brought up my breakfast when I saw our morning snack. It was 'African sausages'—otherwise known as goat's intestines. The boiled intestines, which were grey and slimy, came out dangling daintily from a stick. This was accompanied by a mug of soup that I'm pretty sure isn't in the Continental Cup-a-Soup range: Hearty Goat with Fat Globs and Grey Sludge. I will try to eat most things, but after the first sip left a thick layer of grease on the inside of my mouth I sheepishly (if that's the word) pushed it aside.

'Because you are a special guest we have a surprise for you,' Mutisya said, rubbing his hands together excitedly. It certainly was a surprise. Mutisya's uncle plopped a rather grotesque-looking boiled and blackened goat's head down on the table. At least we didn't have to eat it by ourselves, since a crowd of men appeared and began something of a feeding frenzy as they pulled off ears, eyes, cheeks and lips. Being the special guest, I was handed the 'choice' portions, but God knows what I ate. I sampled all sorts of squishy white, brown and pink chunks of meat. And something that looked like grey jelly. Admittedly, some of the bits were quite tasty, but others tasted not unlike rancid shark meat.

When the skull had been picked bare, Mutisya's uncle produced a huge machete and smashed it open, splattering bits of goat's brain onto my face and clothes. The rest of the grey mush was devoured in less than three minutes. All that was left on the table was the skull, jawbone and teeth.

We spent most of the afternoon driving from house to house through heavy rain and thick mud on The Great Relative, Cow, Goat and Chicken Tour. With an ever-changing entourage of relatives joining us in the car, we visited a brother, an aunty and a third cousin and they all seemed to have large broods of humans, goats and dogs.

On the way out of Nairobi we'd passed shop after shop selling couches and now I knew why. Our last call was on Uncle Peter, who had five couches and six lounge chairs squeezed into his living room. Peter needed plenty of space because he had nine children and fourteen grandchildren, and he himself was one of ten brothers and five sisters.

The most comfortable chair was reserved for Nzioka, Peter's 103-year-old father. 'He has lived so long because he had three wives,' Mutisya told me. Nzioka, who still looked incredibly sprightly for a centenarian, had served in the British Army during the First World War then worked as a butcher until he retired at 89. Peter was also retired after working as a policeman for 36 years.

All the men were kicking back in the lounge room while the women scuttled about preparing dinner—which I guessed would be chicken after I'd spotted aunty chasing one around the yard as we'd arrived. That chicken may have also been past retirement age. Although it was tasty, it was a bit like trying to eat a rubber novelty chicken.

After dinner, the men discussed village politics. Or rather Mutisya did all the discussing while the others listened. Peter told me later that Mutisya was a budding politician and that one day he would be Prime Minister.

I was having a lot of trouble staying awake. I'm pretty sure I was in the advanced stages of CSFS (Couch Surfing Fatigue Syndrome). It wasn't even eight o'clock and I couldn't keep my eyes open. I even tried to write some notes, but I dozed off mid-sentence. I woke up almost an hour later with a long black pen line scrawled down the centre of my notebook.

'Have you got a gun?' I asked Mutisya.

'What for?'

'So I can shoot whatever was making that "ERRRGGG-OOOHHH" noise at four o'clock in the morning.'

'That is the cows.'

'If William does marry Jasmine, you can keep the cows,' I said.

The moaning cows did bring the couch rating down a fraction:

Couch rating: 6/10

Con: The room was dark

Pro: The room was so dark that I couldn't see how dirty the sheets were

It was still raining, so we dropped into the 'hotel' in the main street of the village, which was run by Mutisya's brother Francis. A 'hotel' in Kenya is traditionally a teashop. Because of the rain the place was full of men drinking milk tea and eating *chapatis*. Francis's wife served us our tea and Mutisya told me that she got up at 4.30 every day of the year to milk the cows and then worked at the hotel all day serving tea.

'Milk was our incentive to go to school when I was young,' Mutisya said as we sipped our hot tea. 'We were given milk at the end of class and all the kids would come to school because not many families could afford to buy milk.'

Mutisya, Willy and Francis had a funeral to go to, but because it was still raining they decided to go to the pub instead. Although it wasn't quite midday, the pub was full of drunk men, including a few who had already passed out slumped in their chairs.

Just as we sat down, the chief of the village arrived. When Mutisya introduced him to me, he took off his hat. 'It is a sign of respect to take off your hat,' Mutisya said.

'Oh, should I take off my hat? I asked, reaching for my cap.

'No, no,' Mutisya said, shaking his head. 'He is taking off *his* hat as a sign of respect for you because you are a world-famous author.'

When the rain finally cleared we headed out in the car to see a 'much nice view' from the top of Yatta plateau. As usual the 'we' also included an entourage. Joining us this time were a young lady named Catherine and some old bloke from the pub. We drove for 40 minutes up a steep dirt road and then continued by foot up a narrow track through a eucalyptus forest that smelt just like the Australian bush and, very tentatively on my part, along the edge of a steep precipice with a sheer drop down to vast brown plains running away to a far-off horizon.

I was even more cautious when we shuffled out onto Thui Rock lookout, which hung precariously over a jagged rocky outcrop. It was worth it, though. The view was spectacular as the late afternoon sun cast long shadows that seemed to stretch right across the continent. We were so high up that hawks were circling far below us in the thermals.

'This is not in any guide book,' Mutisya said proudly.

Mutisya pointed out a series of caves below where 'men bring women for to have them'. These women were usually someone else's wives. 'The women say that they are going out looking for firewood,' Mutisya said with a wink.

The old fellow said something to Mutisya who translated: 'He told me that the last time he came up here was in nineteen-sixty.'

'To help a woman look for firewood?' I said, returning the wink.

On the way back to the village we dropped into the Backyard Bar for dinner and *cold* beers. The bar was chock-full with locals watching an English Premier League match on a big-screen TV. When we went to sit down there weren't enough spare chairs, so Willy grabbed a seat, then grabbed Catherine and sat her down on his knee.

'We call him Mr Smooth,' Mutisya said. 'You know he once had sex with one of my couch surfers.'

After dinner Mutisya stood up and announced, 'You must see a Kenyan nightclub.' I would have passed if I'd known getting to this Kenyan nightclub meant a 50-minute drive in pitch darkness on a rough dirt road, all the while getting tossed around in the back like a rag doll. I was exhausted by the time we got there just from holding on for dear life.

The busy main street of Machakos town was crammed with bars and nightclubs, including Hot Babe Nightclub and one rather subtly named 'Drink Here'. Since there were plenty of menacing-looking youths milling about, we opted for the one place that I figured should be safe from any trouble: the Peace and Love nightclub.

Inside, a Kenyan UB40 cover band was bouncing around on stage while a big-screen TV was showing a video of various African animals copulating, or 'animals getting married' as Willy described it. The old bloke from the pub immediately fell asleep in the corner.

I was tired and didn't really feel like partying, but I ended up having a fun night after a few beers and quite a bit of dancing. At one point I noticed someone staring at me. And no, it wasn't my terrible dancing. It's funny, but I hadn't even noticed that I was the only *mazungo*, or white man, in the nightclub.

Mutisya drove back at breakneck speed. And it wasn't because he was in a hurry to get home. He was just drunk.

'The Kamba people are the best woodcarvers in the world,' Mutisya boasted. 'Not just in Kenya, but the whole entire world.'

We were driving through hot dusty plains near the village of Wamunyu, which is home to what looked like just about every woodcarving workshop in Africa. 'Most of the wooden giraffes in people's homes around the world comes from here,' Mutisya told me as we passed a fourth large gang of woodcarvers sitting just off the road, on top of a mountain of yellow wood chips, carving out wooden giraffes. In fact, all four workshops we'd passed were full of folk knocking out wooden giraffes and nothing else.

We stopped at the region's largest workshop, where around 40 old men were squatting in front of a long, open-sided tin shelter roughly chiselling out entire herds of giraffes (or corps of giraffes, which is apparently the correct collective noun). 'Older men do the first and most important part of the carving,' Mutisya said as we negotiated our way over the wood-chip minefield. 'It's because they are the most experienced and fastest.' Inside the shelter, long lines of younger men were sitting cross-legged on the dirt floor fervently filing and sandpapering. Although it looked like incredibly delicate work, they were extremely quick. Right at the very back of the shelter a giggling group of young women was painting the giraffes. 'The longer and harder you work, the more money you make,' Mutisya said as we stepped around a massive pile of giraffes waiting to be painted. Everyone was so diligent because they all had a stake in the business. Each artisan was a member of the 3000-strong Wamunya Co-operative Society that owned and ran the workshops.

They certainly were devoted. Although it was Sunday the workshop was full and most of the workers had started at 6.30 in the morning and would work for twelve hours or more. Mutisya asked one of the carvers why they were so busy.

'A huge order from America came in,' he said.

In the adjoining co-op shop was a large display of just about every animal you can think of carved out of wood, ebony and mahogany. There was also a small army of 2-metre high African Blackwood Masai warriors.

'You can get thousands of dollars for one of those on eBay,' Mutisya whispered. 'I'm saving up to buy a few.'

Mutisya really was quite the entrepreneur. On the drive out to visit his brother Vincent's farm he told me that he owned the farm. 'The farm was empty when I bought it,' Mutisya told me. 'But local people began moving in and cultivating the land, so I built a house for my brother to live in so he could run the farm for himself.'

I asked Mutisya if he was considered well off in Kenya and he said, 'I am very lucky. Compared to other Kenyans I have a very good life. My family has a house, we eat very well and I have a car. The people in my village are shocked that I even buy a newspaper every day. Many people could feed their family for the day for the price of a newspaper.'

Mutisya had worked hard to get to where he was. After finishing his O levels in high school, he took a course in tourism before landing a job as a waiter in a Mombasa hotel. After two years he was moved to the travel desk and also began studying marketing part-time. This led to a job as a marketing manager and eventually general manager of a travel and tour company. In 2004 he set up his own travel/safari company and subsequently hired three of his relatives to work for him: a brother and sister in the Nairobi office and cousin Willy as the company driver.

Mutisya's brother Vincent, on the other hand, didn't have much work. He had planned to grow maize and beans on the farm, but the land had been too dry to plant. Instead he was hunting small animals with a bow and arrow to sell at the market. Vincent told me that a few weeks earlier Mutisya had sent him an Irish couch surfer who stayed for two days. 'He went hunting,' Vincent said. 'And he killed three doves and two hares. We had a very nice dinner that night.'

We had a huge lunch of *ugali* with cabbage and onions while sitting under the shade of a tree overlooking the parched yellow dust bowl that Vincent was hoping to cultivate. After I'd barely touched my meal, Mutisya gave me a lecture. 'You don't eat enough like an African man. Your metal is much bigger and harder when it's heavy,' he said, gesturing towards his groin. Thankfully, before Mutisya could go into detail about his heavy piece of metal, he changed the subject.

'Vincent's other name is Mutuka,' Mutisya said, 'which means "It was dark" because it was dark when he was born.' Mutisya's older brother's name is Mutunga, which means 'looks like grandfather', while Francis Wambua translates as 'born in heavy rains'.

'My name means "too long to be born"', Mutisya said proudly. 'Because my mother had very long labour pains.'

After lunch we headed west to Fourteen Falls, which was on the border of Oldonyo Sabuk National Park. Fourteen Falls only had twelve waterfalls, but I won't quibble—one of the major tourist attractions near Melbourne is called the Twelve Apostles although there are only nine of them.

To get near the falls we had to leap over a series of rock pools and clamber up and over steep ledges. This proved to be almost fatal. As I leapt onto a boulder I failed to notice a protruding rock ledge. A perilously sharp protruding rock ledge. I slammed my head into it with a sickening thud and blacked out for a few seconds. If Mutisya hadn't caught me, I would have tumbled over the edge. When I regained my senses blood was trickling down my forehead, but I didn't feel it. What I could feel, or more accurately *not* feel, was my back. It had gone totally numb and I could barely walk. I had to be helped to the car and on the subsequent long drive to Lake Naivasha the roads were so bad that I would squeal with pain every few seconds as we went over a bump.

We arrived in Naivasha town at nightfall and the main street looked decidedly seedy under the cloak of darkness. 'This place is very famous in Kenya,' Mutisya said. The area did have a claim to fame, but I doubt if it would make a great tourist slogan. 'This area has the highest amounts of rape in *all* of Kenya,' Mutisya said.

We were staying with a 'sometimes friend' of Mutisya's who owned a restaurant and small guesthouse. After having a bite to eat we were shown to a few old lumpy and soiled mattresses on the floor in the back room. I decided, however, to pay 5 dollars for an upgrade to one of the guestrooms. Yes, it's not technically couch surfing because I paid for my bed, but I think my back would have disowned me if I'd slept on one of the lumpy mattresses.

A large sign on the side of the road read: ANIMALS HAVE RIGHT OF WAY. There were certainly plenty of them to exercise that right if they wanted to. In the space of only a few kilometres, we passed [insert appropriate collective nouns] of zebras, warthogs, antelopes, buffalos and black-and-white colobus monkeys.

'Most Kenyans have never seen a giraffe or a lion or an elephant,' Mutisya said as he turned around to point out another herd of zebras. The whole turning around thing was worrying me because Mutisya was driving. Willy had been called back suddenly to Nairobi to do another driving job, so he'd got up early to catch a bus.

We were on our way to Crater Lake Game Park to 'see some animals up very close'. When we pulled into a car spot in front of the stone-hut ticket office, we almost ran over two vervet monkeys who were very close indeed. Without losing rhythm for a second the copulating monkeys looked up at us as if to say 'Do you mind?' Mutisya waltzed straight past them in the middle of their lovemaking and into the ticket office.

While Mutisya was inside the ticket office, one of the formerly amorous monkeys leapt through the driver's window and casually hopped onto the back seat. He got himself comfortable then gave me a look as if to say 'Right, so when are we going then?' When a ride wasn't forthcoming, he snorted at me and jumped back out.

'You are a famous author!' Mutisya barked angrily when he returned to the car. 'And they will not give us a discount, so we will not pay!'

We snuck in instead.

Mutisya drove off the main road down a dusty track, then slipped through a side gate. It was even dustier in the park and after only a few minutes we were both covered in dust. Not only was it too hot to close the windows, but if we had I wouldn't have been able to see the grazing herds of giraffes, buffalos and zebra; or the elands, gazelles and impalas sashaying silently through the bush; or the troupes of playful monkeys leaping between tree limbs. And that was all in the first fifteen minutes in the park.

We were driving along the designated track when we happened upon a walking group being led by a park guide—Crater Lake Game Park is one of the few national parks in Kenya where you can wander around because there are no big cats that may consider you a tasty afternoon snack. Instead of slowing down when we got near the group, Mutisya thundered past, blanketing them all with dust.

Luckily for us, after the great dusting we didn't see any more people—or more specifically any park guides on the lookout for freeloading hoons. We spent the next hour driving around, stopping now and again to get out and take a photo of loping giraffes or gambolling gazelles. Except they all kept scampering away when we got too close.

'I'll get you a good photo!' Mutisya bellowed, after yet another unsuccessful attempt to get close to a herd of animals. Mutisya hit the accelerator then spun the steering wheel wildly, sending the car lurching and rattling off the designated track towards a family of giraffes. The old Toyota bounced around like a tin can tumbling down stairs. And so did my head cannoning repeatedly into the roof. Mutisya chased the giraffes and then some zebras around an obstacle course of acacia trees, then sent some dementedly frightened impalas leaping over bushes. I didn't get any good shots, but we did almost collect a family of antelopes.

I was just happy that we finally left the park before a park guide got a good shot at us.

At least we didn't have to sneak into the Crater Lake reserve. Entry was free. We parked the car and clambered on all fours up a steep incline to a lookout on a rocky outcrop. Below was Crater Lake, which was emerald green with a pale pink fluffy fringe around it. The pink fringe turned out to be thousands of flamingos wading in the shallows.

On the edge of the lake was Crater Lake Camp. It wasn't a two-man tent, shared shower-block type camp, though. It was more your five-star type camp with shaded lawns and neat curved stone paths leading to secluded tents in the lakeside forest with sweeping views over the flamingo-lined waters. Each tent was furnished with giant four-poster beds and ensuite bathrooms with hot showers—but you'd hope they would be at US$250 a night.

We had an expensive, but desperately needed, cold drink overlooking the lake in the open-sided dining/bar pavilion, which was made of rough-hewn stone and dark wood. While I was sipping my iced tea, I noticed a very odd sight. A man in black pressed pants, white shirt and bow tie was standing on the edge of the lake casually pulling dead flamingos out of the water with a long pole. After we'd finished our drinks we wandered down for a closer inspection. The plucky flamingo plucker was one of the waiters. 'It is not good for the guests to see lots of dead flamingos,' he said, throwing another large flamingo into an already laden wheelbarrow. The flamingos had died, he told us, because the water was too low so there was not enough algae for the birds to eat. Or there was too much algae to eat. He seemed as confused as we did.

Another waiter came to collect the full wheelbarrow and headed back in the direction of the dining pavilion.

I had a sneaking suspicion that there might just be Fricasseed Flamingo Pie on the menu that night.

On the drive back to Nairobi we stopped for a late lunch at a hot dog stand, which had been set up next to a petrol station. A troupe of blue-bottomed baboons joined us for lunch. I'd just started on my hot dog when the largest and meanest-looking one tottered over towards me, then, in a furry flash, wrapped its fat little fingers around my hot dog and wrenched it from my grasp. He gulped it down in one mouthful then looked at me as if to say 'Go on then, go get me another one'. I did get another hot dog, but I ate it in the car.

'I'm very tired,' Mutisya said as we were about to leave. 'Can you drive?'

If you asked any of my friends if I can drive, they would probably say not very well at all. So it was with much trepidation, and a powerful surge of sheer panic, that I took over the driving on possibly the worst roads that I'd ever experienced in my life. I could just about handle dodging the oncoming trucks (I simply swung onto the dirt shoulder, which was often in better condition than the road anyway), but I also had to dodge people, goats, cows, donkeys and the odd baboon wandering across the road. Oh, and potholes the size of bathtubs. It couldn't possibly have been any worse. Then it started raining. It did make dodging all of the above easier, though. That was because I couldn't see a thing. I spent the entire time clutching the steering wheel like I was on the world's scariest rollercoaster. Actually, it was a lot scarier than that.

'Pull over up ahead,' Mutisya said. The rain had cleared now, so at least I could see the hordes of people standing on the side of the road holding up bags of fruit and vegetables to the passing traffic.

'This is called the Crazy Market,' Mutisya said.

'Why?'

'You'll see.'

When I pulled off the road, a gang of screaming people clutching bags of carrots, peas, onions, potatoes, leeks and cabbages converged on the car and pressed their faces up against the windows. My window was only open a few centimetres and one of the insistent vendors tried to force a bag of carrots through the tiny gap. 'You buy carrots!' he pleaded. 'You must buy carrots.'

'I'm leaving the country tomorrow,' I screamed back. 'I can't take carrots with me.'

'How about onions then?'

Mutisya very bravely jumped out to buy some cabbages. When he opened the boot, ten different cabbage sellers shoved their bags inside. It took ten minutes of arguing and shouting before we could finally drive off with only one bag.

For more than an hour we'd been climbing steadily, but I hadn't realised just how high up we were until we rounded a bend and the ground next to the road fell away to the Great Rift Valley far below, an immense plain that spread out as far as the eye could see. At the highest point—more than 2500 metres above sea level—was a long row of souvenir stalls. When we pulled into the empty car park, a legion of hawkers bounded over to greet us with armfuls of trinkets.

'I have no money,' I said gravely.

'He is my driver,' Mutisya said. 'He is very poor.'

We were then left alone to admire the view—although the hawkers did grill Mutisya on why I was so poor. He told them that I was from Mongolia and that we are not allowed to take money out of the country.

Driving into Nairobi I almost wet my pants a number of times. I had to constantly slam on the brakes to avoid crashing into the buses and cars that kept cutting me off. At one point I gave the locals a taste of Australian road rage. When a small van cut me off, sending me up onto the traffic island, I stuck my head out the window and yelled 'You're a FUCKIN' MORON mate!'

'Don't do that. He will kill you,' Mutisya said matter-of-factly.

When I finally, thankfully, mercifully, pulled over in Kenyatta Avenue, I leapt out and gave Mutisya a high five. 'I didn't get us killed,' I yelped with delight. Neither by getting hit or by getting shot.

I offered to take Mutisya to a restaurant for our final night's meal and he said, 'I will like to show you where every tourist in Nairobi goes to'. As he told me its name, I shrewdly guessed that it was unlikely to be a vegetarian restaurant.

Carnivore was massive. And that was just the car park, which was full of tour buses. The restaurant catered for more than 500 people at each sitting. The building itself was a monolithic modern place with a few rough wooden poles added to make it look rustic. Just inside the entrance was a massive charcoal fire pit surrounded by a dozen chefs in ridiculously tall hats and enveloped in barbecue smoke.

We were escorted to our table past large herds of tour groups, mostly of the Japanese and old-folk variety. Sitting next to us was a bunch of oldies wearing safari vests (with lots of pockets), loud shorts, white socks and white runners. I wasn't that surprised when I heard their American accents.

As soon as we sat down, the waiter hoisted a small cardboard flag up in the centre of our table, which we were to put down when we'd gorged ourselves enough.

'Soup, sir?' the waiter asked, holding a wooden tray laden with bowls of soup.

'Don't have any soup,' Mutisya barked. 'Save your stomach for the meat.' Mutisya said the same thing about the bread and the potatoes.

'I don't want any of that,' Mutisya spat at the waiter when he appeared with a tray of salad. 'Where's the meat? Bring me some meat!'

What followed next was a procession of charred flesh on skewers, including beef, chicken, lamb, lamb chops, pork sausages, chicken livers, camel, crocodile and ostrich. You can take the boy out of the village, but you can't take the village out of the boy. Mutisya ate with his hands while spitting fat and bones onto his plate.

When I finished my last morsel of ostrich, I was so full I couldn't even face dessert—and that's very unlike me.

Mutisya, on the other hand, refused to put the flag down. When the waiter came around asking if we wanted dessert, he said, 'We're taking a commercial break, we'll be right back.'

The rest obviously did Mutisya a power of good. He had three serves of dessert.

By the time we got to Mutisya's house in town, it was after eleven and Terry and the kids were asleep on the double bed. Mutisya gave me the fetching brown velvet couch, while he slept on a thin mattress on the floor. I went to bed still covered in dust. It was caked on my skin and my hair was like straw.

Even though I was exhausted I had trouble getting to sleep. It was stiflingly hot in my sleeping bag, but it was a choice between melting or malaria. A crack squadron of mosquitos was hovering above just waiting to devour me. At one point I seriously contemplated jumping in with Terry and the kids under the mosquito net.

I woke up at five. Well, technically I didn't wake up, because I hadn't ever been to sleep. I spent most of the night swatting mosquitos. I feel a little guilty doing this because Mutisya was such an accommodating and generous host, but—I'm sorry, Mutisya—I've given your couch a rating of 2/10. And I won't do the pro and con thing because there wasn't a single pro. Oh, there was one. I didn't get malaria.

SOUTH AFRICA

16

'You can stay only after being screened and approved and authorised by my mum.'
Walindah Mosia, 25, Soweto, South Africa
CouchSurfing.com

My next couch-surfing host didn't live in a tin shack. Not that I was really expecting my host Walindah to live in a rundown lean-to, but the images beamed around the world of Soweto tend to only show a scruffy, littered and crowded shanty town full of rusty shacks. Then again, I also hadn't expected to find that Walindah lived in a nice brick suburban house in a nice quiet suburban street. The only stereotypical sign that I was in Soweto was Walindah's brother's car in the driveway. It had been totally trashed during a recent carjacking. 'They put a gun to my brother's head,' Walindah said somewhat casually, as we walked up the driveway, 'and threatened to "blow out his brain" if he didn't get out of the car.'

'Is it, um . . . dangerous around here?' I asked a little nervously.

'No, not at all, it didn't happen in Soweto,' Walindah explained cheerfully. 'We feel safer in Soweto than we do in Johannesburg. They've got the highest murder rate in the world, you know.'

So you may well wonder why I chose the murder capital of the world as my next couch-surfing destination. I chose Johannesburg because, as with Belgium, I'd been there before without having seen any of it. All I had seen in my very brief previous stay was the heavily fortified hostel next to Johannesburg airport where I stayed while in transit to West Africa.

There were plenty of couch-surfing hosts to stay with in Johannesburg, but after reading a bunch of profiles I decided that I didn't want to stay in a nice white neighbourhood and eat barbecue steak in a nice white restaurant and sit in a bar surrounded by locals boasting that 'South Africa has the best rugby team in the world'.

But I only had a short time in Johannesburg (due to a short connecting flight), so if I wanted to experience South Africa with an African South African, then Soweto, the black township southeast of Johannesburg, was the place. It wasn't easy finding a host in Soweto, though. I scoured all three websites and found only four potential hosts. But as it turned out I received a reply and a couch invitation in response to my first request—on the proviso that I had been screened, approved and authorised by my host's mum first.

Walindah gave me directions from the airport, which involved catching a bus into the city then an overcrowded taxi-bus to Soweto. My first introduction to Soweto was when my taxi-cum-bus-cum-sardine-tin pulled into the chaotic Baragwanath taxi-rank-cum-market-cum-fast-food-outlet along with hundreds of other mini-buses. The market stalls were mostly manned (or should that be womanned?) by women selling fresh fruit, vegetables, clothes and lots of plastic junk. In between the market stalls were chickens and chickens' feet being roasted on roadside barbecues while butchers were brushing away flies from sheeps' heads. There were constant clashes between the First World and the Third, as when I watched a Zulu witchdoctor sell medicines and animal skins to a man in a suit who was speaking loudly into a mobile phone.

'I will find you,' Walindah had said in her email.

How would she ever find me in a crowded bus station? It didn't take long to figure out how. I was the only white person. Walindah, who was a petite thing and wearing a pretty bright red dress, found me within a minute of me stepping off the bus. There was a bus to Walindah's house, but I said I was happy to do the 30-minute walk—which, with a big backpack, only seemed like a good idea for the first four minutes.

Walindah was very shy and I seemed to do most of the talking. 'There's, um, lots of people here in Soweto,' I said as we weaved our way through the crowd.

'Yes, but no one knows how many people live in Soweto,' Walindah shrugged. 'The government says one million, but it's more like four million. People do not want to do a census because they don't trust the government, so it is impossible to find out how many people there are.'

It was hard to hear Walindah. Not only was she softly spoken, but there was also loud, bass-heavy, tribal-type house music blaring out from shops and cars and market stalls. Walindah told me that the music is called *kwaito*, an Africanised version of hip-hop that started in Soweto and is now the most popular form of dance music on the continent.

Even every inch of space on the narrow footbridge that spanned the main road was taken up with market stalls. Well, when I say 'stalls', I mean people sitting behind cardboard boxes. This was obviously the place to sell illegal substances and shifty-looking folk were either selling blocks of hash, dried bunches of marijuana leaves, pills or—I wonder if they smoke 'em or sniff 'em—pairs of socks.

'That is where I work,' Walindah said, pointing across the road to a collection of large ugly buildings that looked like a rundown council estate. 'It is Chris-Hani Baragwanath Hospital, the largest hospital in the world. There are over three thousand beds and seven thousand staff members.' Walindah was one of two thousand nurses.

'More than two thousand patients check in to the hospital every day,' Walindah continued. 'And over half of them are HIV-positive.'

Walindah then reeled off some stats that were just staggering. One in five people in South Africa, which has the most severe AIDS epidemic in the world, are infected with AIDS. That's more than 6 million people. Around 260 000 of them are children under sixteen.

'There are about one thousand AIDS deaths every day,' Walindah said matter-of-factly. Although Walindah worked in the maternity ward, she still witnessed the effects of AIDS every single day—30 per cent of pregnant women in South Africa are living with HIV.

'We only started to supply drugs to help people with AIDS two years ago,' Walindah said. 'And this is many years after most other countries have had them.'

As we walked past the hospital entrance we had to sidestep a line of folk waiting to enter. Although we all know that you can't catch AIDS through casual contact, it was a bit unnerving just to think how likely it was that a lot of them had AIDS.

We walked in silence until we'd finally passed the last of the hospital buildings.

'So, were you born in Soweto?' I asked Walindah.

'Yes, and so were my mum and dad.'

Walindah was proud of being a Sowetan and as we trudged, or at least *I* trudged, through the suburbs, Walindah filled me in on the history of the 'township'. The city of Soweto (a contraction of South Western Townships) was established in 1930 when the government decided that the black suburbs in Johannesburg were getting too close to the white suburbs. The blacks were given eviction notices and were moved to a farm 18 kilometres from the city. It doesn't sound as if they got a very good deal, though. It took the new residents of Soweto three hours to get to work because there were no roads—or shops, parks, electricity and running water. Over the next twenty years the population of Soweto exploded, with large numbers of Zulus and others driven to the city in search of work and a better way of life. The 'better way of life' turned out to be in overcrowded slums. Eventually the municipal authorities decided that if they built 20 000 low-cost houses then they would have better control of their low-cost workers.

'There are only two roads in and out of Soweto,' Walindah said. 'The road was built this way to control the people. The police could just cut off the two roads and stop people moving in or out.' The locals had their own way of outsmarting the police, though. Under Apartheid Soweto didn't have street signs to make it hard for the police to know where they were.

We were now walking past the endless rows of low-cost houses and, although they were actually more like tiny brick matchboxes with a window and a door, it still wasn't how I imagined Soweto. It was a far cry from a shantytown and many of the homes had lovingly tended gardens, fresh paint jobs and satellite dishes.

Walindah's neighbourhood was much the same except with much larger homes and much larger satellite dishes.

Walindah's mum Yolanda, a robust and jolly woman, greeted us at the door (I still had to pass the final inspection before I was allowed to enter the house). Yolanda was a high-school teacher and—making me feel very old indeed—was a year younger than me. Walindah gave me a brief tour of her home, which looked pretty much identical to any average suburban home, then showed me to my room. 'No, no I can't sleep here,' I protested. Walindah was giving me her room and she was going to sleep with her mum.

'No, no,' she replied. 'You are our special guest.'

There was no mention of Walindah's father, so I subtly brought him up in conversation. 'So, where's your dad?' I asked.

'He just . . . disappeared one day,' Walindah shrugged.

While Yolanda cooked dinner we sat on the front steps watching the passing parade of folk walking home from work or carrying bags of shopping while laughing children played football on the street.

Walindah asked me lots of questions about my life in Australia. She told me that she had hosted a few couch surfers and because she probably would never travel, it was her way of 'seeing the world'.

'This way I have the world coming to me,' Walindah said with a beaming smile.

Walindah's younger brother Elijah turned up just as dinner was being served. Elijah was unemployed and had been out looking for work. He was even more shy than Walindah. 'It is hard for Elijah,' Walindah said, as we sat down for dinner. 'Eight million people are unemployed in this country, which is almost forty per cent of the population.'

Dinner was a delicious spicy chicken stew with rice and mashed pumpkin. Nobody talked much during dinner because they were all glued to the television getting their daily fix of the soap *Egoli: Place of Gold*.

'South Africa didn't get television until nineteen seventy-six,' Walindah said during the commercial break. The main reason for the delay was that the white minority regime saw television as a threat to Afrikaans by giving undue prominence to English. There was no undue prominence to English in *Egoli: Place of Gold*. The show was quadrilingual, and the characters would suddenly switch in mid-sentence from English to Zulu or Afrikaans to Xhosa.

'It is a very popular show,' Walindah said. 'There has been over four thousand episodes.'

I often feel like a linguistic dumbass when I travel, but even more so on this trip. Everyone I'd stayed with so far spoke at least two languages fluently. Walindah spoke five languages: English, Afrikaans, Setswana, Xhosa and Zulu.

Walindah and her mum sure loved watching TV. After *Egoli: Place of Gold* finished, we watched South African *Big Brother* followed by South African *Who Wants to be a Millionaire*. It was exactly like TV at home—I picked up the TV guide and was mortified to see that they also had South African versions of *Idol*, *The Weakest Link*, *Deal or No Deal*, *Temptation* and even a *Survivor South Africa*.

'More people vote on a reality TV show than in an election,' Walindah told me proudly.

When Walindah turned over to *South Africa's Biggest Loser* I feigned a large yawn and slunk off to bed.

It really was like being at home. At 6.30 the next morning, I woke with the same startled fright that I have at the same ungodly hour in Melbourne. I never would have imagined that I'd hear the hissing and humming hydraulics of a hi-tech garbage truck as it picked up wheelie bins from the street in Soweto. The Sowetan suburbs so far seemed amazingly normal.

The loud garbage truck did bring the couch rating down a bit, though.

Couch rating: 8/10

Pro: Walindah's bed was comfortable

Con: I felt uncomfortable about stealing Walindah's bed

After breakfast, Walindah's mum said that we could borrow her car (bless her, she caught the bus to school instead). I'd timed my visit well because Walindah had a day off—and to be quite honest I was a little bit worried about the idea of wandering around the back streets of Soweto by myself.

Our tour began on a somewhat sombre note. Our first stop was the suburb of Orlando West, which is home to the Hector Pieterson Memorial and Museum, a monument to Soweto youth named after the schoolboy shot dead in the infamous 1976 uprising. What started as a peaceful protest march by youths against the use of Afrikaans as a medium of instruction in Black Schools in Soweto escalated into bloody violence as police opened fire on 10 000 students marching from Naledi High School to Orlando Stadium. Walindah's mum was one of those students.

'She was fourteen years old,' Walindah said, as we stood in front of a photo of terrified school kids screaming under a cloud of tear gas. 'She got away before the police started shooting everyone.'

Inside the museum was a series of moving photographs and multimedia presentations showing the conditions that led to the student strikes and the subsequent white minority's violent reaction. The most disturbing, yet poignant, photograph was the iconic shot that sparked the world's outrage. Running through a suburban street is Mbuysia Makhubu, his face contorted by grief and disbelief, with the bloody and lifeless body of 12-year-old Hector Pieterson in his arms. Hector had been shot in the back while he scurried away towards safety. Hector was just one of 556 who were killed by the South African police.

The impact of the Soweto protests reverberated through the country, drawing the world's attention to the plight of black South Africans, resulting in international sanctions and eventually the end of Apartheid.

Outside the museum was a memorial stone where Hector Pieterson had fallen.

'That could have been my mum,' Walindah said. 'She was a lucky one.'

We drove around the corner from the museum to Vilakazi Street, a normal suburban street with one mighty claim to fame. This small street has been home to two Nobel Peace Prize winners: Nelson Mandela and Archbishop Desmond Tutu. Nelson Mandela's old house is now a museum run by Winnie Mandela. Walindah told me that she lives in a secure mansion two blocks away and can occasionally be seen cruising the area in a white Mercedes with bulletproof windows.

Inside Mandela's house the walls were adorned with photos and tributes, including countless honorary degrees and a formal apology from America's Central Intelligence Agency for its involvement in his persecution. To be frank, though, I thought most of the house, like the jackal bedspread and Winnie's army boots at the end of the bed, was all a bit tacky—particularly the hawkers out the front selling Nelson Mandela T-shirts, Nelson Mandela mugs and plastic jars filled with 'dirt from Nelson Mandela's backyard'.

Archbishop Tutu still lived in his grey, two-storey house, but he must have felt a little jealous. No one was selling Archbishop Tutu mugs out the front of his house.

'This is the most dangerous part of Soweto,' Walindah said, as we later drove through the middle of the ghettos of Zola and White City past impoverished street traders with scant arrays of truly pathetic produce laid out before them on the sandy footpath in front of their homes. Their 'homes' were self-made shacks of corrugated metal and wire.

'This area is notorious for gangs of armed car hijackers,' Walindah said without even a hint of panic in her voice.

'Should we be here in a . . . in a car then?' I said with quite a bit more than a hint of panic in my voice.

'It's okay,' Walindah assured me. 'But, we'd be mad crazy driving through here at night.'

I wasn't that surprised when Walindah then said, 'The tour buses don't come here.'

'Where do the tour buses go?' I asked.

'I will show you the tourist slums,' Walindah said brightly.

We pulled into the small gravel car park for the 'tourist slums' next to a small tour bus and a few souvenir stalls. One stall was selling 'Authentic South African wood carvings'. Most of the woodcarvings were of giraffes and looked suspiciously as if they came from the Wamunyu collective in Kenya.

Walindah arranged with a local boy named 'Brilliant', after a somewhat hefty donation from me, to view the shack that he shared with his mother and sister. Although I knew the 'donation' was well needed, I felt uncomfortable about having a gawk at a stranger's poverty.

'It's okay,' Walindah whispered as we were led down a dirt track lined with tiny shacks that had stones holding the roofs in place and were covered in plastic sheeting to prevent the rain turning the dirt floors to mud. 'This is how they make their living.'

Women in large bright dresses flashed us large bright smiles as we wandered past yards filled with rows of maize drying in the sun next to piles of rubbish and old rusted cars. Brilliant's shack was painted bright red and had lovely lace curtains in the window. Inside, the family shared a few square metres with one table and one bed. With no electricity or running water in the area, the house was heated with a paraffin stove and they used buckets for showers. They did have a television set powered by a car battery, though. 'See, they can watch the soaps, too,' Walindah said.

On the way back to the car we strolled past a church, which was more like a large tin shack. We only knew it was a church because we could hear the service inside, where a gospel choir was singing joyous hymns in Xhosa and English. We peeked through a gap in the door and were immediately dragged in and welcomed by a grey-bearded priest in a bright yellow flowing robe and large red cape decorated with white tassels. Although the room was dark it was virtually aglow with a flock of women in long white robes and white hats singing, wailing, clapping their hands and swaying with an outpouring of devotion. It was like a sauna in the tin shed and after a few minutes the sweat was pouring off me in buckets.

When we stepped back onto the street, Walindah told me about the time Bill Clinton came to visit Soweto and went to a church service. 'The priest gave the sermon,' Walindah said with a giggle '. . . about adultery.'

By way of contrast, we then drove to Diepkloof where 'the millionaires and crime bosses of Soweto live'. This was the posh part of Soweto, with three-storey mansions behind high walls and electric gates that looked just like the fortress homes of the white suburbs I'd passed in the city. All the roads were freshly tarred and there were BMWs in the driveways and well-dressed children playing in the gardens.

There were more glistening BMWs and chrome-plated Toyota four-wheel drives lining the street outside Sakhumzi Restaurant, a few doors up from Archbishop Tutu's house, where we stopped for dinner. We sat outside in the garden, where young men in designer suits mixed with young men in trendy ghetto gear.

'Would you like me to order some traditional South African food?' Walindah asked, after we were shown to our table.

Our traditional South African entrée was a plate of fat black slimy worms that were 'gently simmered' and came served with peanut butter and tomato relish. I may have grimaced a bit because Walindah said, 'They're not really worms, they're Mopani worms which are actually the caterpillars of the emperor moth.'

Oh, that made me feel much better.

'Mopani worms are very nutritious,' Walindah said, as I very, and I do mean very, tentatively picked up a worm. 'They are sixty per cent protein and have lots of calcium,' Walindah added. When I popped the worm into my mouth, the first crunch wasn't so bad. It tasted like burnt sausage. Then the second crunch let loose the slimy insides which tasted exactly as I had feared a worm would taste like. As if someone had blown their nose into my mouth.

It wasn't until I'd eaten a couple that I noticed Walindah hadn't touched them.

'I'm not eating them,' she said, screwing up her face. 'They're disgusting.'

I didn't think I could stomach the traditional main course, either. It was *umgodu*, otherwise known as stomach. The plate of white rubbery-looking tripe came with *umxushu* (beans), wheat bread and crushed corn. The crushed corn and beans were delicious. I pushed the tripe around the plate, so it looked as if I'd eaten some.

'Can we go to a *shebeen*?' I asked Walindah when we got back to her house. I'd noticed that there was a *shebeen* (which is an illicit bar) only a short walk up the road from Walindah's house.

When we got to the *shebeen*, Walindah said, 'I won't stay. This is a man's bar, but I will find someone to look after you.' She scanned the small crowd sitting out the front and walked over to a young fellow with arms as thick as my thighs. 'He is my friend's cousin. He will look after you and walk you home later,' Walindah said. 'It is probably not a good idea to go inside,' Walindah added before she turned to head back. 'There are a lot of drunk crazy people inside.'

As soon as Walindah left, my new friend said, 'Come inside.'

When I walked in many of the patrons stared at me as if to say 'What are you doing here?' It wasn't an angry 'What do you think you are doing here?' It was more of a 'How have you managed to get so completely lost as to end up here?' Not surprisingly I was the only *umlungu* or whitey in the *shebeen*, and probably the first to ever to step foot into the bar.

One man with bloodshot eyes and sporting a blue work suit staggered over and shook my hand. 'I am your friend,' he spluttered.

We grabbed a beer and sat outside and I was immediately surrounded by a group of young men. They were all talking at once, asking me to buy them beer, and if I 'want an

African girl'. Two handed me bits of paper with their addresses on them so I could write to them and then 'sponsor' them to come to Australia. My 'minder' went back inside the bar, leaving me with a large but quite effeminate young fellow to 'look after me'. 'Did you know that South African men have the biggest dicks in the world?' my new minder said, giving me a wink.

'You're back early,' Walindah said. I hadn't even waited for my minder before trotting rather briskly back to the house as soon as I'd finished my beer.

'Oh, I have to get up early to get to the airport anyway,' I muttered.

'*Survivor* is just about to start if you'd like to watch it,' Walindah said, before turning back to the TV.

INDIA

17

'Our colony of cows will greet you at the front gate . . . along with our 24hr security guard who tends to nod off during his shifts.'
Penelope Walker, 26, New Delhi, India
GlobalFreeloaders.com

'Where is the house?' my grumpy taxi driver asked after he'd driven around the same block four times.

'I don't know, I haven't been here before.'

'I don't know, either,' he huffed before dumping me in the middle of a dark and dusty lane somewhere in the back streets of Kalkaji in South Delhi.

The houses and apartment blocks in the street were hidden behind high brick walls. But that wasn't the problem. The problem was that there were no numbers. I really had no choice. I would have to ring every bell until I found the right block. I wasn't going to be very popular either. It was after midnight. With a large sigh I tottered a few metres over to the nearest apartment and rang the bell next to the high iron gates. There was no answer so I rang it again.

And again. When a somewhat groggy security guard finally appeared, I asked, 'Do a Penelope and Sarah live here?'

'Yes.'

Yes!

I'd found it on my first go and this was the famed security guard who 'tended to nod off'.

Penelope and Sarah don't sound like Indian names, but that's because their owners were two Australian girls from Sydney working in Delhi. When I stumbled upon their profile I decided it might be interesting to see what expat life was like in one of the biggest, noisiest, smelliest, hottest, dirtiest and most crowded cities in the world. Plus I couldn't pass the opportunity to stay in a palatial mansion:

> Comfy velvet bottle-green couch in a palatial mansion with marble floors and high ceilings. We're working in a call centre in Delhi full time, and we go out for dinner or drinks pretty much every night of the week because everything here is so cheap.
> Penelope, 26

I sent out some requests to a few locals as well in case the comfy velvet bottle-green couch was otherwise occupied. It was a pity I'm not a female, though, because I found some other great potential hosts:

> Our house is not in an excellent shape, however all the conventional facilities are there. I live with my family so you have to be a girl and you have to

behave. I also expect decent standards of hygiene
from you (ie. no piddling on the floors).
Shashank, 25

Gender of Guest: Female only
Sleeping place I can offer: My King Bed with me!
Suresh, 43

I'd like to spare room with some not smoking girl. i
can provide a lot of things from cooking dishes till
mattress and pillows. illegal sex is strictly not allowed.
Praveen, 30

Penelope and Sarah welcomed me at the door of their apartment. 'We're so happy to see you,' they giggled. 'We're a bit drunk.' Both girls were incredibly tall and slim. Sarah had blonde hair and blue eyes and Penelope had freckled cheeks and long auburn hair. They couldn't have stood out more in India if they tried. 'Come on in,' Penelope said, grabbing my hand and escorting me down a long corridor to a dimly lit lounge room. The lounge room did have marble floors and high ceilings, but it wasn't looking very palatial. Littered around the room were empty beer bottles, pizza boxes, overflowing ashtrays and empty chip packets. And slouched on my comfy velvet bottle-green couch behind a thick haze of smoke were two fellows smoking a whopping joint and tipping ash all over the comfy velvet. I was introduced to 'John from England' and 'the Dutch guy'. They didn't look as if they were leaving, or capable of leaving, my 'bed' anytime in the near future.

Then Penelope said something that made me want to hug her with joy. 'You don't have to sleep on the couch,' she said. 'We've got you your very own apartment.' Another expat had recently moved out of one of the upstairs apartments, so the girls had sweet-talked the security guard into unlocking it for a 'special guest'.

On the way up to the apartment Penelope told me about her job in Delhi. Both girls and 'John from England' worked in a call centre for a UK-based travel agent selling Australian package tours. 'It suits us perfectly,' Penelope beamed. 'We start at one in the afternoon and finish at nine.' The reason for the odd hours was that they worked on UK time. Callers were then under the assumption that they were calling from somewhere in the UK. Penelope had been manning the phones for six months, and had only recently talked her best friend Sarah into joining her in India. 'I'm here for another six months then I'll go home and get a real job,' Penelope said. 'The job here is not bad, though. We have a driver who picks us up and drops us off every day and the company has a chef who makes us curries for dinner every night.'

'You're our first house guest from GlobalFreeloaders,' Penelope said, when I asked if they'd had anyone else stay with them. 'We've had lots of requests, but they've all been from sleazy Indian businessmen.'

My very own apartment was huge. I had three bedrooms to choose from, plus my own lounge room, kitchen and two bathrooms. Just when I was longingly eyeing off one of the beds, Penelope said, 'We've been waiting for you to arrive, so we can all go to a party'.

The party was taking place in another block of apartments shared by expats. There were around twenty people at the party, including Swedish, Irish, French, Spanish and a couple of Indian fellows. All of them were drunk. It really is not that much fun being the only sober one at a party and I didn't feel at all like trying to 'catch up'. I had a whole bunch of those wonderful conversations with seriously intoxicated people who either didn't make any sense or did make sense, but told me the same story five times.

When someone dragged out a guitar at least it gave me something to do. I was the only one sober enough to play.

It was a bit creepy going back to my empty apartment. The apartment was fully furnished, so it looked as if someone had left in a hurry—or their dead body was stuffed in a wardrobe somewhere.

Before I hopped into bed I went through all the rooms and turned on the lights. And checked inside all the wardrobes.

'You're up early,' John said when he saw me traipsing down the stairs to the girls' apartment.

It was ten-thirty.

'The girls don't get up until after twelve,' he said, after inviting me up into his apartment.

John's apartment floor was totally covered with newspaper. 'I'm house-training Vindaloo,' John said, as an almost hairless, ratty creature that vaguely resembled a puppy timidly tottered into the kitchen. John had found him cowering in a pile of rubbish by the side of the road. He had already spent a fortune, or an Indian fortune at least, on vet bills to simply keep the poor thing alive.

The girls wouldn't be up for a while, so I joined John who was heading out for some brunch. My first view of India in daylight was of the upscale but somewhat fading neighbourhood we walked through on our way to the main road to get an auto-rickshaw. As a total contrast to the large upper-class homes and apartments that I'd just walked past, families had set up their homes, which were made of corrugated iron and plastic sheeting, on the median strip of the busy main road.

This glimpse of destitution was only a brief interlude, however. Our auto-rickshaw soon turned off the main road and pulled up in front of a trendy cafe full of Indian girls in designer jeans clutching mobile phones. Although most of the girls were in their twenties, they were talking and giggling like young teens. When we sat down at our table, a group of girls behind us were whispering about which boys they liked, and when one of the girls said that a boy had held her hand the others went 'ohhh'.

'They may dress and act like Western girls,' said John, 'but they still follow strict Indian traditions. They don't even kiss their boyfriends and don't have sex until marriage.'

John eyed off the pretty girls next to us. 'It's a pity 'cause I'd love to get into an Indian girl's pants.'

While we ate our delicious omelette and drank our huge mugs of spicy *masala chai,* John told me that he'd been travelling and working his way around the world for six years. 'I don't know if I'll ever be ready to settle down,' he shrugged. 'I like to live on the edge.'

Before we headed back to the apartment, John had a bit of shopping to do. Not far from the cafe was an arcade of elegantly shabby shops selling clothes, kitchenwares, shoes, electrical goods and flea collars. We went into a pet supplies shop and John bought a flea collar, two giant bags of dog biscuits, a leash and some squeaky dog toys. I couldn't help thinking that the money John spent on his scruffy street dog would probably feed one of those families on the median strip for a month.

John still had one more bit of shopping to do on the way back. 'I need to buy some dope,' John said, as he hailed an auto-rickshaw. Twenty minutes later we climbed out of the auto-rickshaw and into another world. We'd entered the slums. We walked briskly across a small bridge over a stream that was grey with oil and filth. Fetid rubbish piled a metre high lined the banks as naked laughing children splashed in the knee-deep water next to a bloated floating dead dog. It was a dismal assault on the senses. This was like the slum of slums. The 'slums' in Soweto looked like middle-class suburbia compared to this. As soon as we entered the squalid maze, bedraggled children followed behind us while feckless youths threw us furtive looks. 'Hello, Mister John.' Mister

John had obviously done a bit of business here before. Five minutes later we were back in the auto-rickshaw and John was tucking a large bag of hash under his jacket.

When we got back to the apartment, the girls were just getting out of bed. They were looking a bit dishevelled, but the apartment was absolutely spotless. All the pizza boxes and beer cans were gone and even the comfy velvet bottle-green couch looked like new. 'As part of the deal for our job we get a magic cleaning fairy who comes every morning,' Penelope said.

The girls had the weekend off and they were excited about showing me around Delhi—or showing me around the bars of Delhi, which seemed to make up the bulk of their itinerary for the next two days.

The main thoroughfare into Old Delhi was a wild and clamorous confusion of ox-drawn carts, motorcycles, auto-rickshaws, bicycles, cars, horse-drawn carriages, cycle-rickshaws, trucks, buses and the odd roaming totally nonchalant cow. I've been in huge cities where you are confronted by inconceivable masses of people, but I'd never seen anything like this. There was a barely an empty space anywhere. Everywhere I looked there was someone standing, squatting, walking, lying down or tripping over someone standing, squatting, walking or lying down. The footpaths were so packed in Old Delhi that folk were just wandering on the road in between the crawling traffic. But if they weren't flirting with death, we certainly were. As we crept at an excruciatingly languid pace through the virtual gridlock, we were slowly getting choked to death. The exhaust pipes on the ancient buses were at a perfect height to blow black toxic smoke right into our faces. Then every time we stopped, even for only a second, a bevy of beggars, often with some body part missing, would rush up to our auto-rickshaw not pleading but demanding that we buy newspapers, matches or toys, or simply asking for money. I'm pretty good at ignoring beggars, but the Delhi expat gang had it down to a fine art. They didn't even blink when flapping plastic birds were just about shoved up their noses.

At length we reached the Red Fort, whose high red sandstone walls rose above the surrounding chaos of Old Delhi like a proverbial red beacon. 'The Red Fort was the palace for Mughal Emperor Shah Jahan's new capital Shahjahanabad, after he moved his capital from Agra in the seventeenth century,' John said as we walked up to the imposing main gate. 'The fort was captured by Britain in 1857 and was made the headquarters of the British Army until India gained independence in 1947. It wasn't until December 2003 that the Indian Army moved out and let the tourists in.' John wasn't actually an authority on Indian forts. He'd brought along a guidebook. Inside the fort was teeming with families and couples, but it was just lovely to wander around the peaceful gardens and pavilions, breathe the non-toxic atmosphere and enjoy a brief respite from the utter madness outside.

It was getting near dusk when we climbed the broad and steep steps to Jama Masjid mosque, the largest mosque in India. The courtyard inside the mosque may hold up to 25 000 worshippers, but the steps leading up to it can hold up to 2000 beggars. I have never seen so many skinny people with skinny hands reaching out and demanding money. 'It's actually illegal to give money to beggars in India,' Penelope said, brushing a withered hand away from her face. 'The "giver" can be given three years in jail if they are caught.' The threat of our possible incarceration certainly didn't deter the beggars.

After just about every beggar in Old Delhi had asked us for money, we headed into the old town and John led us up and down narrow lanes then back up and down the same narrow lanes in search of a restaurant that he'd been to 'a hundred times'. Karim's Restaurant should have been easy to find. You could probably see it from the moon. The banks of fluorescent lights inside were so bright that it felt as if you were about to dine while undergoing police interrogation. The restaurant was full of men, and men only, sitting at large communal tables sharing metal plates and bowls filled with intensely coloured and intensely aromatic food.

We ordered a selection of dishes, including a rich mughlai chicken, mutton qorma, a sweet chicken jahangiri, goat curry, romali rotis and rice (sadly we couldn't have the tandoori bakra, which is an entire goat stuffed with dry fruits, basmati rice, minced meat and spices and costs around $A100, because you had to order it a day in advance). John, who must have also liked to live on the culinary edge, ordered 'brain curry' as a side dish.

While we were digging into our food, I noticed that Sarah was only eating the rice and rotis. 'Are you vegetarian?' I asked.

'No,' Sarah shrugged. 'I just can't stand curry or Indian food.'

'What about at work? Don't you have curries everyday?'

'Um . . . yeah, but I just eat a bit of rice, then order pizza when I get home.'

I didn't want to sound rude, but you'd think Sarah may have guessed there would be a fair bit of Indian food in India before she decided to come live in the country for six months.

After dinner we plunged into the crowded medieval labyrinth of Chandni Chowk where there were narrow alleyways given over to an extraordinary array of jewellery, perfumes, spices, carpets and lurid textiles. The girls got quite excited as they pored over exquisite gold, pearl and ruby jewellery, but nowhere near as excited as John and I became when we found an entire street devoted to fireworks. We both regressed to mischievous 10-year-olds as we pulled out boxes of Catherine wheels, ground spinners, fountains, Roman candles and rockets. John got a little carried away, however, and bought a 'MEGA WOW' box of gargantuan rockets from a stallholder who said 'I am making you a special price'.

'How much to Kalkaji?' Penelope asked an auto-rickshaw driver who was about half her height.

'One hundred and fifty rupees,' he barked.

'We'll pay you fifty rupees.'

'No,' he said, shaking his head vigorously. 'It is one hundred and fifty rupees.'

'Put your meter on then.'

'No. It is broken.'

'Take us there for fifty or I'll get the police,' Penelope glowered.

'Get the police then,' he sniffed.

A few minutes later Penelope returned with a big smile and a policeman in tow.

'You must take them for fifty rupees,' the policeman told the driver.

John thought it would be a good idea to wait until he'd smoked a huge joint and downed a few glasses of whisky before he set off the rockets. We were all a little wary of the 'MEGA WOW' rockets, so when John lit the first one in an empty beer bottle in the front garden we all scampered behind a large tree. But it wasn't our safety that we should have been worried about. The bottle tipped over during take-off and the rocket shot over the fence towards the apartment across the road and straight into their security guard's open booth. When the rocket exploded with an almighty BANG! on impact, the guard's heart probably did the same.

John was undeterred, however. The next rocket also tipped over and hit the side of the house next door with a horrendous BOOM. 'Fook that!' John bellowed as he picked up the next rocket, lit it and held it up in his hand.

'I don't know if you've figured it out yet,' Penelope said, 'but John's a bit mad.'

A deluge of sparks poured down John's arm just before the rocket shot into the air, but he still had the same demented smile on his face.

Being a human rocket-launcher must have hurt because he let the next one go too early and it shot over the fence again. This time it hit the windscreen of a passing car. The driver slammed on the brakes and the screaming from inside the car was almost as loud as the BANG.

Just as John finished tormenting and petrifying the neighbourhood, Sarah's 'hot fashion model' boyfriend Shiv turned up. He certainly was a tall, dark and handsome model, but I wouldn't have called him fashionable. When he found out that I was an ex-advertising art director, he went back to his car to get his 'model' folio.

As Shiv set it down on the coffee table, Penelope whispered, 'Try not to laugh'.

It was very hard not to.

Not only did the poses he was striking look like they were either straight from a 1950s Sears catalogue or from an issue of Gay Weekly, but the 'fashion' was things like a crocheted waistcoat revealing a bare chest and silk baggy pantaloons.

John didn't care. He laughed his head off as Shiv turned over each page of his folio. John almost fell out of his seat at one fashion spread. Shiv was wearing some sort of military garb and was trying so hard to look earnest it looked as if he had a serious case of constipation.

Shiv, who was wearing very normal jeans and nothing crocheted at all, had come to pick us up and take us to a nightclub where all the 'fashionable people of Delhi go'. I didn't have any items of clothing that were crocheted, so I hoped I was considered fashionable enough.

The nightclub, which was in the basement of some flash hotel, didn't consider the country's traditional and centuries-old sari fashionable, though. A large sign at the entrance read 'NO SARIS'. The interior was like any fashionable nightclub and the drinks were fashionably unaffordable. Every girl in the club was stunning, with huge brown eyes and perfect skin, and they were all wearing the latest and sexiest designer wear. It still felt like an under-16s disco, though. The girls mingled, chattered and danced amongst themselves while shyly shooting passing glances at the men and giggling.

This was a far cry from a Brazilian or Icelandic nightclub. There was no snogging or dirty dancing here. It was all very nice and very tame. The only fellow dancing with a girl was a smiling Shiv tripping the light fantastic with Sarah.

Later in the evening I was speaking to an Indian guy at the bar who told me that he'd been with his girlfriend for two years and he hadn't kissed her yet. No wonder Shiv looked so happy. He'd slept with Sarah on their second date.

I had a terrible dream that the dead bodies in the wardrobes had all risen and were dancing about in the kitchen. That did bring the couch rating down a little bit.

Couch rating: 8/10

Pro: An entire apartment to myself

Con: The dead bodies in the wardrobes

In the morning I waited for more than an hour for a sign of life from the other apartments, but gave up and headed into the city by myself. I didn't really have an idea of where to go, but Penelope had mentioned that there was some sort of large underground bazaar at Connaught Place.

Connaught Place reminded me of England with its concentric circular roads lined with Victorian terraced buildings housing Pizza Hut, Dominos, McDonalds, and Wimpy's. The only difference was that there were Indians and Indian restaurants everywhere. Hang on a sec, that's exactly like England. As soon as I stepped out of the auto-rickshaw, a tout latched onto me. 'I'll be your very good guide,' he announced. 'And I will take you to a very good shop.' He harassed me for ten minutes and when he gave up another annoyingly persistent tout took over. I was okay with it, though. I figured I couldn't really have an authentic Indian experience without being hassled incessantly.

There was more persistent pestering in Palika Bazaar, the huge sprawling shopping centre underneath Connaught Place. Without fail, every single stallholder would say something like: 'Hello mister, you buy something. I have a very good price for you.'

Apart from a few stalls selling saris, most were filled with exactly the same global mega-brand T-shirts—Levis, Nike, Adidas, Ralph Lauren, GAP etc., etc.—that I'd seen in every market in every country I'd been to. What moronic carbon-copy consumers we've all turned into.

In the next hour I did buy a couple of global mega-brand T-shirts for a little bit more than a very good price and also spent ten minutes arguing with a fellow who followed me. If I told him once I told him a thousand times, I didn't really need to buy a bright orange silk dressing gown.

After a kwality lunch of tandoori prawns and rice at Kwality Restaurant back above ground, I stopped at an internet cafe to search for a couch in Agra. John had told me: 'You have to go to the Taj Mahal. It's foockin' mad.' I said that I would go to Agra if I could find a couch. 'There must be a few nice ones in the Taj,' John said.

There were only a few couches to choose from in Agra, and some of the profiles weren't that inviting:

> Guests should be tolerant. Be aware, I am a heavy smoker.
> Arijit, 27

> I live with my mother who is a terrible nag—so be warned!
> Mukesh, 48

> I love to talk about God all the time. We can talk about his great love for mankind, his great plan of salvation and redemption of fallen mankind. I wish to explain this to people and bring them to God's way so their life will be bright and peaceful. He loves you and wants to take control of your life.
> Subash, 45

I sent off some requests, then jumped in an auto-rickshaw for the long, hot, dusty and smelly ride back to the apartment. As soon as I stepped through the door, Penelope said, 'Let's go. We're going to some bars in Connaught Place.'

John tagged along as well and he told me that we were going to 'run amok'. I had a close look at his pockets to make sure he didn't have any rockets with him. The first bar we went to looked much the same as the second and the third ones. They all had that 'hotel bar' feel, with lots of panelled wood and chrome and were full of barmen in starched jackets who put down little paper coasters with your beer. They also all had 'hotel bar' prices.

Sarah was very happy with the first bar we went to, though. Like any good panelled-wood-and-chrome bar, they had hamburgers on the menu.

While we were sitting in our third indistinguishable bar, John suddenly announced, 'I'm going to steal the motorbike'.

John had been eyeing off the large-scale model of an Enfield motorbike that was sitting in pride of place on a sideboard next to us.

John was serious. 'What do you want the motorbike for?' I asked.

'It will look good in my apartment.'

John downed the rest of his beer then stood up.

'I need one of you girls to attract everyone's attention in the bar,' he said.

The girls were right. John was mad.

'Is this really a good idea?' I asked nervously.

John asked me if I'd like to help. In my youth I was an accomplished shoplifter, but I'm sort of past that. 'Just stand by the door and get ready to run then,' John said, getting himself into position.

Sarah stood up on top of the bar and announced that it was an Australian national holiday then started belting out *Advance Australia Fair*.

I was running up the street when John bolted past me with the motorbike under his arm. I stopped dead in my tracks when I heard a booming male voice and both the girls calling us back.

'Go find John and bring him back,' Penelope hissed as Sarah was trying to talk the very irate manager out of calling the police.

'He only did it for a prank,' Sarah pleaded. 'He's a bit mad.'

I found John around the corner puffing and panting. 'That was foockin' brilliant,' he gasped.

'You have to take it back,' I said.

'No, I want to keep it.'

'No, you have to take it back,' I protested. 'The manager and a big security guy have got the girls.' It took me a few minutes to talk him into going back, but that worked out well. It gave the girls enough time to convince the manager that John was mentally deranged.

18

'Maximum Surfers Per Night: 99.'
Vikram Gupta, 29, Agra, India
CouchSurfing.com

I thought Vikram might have been a tad ambitious thinking of fitting 99 surfers into his one-bedroom apartment, but then I saw that many people trying to squeeze into one small second-class compartment on the train. As I watched I was quite happy that I'd waited over two hours in the 'foreigners' ticket office' to get a First Class ticket for the three-hour trip to Agra, the home of the Taj Mahal.

I only got one reply to my couch requests, but that's all I needed. Vikram's profile sounded relatively normal, although I was a little worried that he lived in a corridor:

> I have a hall with a couch. I am very positive and open mind guy who mix with other peoples very soon and want to listen about them what they want to tell us. I don't smoke or drink, but enjoy hanging around while others are drinking.

There probably wouldn't be much time for Vikram to hang around me while I was drinking because I wasn't going to be hanging around long enough. By the time I'd crawled out of bed and got to an internet cafe to check my emails, it was almost midday, so that meant I wouldn't get into Agra until after five. I planned to get up before dawn the next day to see the Taj, then hop straight on a train back to Delhi.

I was tempted to sleep on the train (I had my own bunk bed), but there was just so much to see out the window. Although the passing landscape itself was nothing exciting—endless dusty fields and shantytowns of flapping sheets of plastic—there were people everywhere. Which, with India's population being 1.3 billion, really wasn't that surprising. There were barbers and hairdressers working away on the roadside, mothers bathing their babies and doing laundry in brown rivers, women traipsing through fields with bundles on their heads, cyclists on rickety bicycles trundling along dirt tracks and lots of folk just wandering about. Mostly, though, there were men sitting everywhere and men shitting everywhere. India, it seems, is one big open latrine. I have never seen so many bottoms—and I've been to the Sydney Gay and Lesbian Mardi Gras after-party. All along the side of the train track, lines of men were casually squatting down and fertilising the plants, so to speak. A friend who'd been to India had told me that 'Most of India is a shithole'. I now realised he had meant it literally.

I got the shits too when I got off the train in Agra. The cycle-rickshaw drivers were so fiercely relentless in their persistence that even my time-tested ploy of ignoring them didn't work. I ended up picking the one and only person who didn't hassle me. Mind you, that was more to do with the fact that he couldn't see me. The Professor, as I immediately dubbed him, was wearing mega-size Coke-bottle glasses that made his eyes look as big as saucers. The only small downside was that he could hardly see all the other traffic on the road as he pedalled slowly through the dusty, dirty and rather charmless city streets of Agra.

'Which hotel?' the Professor hollered over the traffic.

'I'm not staying in a hotel.'

'I know very much a good nice one for you.'

'I'm not staying in a hotel.'

'Where are you staying then?' he asked, looking somewhat perplexed.

'I'm staying on someone's couch.'

That only threw him for a second. 'I will take you to the Taj Mahal tomorrow. What time do you want to go?'

I decided I quite liked the Professor. He was almost the spitting image, albeit an Indian image, of Jerry Lewis in *The Nutty Professor*.

'Pick me up at five o'clock tomorrow morning,' I said to the Professor when he dropped me off out the front of Vikram's apartment block, which looked as if it was made from papier-mâché.

Vikram looked like an Indian version of a younger Danny De Vito. 'Welcome to the city of Taj Mahal, the great symbol of love,' Vikram said as he greeted me into his tiny and sparse apartment. 'This is your couch,' Vikram said, pointing to a couch that would struggle to hold one person, let alone 99.

It was getting late, so we headed straight out to dinner (Vikram had seemed very excited in the email he sent back when I said that I would take him out to dinner).

'So, what do you do for a job?' I asked Vikram as we walked down the street dodging potholes and broken bits of concrete. On Vikram's profile under 'occupation' he had put 'business'.

'I work in restoration and artisan objects,' he said. 'I will like to show you something very good.'

The something very good was his family's large 'marble emporium' where he then tried to sell me some 'unique marble works'. Including a large marble table for a thousand dollars. After explaining that I'd have a bit of trouble fitting it in my backpack, he passed me onto his uncle who tried to flog me cheap marble ornaments for 50 dollars. It was obvious that I was being taken for a bit of a shopping ride. Even as I tried to leave I was ushered into the 'last chance bazaar', which was chock-full of cheaply made crap—except that they were not cheap.

This definitely wasn't in the spirit of couch-surfing and I was already drafting the 'Negative' reference for Vikram's profile in my head. Vikram seemed nice enough, but this obvious ploy to get me into his shop had definitely put a red mark against his name. Mind you, Vikram's couch-surfing 'scam' was modest compared to some of the 'negative', or even 'extremely negative' references I found.

Among the worst hosts were a rip-off travel agent masquerading as a couch-surfing host, sleazy men, stalkers and someone who was dubbed 'a clown, a liar and fucking stupid'. However, most of the 'negatives' were for couch surfers who hadn't bothered to turn up, leaving hosts waiting at train stations or airports—or vice versa.

I should point out though that I did an extensive search to find these very few bad references. To be fair there is only a tiny, tiny minority of bad seeds out there in the big wide world of couch surfing—in fact, 98.8 per cent of users have rated their couch-surfing experience a positive one.

By halfway through dinner Vikram was on his way to earning an upgrade from 'Negative' to 'Neutral'. He was actually quite pleasant company when he wasn't trying to sell me 'unique marble works'. Also, Dasaprakash restaurant where he'd taken me to was nice—and nice and cheap. We ate *thali* (Hindi for plate), which was a large round steel tray with multiple compartments filled with rice, dal, *sambhar*, curried vegetables, chapatti, yoghurt, chutney and pappadums. Vikram still couldn't enjoy watching me drink, though. The restaurant didn't serve alcohol.

As our waiter kept topping up the 'bottom-less' refills, Vikram talked about his family and life in India. Vikram was one of five children and his family had been in the marble business 'since they built the Taj'. Vikram was considered quite a rebel for moving out of home at 28. His older brother, who was 35, was still living at home. 'You usually don't move out until you're married,' he said. 'But I wanted to be free.'

As I was digging into my third or fourth helping, Vikram said, 'Did you know that Agra was very famous for food poisoning?'

'Um, no,' I mumbled through a mouthful of dal.

'Tourists were given poisoned food in some restaurants and then taken to a private clinic for treatment. Then their insurance company would get a bill for thousands of dollars.'

Vikram noticed me looking somewhat horrified as I stared at the remaining food on my plate and thought about how much I'd already eaten. 'It has not happened for quite a while,' he said—not totally reassuringly.

I thought I'd better just check. 'Was this restaurant involved in the poisoning scam?'

'No!'

Good.

'Well, I don't think so.'

Thankfully, I didn't collapse on the walk back to Vikram's, although I wouldn't have minded just a little bit of poisoning to knock me out when I tried to go to bed. The couch was way too small and the room was way too hot. Vikram may have elevated his reference back up to 'Neutral', but his couch rating took a beating:

Couch rating: 5/10

Con: A very short couch

Pro: A very short stay on the very short couch

The Professor turned up promptly at five o'clock and immediately tried to drum up some more business. 'After the Taj Mahal we go to the Red Fort.'

'No, I go back to Delhi.'

'Ah yes, then we go to Akbar's Tomb. It will be very much nice for you.'

The streets were dark and deserted as we made our way towards the Taj Mahal. My plan was to be the first through the gates. John had told me that if I bolted through the walled courtyard inside to the Taj gate, I would have the entire Taj Mahal to myself. Well, for a few minutes at least.

I had to walk the last few hundred metres to the entrance and I was delighted to see that it was too early for the rows and rows of tourist shops (and rows and rows of accompanying hawkers) to be touting their 'unique' marble works.

When I paid the 'foreign nationals' 20-dollar entrance fee I was given a 'free' bottle of water. I doubted if the 'Indian nationals' got a free bottle of water, though. That would have cost more than their 50-cent entrance fee. I also purchased a small guidebook. I wanted to know a bit of the history and couldn't face the thought of a guide following me around all morning.

Here's the history for you in a nutshell: Shah Jahan built the Taj Mahal in the seventeenth century as the mausoleum for his favourite wife, Mumtaz Mahal, who died soon after giving birth to their fourteenth child. Work started in 1641, and the structure took 20 000 labourers 22 years to complete. Legend has it that Shah Jahan cut off the hands of the architect (Persian-born Ustad Ahmad Lahori) and his labourers to ensure that they would never build another.

When I got inside I ran like the wind. A red sandstone gateway blocked off all sight of the Taj until the very last moment. Then it was like a cymbal crash as I caught my first real-life glimpse of its striking beauty. It's almost as if you expect to be disappointed when coming face-to-face with such a famous landmark, because of the gap between the two-dimensional iconic image—which is like a supermodel, always shot from her best angle—and the three-dimensional warts and all reality. But nothing can really prepare you for the exquisiteness of the Taj Mahal.

My timing was perfect. The first rays of morning sun were just hitting the white marble, turning it from blue to orange to yellow. And best of all, I had the entire dream-like setting to myself for all of nine-and-a-half-minutes. That also gave me the chance to take away something that not many visitors to the Taj can capture: a photo of the Taj Mahal without a single person in the shot.

Up close, it was just as breathtaking. The interior marble surfaces were glowing with flowers made of inlaid precious stones. I often went back to the same spot over and over again as the colour of the marble changed with the rising sun. I thought I'd only need an hour or so there, but by the time I dragged myself away it was more than three hours later.

On the way out I could barely move through the hordes of tourists.

The Professor was waiting for me. Well, actually, I walked right up to him and waved my hand in front of his face so he knew it was me.

'We just have to stop somewhere,' the Professor said as he turned off the road to the train station and up a long driveway.

'This is my friend's marble shop,' he boasted. 'It is very much good for you to buy something.'

I told the Professor that it would be very much good for me if we went straight to the station.

It looked like I might have to spend another night with Vikram. There were no tickets for the train to Delhi. Well, no First Class tickets at least. 'You must pre-book at least three hours before,' the ticket master grunted at me. There were only Second and Third Class (with the goats and chickens) tickets available.

It's handy being a foreigner in India. I purchased a Third Class ticket (for around a tenth of the price of First Class) then simply sat in First Class. There were plenty of empty bunks and everyone just assumed that I was in First Class because I was a foreigner. Everyone, that is, except the conductor. I tried feigning a deep sleep, but he kept poking me until I 'awoke'. Although he was quite surprised to see a Third Class ticket, he ordered me out of First Class. I hid in the First Class toilets until he'd gone—which I figured at least gave me some experience of being in Third Class since that was just how I imagined Third Class would smell.

It was raining when I stepped out of Delhi train station. No, raining is probably the wrong word. It was more like a Biblical deluge. Although the auto-rickshaw was 'covered', I was drenched within fifteen seconds of us driving off down the road. The girls were working, so Penelope had recommended a 'Moghul and Afghani cuisine' restaurant that was 'sort of on the way back' to the apartment. I was impressed that the auto-rickshaw driver even knew where it was, but then I wasn't that surprised when I saw the sign at the entrance gate to the restaurant: 'Two times National Tourism Awards winner for Best Restaurant in India.' Park Balluchi Restaurant was in the grounds of leafy Deer Park and as I trudged along the winding path through the rain, peacocks, rabbits and deer scampered about in the gardens next to me.

A squad of turbaned waiters in waistcoats and long shirts greeted me at the door and showed me to my very salubrious table. Before I sat down I checked to make sure I'd brought my credit cards. The meal was a little expensive by Indian standards, but well worth every single rupee. For entrée I had *khumbh bharwan*, which was large fresh mushrooms stuffed with fresh coriander, cheese and spinach then grilled in a tandoor, and a huge serve of *peshwari naan*, bread cooked with poppy seeds and coriander leaves.

I was full by the time my main course came out it in a blaze of glory. And I mean literally in a blaze. The delectably tasty Afghani-style *murgh-potli* was a tandoori chicken breast stuffed with minced mutton and served flambéed on a sword. After my meal I had a couple of Kingfisher beers while I waited for the torrential rain to subside, but—incredibly—it seemed to get worse.

By the time I'd jumped in an auto-rickshaw, the streets had been transformed into gushing rivers. Then, shortly after we hit the main road, the city suddenly disappeared under a blanket of darkness. A massive power cut turned navigating the already jeopardous streets into a frightening game of blindfolded sink or swim.

Eventually my driver gave up. He'd already changed route a few times to avoid massive puddles, but when he came to a lake in the middle of an intersection he abandoned me on the side of the road. Thankfully, I was at least in the right neighbourhood. And I was also thankful that John had fired so many unguided missiles into the street in front of the apartment. It was only by spotting his burnt-out rockets on the ground that I knew where the apartment block was.

I rang the bell for a while before I realised that, duh, without power it didn't work. So I did what any rational person would do . . . I screamed my head off. Just when I was contemplating scaling the wall, Mr Sleepy the guard appeared. And the reason the girls couldn't hear me was that they were having a 'power-cut party' in the top-floor apartment.

All the apartment block tenants (as in all twelve of them, including Vindaloo) were sitting around by candlelight downing large bottles of beer.

'That guard sure is dozy,' I said as I sat down next to Penelope.

'That's because he has two jobs and works twenty-four hours a day,' Penelope said. 'He finishes his twelve-hour shift here, then goes straight to another twelve-hour guard job in another apartment block. The only time he gets to sleep is on the job.'

What was even more amazing was that he had a wife and young family. The amazing part being that he could get the time to make a family, let alone see them.

As I glanced around the room I noticed Sarah's leg. All up the side of her calf was a huge, nasty, deep-red graze. 'What happened to you?' I exclaimed.

'John tried to kill me.'

John looked over with a sheepish grin.

The previous night they'd gone out for a drink and on the way home John decided that he wanted to drive the auto-rickshaw. That was perhaps a little irregular, but although John was drunk, they are easy to drive. Until you start pretending you're in the Motorcycle Grand Prix. John overturned the rickshaw and Sarah was dragged along the road.

Sarah shrugged. 'What can we do? John's a lunatic.'

'We're going to another party, if you'd like to come,' Penelope said as everyone was getting up ready to leave.

I was just happy to go to bed. Dead bodies and all.

PHILIPPINES

19

'I can guarantee at least one free sumptuous banquet feast at a popular Manila restaurant on my expense to every couch surfer who happens to drop by.'
Jude Defensor, 27, Manila, Philippines
CouchSurfing.com

Well, that had me sold. Even if Jude's references were really bad and said that he was a homicidal maniac, I couldn't possibly pass up a 'free sumptuous banquet feast at a popular Manila restaurant'.

Actually, Jude's references were all 'Extremely Positive' and most looked something like this:

> Sign this man up for a cruise director or travel agent. Jude is 'Mr Hospitality Plus'. He even treated me to a magnificent Filipino feast.

Jude, who listed his occupation as 'writer, student, musician', lived in Malate, 'Manila's bohemian heart'. I caught a taxi there from Ninoy Aquino airport and Manila was just as I imagined it: dusty, humid, hectic and noisy.

'Is the traffic usually this bad in the middle of the day?' I asked the driver.

'No, this is no traffic at all! Today is big holiday. It is All Saint's Day and most people are at the cemetery.'

'The cemetery?'

'Yes, families go to cemetery all day and night to eat and drink with dead relatives.'

'Do you go?'

'No,' he said shaking his head. 'It's not like we can bring them back to life.'

By the time we got away from the airport traffic, the streets were almost dead—so to speak—and when we turned onto the palm-fringed waterfront promenade overlooking Manila Bay we just about had the road to ourselves. Manila looked spotless and decidedly empty after Delhi. Even the battered, rusted, smoke-belching, brightly painted jeepneys looked brand-spanking new compared to Delhi's down-at-heel-buses.

Malate didn't look very bohemian. It was all a little bit rundown and full of mostly seedy bars and clubs. Jude didn't look that bohemian, either. He met me at the door of his 1970s sixth-floor apartment wearing nice slacks and a neat collared shirt. The interior of Jude's apartment was the décor equivalent of nice slacks and a neat collared shirt. There was a place for everything and everything was in its place.

I think Jude perhaps could have added 'being neat' to the extensive list of 'interests' on his profile, which already included: travel, architecture, art, music, food, writing, photography, languages, anthropology, playing the cello, French authors, Siamese cats, dancing like nobody's looking, procrastinating and group texting.

Jude was the editor of *What's On & Expat* magazine where he wrote articles about travel, architecture, art, music—about all of his interests, really (although I'm not entirely sure if he'd get many articles up about procrastinating . . . but then again . . .).

Still thinking of his profile, I asked Jude why he'd described himself as 'embarrassingly overeducated'.

'I studied medicine and worked as an intern for three years, but gave it away,' Jude shrugged.

'Why's that?'

'I worked in a cancer hospital and it was too depressing. Medicine just wasn't for me. My sister is a doctor, though, so my Mum is happy that she got at least one doctor in the family.' Jude also studied the cello and Spanish and had recently been offered the chance to take a Masters degree in Spanish at Barcelona University. 'I still might do that one day,' he said.

We began our walking tour of Manila with a prayer. When we waltzed into the Our Lady of Remedies church, Jude whispered: 'Sit down and pretend to pray.' We parked ourselves on one of the pews and Jude said, 'It's nice and cool in here and this way we've got an excuse to stay a little longer.'

Jude, like most Filipinos, was Catholic and he came to Our Lady of Remedies every Sunday for mass. 'I really don't want to go,' he murmured. 'But mass is only forty-five minutes. It's either that or spend three hours a week arguing with my mum about why I shouldn't go.'

I was feeling a little peckish after our prayers, so we stopped at a traditional Filipino Mini-Stop 24-hour Convenience Store. 'It's our very own Filipino Seven-Eleven,' Jude said, as I squinted under the prerequisite ultra-blinding fluoro lights. We sat outside on bright blue plastic chairs and while I ate my *siopao,* a huge steamed dumpling thing that was stuffed with minced pork, Jude madly texted away on his phone. 'Filipinos are obsessed with mobile phones,' Jude said as he fingered fervently. 'They are very good for us because we are reserved and very shy, so you can text things that you can't say face-to-face.'

Our next stop was, as my dear dad would say, the 'dead centre of Manila'. Paco Cemetery was surprisingly very dead, though. There weren't that many people visiting relatives' graves because most of the departed had departed more than a hundred years ago. 'Most people don't bother about visiting their very old relatives,' Jude said, as we passed an old lady lighting candles next to a faded gravestone.

'The Manila North cemetery will be *full* of people drinking and partying,' Jude continued. 'Except this year they have banned karaoke machines. Sometimes they have a little trouble.'

The next day the *Manila Bulletin* had the headline 'All Saint's Day peaceful and orderly', and the first line of copy read 'At Manila North Cemetery police confiscated 150 knives, flammable materials and some guns.'

We spent most of the afternoon wandering around Intramuros, the walled city built in 1571 for the Spanish ruling classes as their very own little Spain-away-from-Spain with homes, shops, churches, monasteries, schools and hospitals. To get inside we had to walk across an old drawbridge above a moat that the Americans had filled in and turned into an 18-hole golf course. As we ambled lazily up and down worn cobblestone streets full of weeds and past either rundown or knocked-down Spanish colonial buildings, Jude told me that the city survived virtually untouched until the last days of the Second World War. 'During the Battle of Manila the Japanese and the Americans bombed the hell out of it,' Jude said as we strolled past a large pile of ruins. 'Only the city walls and some of the buildings survived. And did you know that more civilians were killed during the battle than in Hiroshima?'

Although most of the city was neglected and falling apart, I loved it. If it had been in Europe they would have rebuilt a sanitised Disneyesque version of the city. There was still plenty to admire, although when I commented on the exquisite street lamps Jude said, 'Oh, they're not the originals. Imelda Marcos took those for her house. These are just copies.'

As we hiked along the top of the crumbling ramparts Jude told me a little about his family's life under Marcos. 'We were better off under Marcos, because Dad was a colonel in the air force,' he said. 'We had a huge house on the base overlooking a golf course, but we lost it all during the People Power Revolution to oust Marcos. When it happened we were trapped in the air force base and couldn't get out to get food, so we ate at the golf clubhouse every night. One night we were walking home, taking a shortcut through the golf course, when helicopter gun-ships began shooting at us. We were only fifty metres from home, so we dashed across the open space. Dad was trailing behind because he was carrying me and bullets rained all around us. Amazingly, not a single one hit us.'

'That is amazing,' I agreed.

'Do you want a coffee?' Jude suddenly asked, pointing down to the base of the wall. Built into the ancient stonework was a Starbucks. Next door, and also built into the wall, was a McDonalds.

'Oh, we absolutely love American food chains,' Jude said when I huffed in disgust. 'You name it, we got it.'

Thankfully we weren't dining at Burger King or T.G.I. Friday for dinner. Jude took me to Kamayan Restaurant, which was owned by his second cousin. His fourth cousins twice removed were the waiting staff. Although it was early, the modern restaurant was full of locals. 'Expats don't come here,' Jude said. 'Most of them eat near their gated communities that look like *The Truman Show*.'

Jude ordered me a local concoction of coconut milk and herbs to start. It tasted absolutely terrible.

'How's your drink?' Jude asked.

'Hmm, nice,' I enthused.

The restaurant served traditional Filipino food, so I was quite disappointed when Jude told me that they didn't have *bopis*, which is pig's lungs chopped and then stir-fried. But

Jude was right when he promised a sumptuous banquet. We had large plates of *kilawin sugba* (pork marinated in vinegar), *rellenong sugpo* (stuffed prawns) and a very squirmy but tasty *kuhol sa gata* (golden sea snails in coconut milk).

'I'd like to buy you dinner,' I said to Jude when we'd finished.

'No, you are my guest. Dinner is on me. You can buy the first beer at the karaoke bar.'

As any of my loyal readers know, I'm a bit of a karaoke addict. I therefore have to admit that, perhaps a bit sadly, I was looking forward to coming to the Philippines because I figured it was the perfect country to feed my insatiable love of a soppy ballad. Like Japan, though, most of the karaoke in the Philippines takes place in private rooms for hire. I told Jude that I preferred to go to a public one so I could showcase my crooning. The karaoke bar that we went to may as well have been a private room, though. There were only four other patrons—a bunch of merry Koreans with ruddy cheeks sitting around a table full of empty San Miguel beer bottles.

'I'll start with my usual opening number,' I said as I perused the song list. 'Everybody's favourite . . . *My Way*.'

'Oh, you can't sing that,' Jude gasped. 'You'll get killed!'

'Killed?'

'Yes, last week a man was shot dead in a karaoke bar singing *My Way*. He was halfway through the song when the bar's security guard yelled at him for singing out of tune. He ignored him and kept singing, so the guard pulled out a thirty-eight-calibre pistol and shot him dead. His defence was that it was his favourite song and he didn't like the way he was singing it.'

It makes 'and now the end is near' rather prophetic, doesn't it?

Apparently, violence is common in Filipino karaoke bars and *My Way* is the most frequent cause of fights and deaths. A few months before another man had been killed and his friend seriously wounded when they sarcastically applauded a student who was singing *My Way* off-key. The student felt insulted, so when they left the karaoke parlour, he ambushed and shot them.

'There have been maybe fifty or more shootings because of *My Way* in the past ten years,' Jude said. 'And after the recent murder many karaoke bars in Manila have taken *My Way* off the song list.'

'So what song did you pick?' Jude asked as I handed my song request to the waitress.

'*My Way*.'

I thought I'd give it a go. I actually won a karaoke competition once singing the song—okay, most of the other contestants were drunk, but that's not the point. Besides, the Korean guys looked friendly enough. There was only one tiny thing that worried me. The security guard at the door was brandishing a rather large shotgun and was wearing a fully loaded ammo belt.

'That was very good,' Jude said with a somewhat relieved smile when I'd finished singing. 'You won't get shot for that version.'

'Let's do a karaoke bar crawl,' I said excitedly. 'Then I can do *My Way* in every one to see if I can get shot.'

There was no one in the second karaoke bar to shoot me. Unless Jude suddenly decided he didn't like my singing. We were the only patrons. I did also sing *You are so beautiful* to the cute barmaid who was the only other person in the bar. 'This is for you,' I said to her as I handed her my song request.

'Be careful,' Jude warned. 'Sometimes they are a man.'

Not that she took any notice anyway. I sang it quite well I thought, but she (or a very beautiful he) ignored me and did the accounts.

On the way to our next karaoke bar, Jude told me that it wasn't just bad singing that got you murdered in Manila. Only the day before a Malate man had stabbed his brother-in-law to death over whose turn it was to wash the dishes.

'Are Filipinos a bit aggressive?' I asked.

'Oh no, we are *very* happy people,' Jude said cheerfully. 'In fact, a survey was done two years ago and the Filipinos were number six in the top ten happiest people in the world.'

I looked it up when I got home and Jude was right.

Incidentally, take a stab at who you think came in at number one. According to the survey the mirthful Venezuelans are the happiest little chappies on the planet. I'd done quite well in the happy stakes myself. On this trip alone I managed to visit six of the top eight happiest nations in the world: Iceland, the Netherlands, the Philippines, Australia, the United States and Turkey. Incidentally, the least 'happiest people' were the Russians, the Latvians and, coming dead last, the poor miserable Bulgarians.

The hosts of 'Let's Have Fun' karaoke bar were definitely full of gayness. Two transvestites—who had lovely long, shapely legs I have to say—were hosting it. Their place was one of many large outdoor karaoke bars on the waterfront promenade. Because of the holiday they were all busy, but we stopped at the largest, which would have had more than a hundred people in the crowd.

I put my name down and had only taken a sip of my beer when 'Miss Diva' called me up onto the stage.

'Where are you from?' Miss Diva purred.

When I told her, the two leggy transvestites hopped around the stage impersonating kangaroos.

'So, what song would you like to do?' Miss Diva asked when she'd finished her hopping.

'*My Way*,' I said brightly.

There was a loud 'Ohh' from the crowd.

'You'll get shot!' Miss Diva said gravely.

I looked out at the crowd. 'Hands up if you have a gun?'

'See, it's safe,' I said when no hands were raised.

Miss Diva smirked. 'Yes, but there's a sniper up in that building.'

Our last karaoke bar was a midget bar. The bar itself wasn't small, but all the staff were midgets—or dwarves, or little people, or vertically challenged folk or whatever is PC and accepted in polite company nowadays. Although the bar was called Hobbit House, Jude didn't tell me about the bar's unique staffing prerequisites and I got quite a shock when someone down at my knees asked if I wanted a drink.

We grabbed a table and when our waiter returned with our drinks, little hands came up and plopped them on the table. The bar may have been run by small people, but they had big prices. Our beer cost three times as much as in the last karaoke bar. I also noticed that they didn't have Randy Newman's *Short People* on the song list.

'How do you say cheers in Dwarfish?' Jude asked, after I'd got through my fourth and final version of *My Way* for the night without a single shot being fired in anger.

Back at Jude's place a short time later, however, I was woken up by what sounded like a gunshot. It was probably the consequence of another bad version of *My Way*. The startled fright I got helped knock the couch rating down a fraction:

Couch rating: 8/10
Pro: The neatest bedroom on the trip
Con: I couldn't get *My Way* out of my bloody head all night

20

'I don't have a couch. Does that matter?'
Elvie Malinao, 21, Siquijor, Philippines
(Cousin of a couch surfer)

In the morning I found myself sitting in a brand new A320 Airbus flying to . . . I'm not exactly sure where.

Jude told me that I couldn't possibly come to the Philippines without visiting one of the islands. 'I'm not going to let you just write about Manila,' he'd said. In between visiting Karaoke Bar One and Karaoke Bar Two the previous night, we had walked into a travel agent and fifteen minutes later I walked out with a return ticket to somewhere called Dumaguete on the island of Negros. From there I was jumping on a boat to the island of Siquijor, where Jude had arranged for me stay on his cousin's couch. He'd been frantically texting her while I was buying my ticket. She texted back and said it was fine, 'But I don't have a couch. Does that matter?'

I was quite impressed with Cebu Pacific Air. Not only did the plane depart right on time, but the crew were cute, considerate and courteous. On the short walk from the terminal building to the plane, they even handed every person an umbrella to block out the hot sun. The view from my window seat was just as impressive as we flew over countless islands—or if you do count them, there are 7107—that looked like green pearl drops in a blue and emerald sea.

I caught a taxi from Dumaguete airport to the port and as we pulled up the driver yelled, 'Quick, quick, there's your boat'. I scampered onto the pier, but it chugged away just as I reached it.

'You can go on that one,' the ticket-seller said, pointing to an abandoned wreck tethered to the pier.

I craned my neck looking for a boat behind it.

'No, that one,' he said, pointing again to the rickety raft.

I had to walk across a narrow and rotting plank to get aboard and then climb over a mountain of bags to get to the top deck. The boat I'd missed was called 'The Fast Boat' and took 45 minutes to get to Siquijor. I dubbed this one 'The Ludicrously Slow Boat'. It took two-and-a-half hours. I didn't mind, though. I lay on the top deck and dozed off in the sun.

Even from a distance Siquijor announced itself as perfectly idyllic: deep green, white-fringed and afloat in a softly glittering vivid blue sea. Its 'ferry terminal' seemed equally enticingly tropical. It was one small wooden pier against a backdrop of white sand and swaying palms. Laughing children were jumping off it and splashing into the clear blue water.

I knew nothing about this tiny island. On the small map of Siquijor in the airline magazine there was good news and bad news. If the name of one of the island's main towns was anything to go by, it would be the perfect place to relax. The name of the town was Lazi. But what was I to make of the fact that it was on the river Poo? 'There's a couple of resorts I think' was all Jude had told me. Elvie worked at one of those resorts—Coral Cay Resort, near the town of San Juan. I caught a tricycle, which was a motorcycle with a sidecar, from the dock and we skirted the coast, past thatched fishermen's huts nestled amongst mangroves. On the twenty-minute drive we passed three cars, a couple of mopeds and a bicycle. Coral Cay Resort was off the main road at the end of a gravel track lined with palm trees. Elvie was waiting for me at the small reception building. 'It is very nice to meet you,' Elvie said with a glittering smile. Elvie was positively tiny and positively gorgeous.

'I'm so sorry, but you can't stay with me,' Elvie said, smiling serenely. 'My room is too small.'

'Oh . . .'

Elvie grabbed my hand. 'But it's okay, because I have got you your own room.'

Elvie led me down a track between huts that were scattered around a picture-postcard-perfect pool, past an empty open-sided beachfront bar and restaurant and onto the beach, a slim arc of soft white sand shaded by swaying . . . you get the picture.

'It's very quiet at the moment, so you can have this,' Elvie said.

Gasp.

'That's a ten out of ten,' I muttered excitedly.

'Pardon.'

'Nothing.'

I hadn't even seen inside, but I was pretty sure I'd found my perfect ten-out-of-ten couch. The thatched beach hut, which also had a large verandah, overlooked my very own hammock that was slung between two palm trees on the water's edge. When I did look inside, I saw polished wooden floors, a huge double bed, marble-tiled bathroom and air-conditioning. Even though I'd only just met Elvie, I gave her a big hug—which left her a little confused about my intentions. She rushed off rather quickly and said, a little nervously, that she'd take me out after work.

So anyway, an Irishman, a Canadian and an Australian walked into a bar.

I wandered into the bar for 'happy hour' at the same time as the resort's only two other guests arrived. Doug, who had a deep chocolate-brown tan, was in his mid-50s and had found out about Siquijor from a work colleague in Manila where he had been for a business meeting. 'I wanted a little break, so he told me to come here. I should have been back in Canada three days ago,' he shrugged, 'but I can't leave.' James was backpacking his way around Asia and had been in the Philippines for a few weeks. 'I stayed with a family in Cebu and they recommended I come here,' he said.

'It's good to have you here,' Doug said. 'There's only been the two of us here all week, so it's nice to speak to someone else for a change.'

'Now we've got only four staff each, though,' James said when the waitress brought us another beer.

'Which room are you staying in?' Doug asked.

'I'm in one of the "Beach Deluxe" huts.'

'Oh, very nice,' James said. 'We're only in the "Garden" rooms.'

I couldn't really tell them that I was getting my 'very nice' room for free.

When Elvie finished work, she met me at the bar. 'So, are you ready to go out?' she asked with a dazzling smile.

'Sorry lads, I've got a date,' I said as their jaws dropped.

'I thought that maybe you would like to see a traditional cultural performance,' Elvie said as we jumped on the back of a passing motorbike that she'd flagged down. It wasn't quite the 'traditional' performance I was expecting, however. I had it in my mind that we'd be going to some little village to witness an ancient, and time-honoured, ceremony. Instead we were going to Coco Grove Beach Resort for the weekly 'Traditional Cultural Show and Buffet'. The resort was a bit more flash than Coral Cay Resort and somewhat busier. Around 40 or so guests were sitting outside around candlelit tables that had been set up in front of a stage. Off to one side a line of chefs and waitresses were manning an impressively laden buffet table—including an entire glazed pig on a spit.

After we'd pigged out at the buffet (well, actually, I did most of the pigging) the show began with traditional Filipino dancing—which was a cross between the Macarena and

Irish dancing. When the third lot of dancers came out in different outfits, but went through identical moves I asked Elvie why she'd left Cebu City to come to Siquijor.

'Cebu City has too much crime,' Elvie sighed. 'Here there is no crime at all. I also like it because it's quiet. The population of Cebu City is seven hundred thousand and the population of the whole island of Siquijor is eighty thousand.'

Elvie also had plenty of work on the island. Not only did she do waitressing and reception work, she was also a 'qualified' foot masseuse.

The 'Traditional Cultural show' went for more than two hours, although by the end it wasn't all that traditional—girls were dancing in hula skirts to the theme tune of *Hawaii Five-O*.

On the walk back we stopped at a newly opened bar on the beach. James, who was the only patron, was drinking whisky with Jurgen, the six-foot-six German barman and owner who towered over his five-foot Filipino wife. I couldn't help notice that large chunks of Jurgen's leg were missing and what was left was nothing more than mangled flesh and scar tissue.

'It's a souvenir from my holiday in Australia,' Jurgen said matter-of-factly.

Jurgen had gone to Australia for a holiday and only three days into his trip he went diving and was mauled by a shark. 'I spent five weeks in a Perth hospital,' Jurgen said, lifting up his leg so I could get a closer look. 'It was fifty-fifty whether I'd keep my leg, but the skin grafts worked.'

Jurgen smiled. 'Now it just looks like the remains of a pork roast.'

When Jurgen brought out a bottle of liquor that smelt like methylated spirits, Elvie called the night watchman at the resort to come pick us up on his moped. As we were leaving James skolled a shot of the firewater and almost fell off his bar stool.

Okay, so my "Deluxe Beach" hut wasn't actually a couch, but it was free so it counts. Drum roll please . . .

Couch rating: 10/10
Pro: Luxurious in every way
Con: Stay too short by many days

I had a taxing morning lounging by the pool. The taxing part was trying to decide which one of the twenty or so empty sun-beds to choose. 'I'll have the other half of the pool then,' Doug said when he turned up in his tiny bathers.

After a delicious calamari salad for lunch, I embarked on an extremely perilous journey to find the most beautiful beach on Siquijor. The reason the journey was so perilous was because Elvie had kindly sweet-talked the night watchman into letting me borrow his scooter. I was quite nervous to begin with—what with my dodgy riding skills and all—but the bitumen road was good and there was hardly any traffic. Or people. As I puttered along the road to San Juan I could only see a distant fisherman lazily hurling a net out into the shallow clear water and a couple of kids playing basketball with a coconut. There was no one else in sight.

The road, which hugged the coastline, was like a necklace strung with small villages with exotic names like Tagibo, Bonga, Dapdap and Bogo. There were a few more people in the villages and as I rode through just about everyone would wave and smile and giggling school children would chase me down the road—which isn't that difficult considering how slowly I ride.

After briefly heading inland through dense jungle, I came to the turn-off for Salagdoong Beach, 'the most beautiful beach on Siquijor.' A steep narrow track wound its way through a forest of molave trees down to . . . paradise. There was a pristine, white-sand cove with crystal-clear water and, overlooking the beach, a thatched karaoke hut. Swimming and singing—now that's what I call paradise.

I spent an hour lazily splashing about in the warm and tranquil water. The only other people were a small group of local teenagers who all at some point paddled over to say hello. After my swim I had a beer at the bar and—surprise, surprise—sang a song. When I'd finished belting out *Sometimes when we touch* a score out of a hundred came up on the screen. I got 98: 'You are a perfect artist!' It was a shame that there was only an audience of eight to witness my exemplary performance. A woman got up after me and sang a Barbara Streisand number. She sounded not unlike a cat on heat. When she got a score of 95 I had to stop myself from screaming out: 'Come on! That must be only worth a sixty at the most.' Now that I had a standard to judge my score against, maybe I'd have to cancel that Karaoke World Tour I'd suddenly started dreaming about . . .

When I got to the jungle on the ride back, I hit the Great Wall of Rain. The monsoonal downpour was so heavy that I couldn't see a metre in front of me. It was like having a strong and warm horizontal shower. Then, when I was only ten minutes from the resort, I rode out the other side of the Great Wall of Rain and into a clear and cloudless day.

'What rain?' asked Doug, who was having a beer at the bar. James was still in bed nursing his killer hangover. 'He tried to keep up with the giant German,' Doug said gravely.

I had dinner at a candlelit table on the beach with the backdrop of a garishly tiger-striped sunset. It was incredibly romantic as Elvie tended to my every need, getting me drinks and an amazing chargrilled fish for dinner. Except that Elvie was our waitress and I was dining with Doug.

'Tonight after work I will take you somewhere special,' Elvie said, when she returned with some lurid cocktail that Doug had ordered for us.

'Gee, you're good,' Doug said, giving me a wink.

When Elvie came back she was all dressed up, which made me feel very dressed down in my shorts and thongs. The somewhere 'special' was a karaoke bar. How did she know? Also joining us was Tey, another girl who worked at the resort. Tey, who had an 8-year-old boy, was even tinier than Elvie. Which was handy, since they were both jumping on the back of the scooter with me. I was already feeling somewhat apprehensive about riding with one person on the back. Now I had two potential hospital bills to worry about.

The karaoke bar was in a small open-sided shack in San Juan. It was so small that there was only enough room for two tables. The bar was dark and the barmaid was asleep behind the bar.

'Is the bar closed?' I asked, waking her up in the process.

'No,' the lady said, as she reached down and turned on the lights and the karaoke machine.

This was hardcore Filipino karaoke. No chatting, just singing. We took it in turns to sing and even so I must have sung twenty songs. I even attempted a Filipino duet with Elvie. In between songs, however, I did manage to sneak in a bit of conversation. I found out that Tey had worked in Hong Kong for a few years. 'Everyone in the world likes to have a Filipino maid,' Tey said.

'Do you know what the Philippines' biggest export is?' Elvie asked.

'No, um . . . karaoke machines?'

'Filipino maids.'

'Really?'

'I don't know,' Elvie shrugged, 'but one in ten Filipinos work overseas, which is over ten million people and it is still the largest source of foreign income for the Philippines. I think last year something like fourteen billion dollars came into the country from workers.'

'That's a lot of money for cleaning toilets,' I said.

Just as I was in the middle of singing a very moving version of George Michael's *Careless Whisper*, four young, tough-looking and very drunk local lads turned up and began talking raucously at the bar. I hope it wasn't my singing, but before I'd finished my song one fellow leant over the wall next to us and proceeded to heave into the flower garden for five minutes.

'I'm so sorry for the inconvenience I have caused you,' he said politely before slumping back into his chair.

The ride back was scary. I don't think the girls quite realised how scary it really was. I'd had a couple of beers, it was dark, I wasn't used to riding with people on the back (let alone two people), but mostly I'm just crap at riding two-wheeled machines. The girls were surprised when I leapt off the scooter with joy once we'd made it back to the resort with all our limbs intact.

Elvie joined me for one quick drink at the bar. She had to get up early for work and I had a ferry and a plane to catch. 'I'm very lucky,' she told me. 'I am happy here. The staff get treated well, I have a nice room and I have this . . .' Elvie swept her arm out towards the beach and water, which were both sparkling bright under the moonlight. 'I think I'll stay here for a while.'

I could as well. I wonder if my family would miss me . . .

21

'Types of people I enjoy:
Manic weirdos, introverts and geeks.'
Leika, 28, Manila, Philippines
CouchSurfing.com

I ended my Grand Couch Surfing Tour of the Globe exactly the same way it started.

Couchless.

And it wasn't as if I didn't try to find a couch. I'd already known for a few weeks that Jude couldn't host me for the last night in Manila, so I'd sent out a whole bunch of requests. I don't know why I didn't haven't any luck, because some of the potential hosts seemed quite accommodating:

> You are free to use my TV, kitchen, laptop and even my clothes (medium size only). You are also free to use the toilet and my shampoo and body soap.
> Jerome, 27

I'd love you to stay and I don't really mind weird, crazy people as long as they're not homicidal and don't trash my place.
Carmela, 23

Still getting no response, in desperation I even sent a request to Rex:

Sorry, I can't offer accommodation because I'm often lying in the gutter.
Rex, 29

Eight different people said they would 'love to have me', but they either had family staying for the holidays or they'd gone away. One girl had five family members staying in her lounge room—another one won't make a difference, I told her.

I did, however, find two girls who said that they would join me for dinner and drinks—even though I wasn't sure I met their criteria as the type of person they liked. Leica was keen on 'manic weirdos and geeks' and Zane preferred 'people with a high tolerance for randomness'. The girls were also excited about meeting up because, quite coincidentally, they were friends. They lived on opposite sides of the city and hadn't seen each other for a couple of months.

I'd finally given up all hope of finding a couch when I checked my emails back in Manila. Just as on the first night of my Grand Couch Surfing Tour, I was going to have to check into a hotel. I rang Jude and he recommended Bianca's Garden Hotel near his place in Malate. It was an inspired choice. The hotel was in an old Spanish mansion filled with antique dark-wood Filipino furniture. It was my last night, and I'd just had nine weeks of free accommodation, so I decided to lash out and took the 'Premier Suite'. The suite, which had a king-size bed and cable TV, overlooked the swimming pool and lavish gardens.

I was meeting the girls at a restaurant in Greenbelt 3 (which sounds like a space station from *Babylon 5*) in Makati, Manila's business district. Greenbelt 3 was part of an immense modern shopping complex with three levels of designer shops, hip bars and restaurants, including the Filipino restaurant Sentro 1771. The girls hadn't arrived when I turned up ten minutes late, so I grabbed an outside table on the terrace looking out across landscaped gardens, fountains and palm trees draped with fairy lights.

Leica was the first to arrive—40 minutes late. 'We call it Filipino timekeeping,' she said bashfully. I could see why Leica liked introverts. I think she was one. Leica was quite shy and would often talk to her hands instead of making eye contact. Her job seemed perfectly suited for her then—she worked as an over-the-phone IT consultant.

'I live with my family, so I can't have couch surfers to stay,' Leica said after apologising for not offering her couch. 'But I love meeting people for dinner.'

After I'd finished my second beer Leica said, 'You may as well order now. Zane is the running-late queen.'

I had marinated monkfish, that although it was delicious, was four times the price of a meal in Siquijor. Zane turned up just as I was finishing my dinner. 'That's okay,' Zane said, then promptly ordered two desserts. Under occupation on her profile Zane had put 'editor, overall critic and frustrated dancer'. Zane was very bubbly and chatty, so I wasn't surprised when she told me that she worked in PR. She also lived with her family and hadn't had any couch surfers stay with her. 'I've met a lot of couch surfers for dinner and drinks, though,' Zane said, with a mouthful of chocolate sundae. 'Last night I took out a tall Swedish gay guy who was wearing pinstripe hot pants and braces.'

The girls hadn't seen each other for a while, so they had a lot to catch up on. 'Did you see *Lost* on Wednesday?' Leica asked Zane excitedly. They also had *American Idol*, *The Amazing Race* and *Prison Break* to compare notes on.

Not only were they talking about US TV shows, they both sounded as if they came from the suburbs of LA.

'It must be a dream come true being a travel writer,' Zane said in her American drawl.

'Yes, it was a silly dream I had many years ago.'

'I have a dream, too,' Leica said.

'What's that?' I asked.

'My dream is to marry Wentworth Miller from *Prison Break*.'

'I think that guy's fulfilled his dream,' I said, nodding subtly to the table next to us. An American guy, who must have been 60, was canoodling with his Filipino girlfriend who looked about twenty.

'That's nothing,' Zane said. 'There's a bar downstairs that's full of them. Do you want to go have a gawk?'

We wandered downstairs to the Havana Club and grabbed a table outside. 'Okay, let's play spot the paid-for girlfriend,' Zane said, eyeing off the crowd.

'Gee, that's hard,' I said. Most of the clientele were old, paunchy, bald men in Hawaiian shirts accompanied by slim, young Filipino girls. At the table next to us an old fellow with white hair and a bulbous beer belly was asleep at the table, while his young 'girlfriend' sat forlornly staring at her drink. When I noticed that a few of the men were staring at me, I realised that they were thinking I was just one of them. Except I had two girlfriends. They were also probably trying to figure out how I managed to get two when I didn't look like I had a lot of money.

Leica was feeling uncomfortable. 'It's just a dirty old man's meat market,' she winced.

'It's fun,' Zane said brightly. 'They all keep looking at Brian thinking that he is some sort of rich stud.'

Zane then started playing gently with Leica's hair.

'This will make them *real* jealous,' Zane smiled cheekily. 'They'll think he's got himself a couple of lesbians.'

After we finished our beers Leica said that she'd had enough. I didn't mind. I was looking forward to my hotel room—and my own space, my own TV, my own shower and my own toilet to make whatever loud noises I desired in. One thing I would recommend for anyone planning a couch-surfing trip would be to break up the couches with a few nights in your own space. In fact, it's more than just having your own space. Your liver will probably need a break as well. One of the great discoveries I made on this trip is that the entire planet seems to be fuelled by alcohol.

On that note I stopped at a bar near the hotel for one final couch-surfing drink just to 'soak in' what had been an incredible and incredibly long journey. My Grand Couch Surfing Tour of the Globe had taken me over 60 000 kilometres on 22 flights through 15 countries on 23 different couches. What an extraordinary and privileged experience it had been being welcomed into people's homes to share, even for a short time, a snapshot of their lives. Yes, I also got free couches to sleep on and a local's perspective, but mostly I'd forged instant friendships.

Couch surfing is such a great way to learn about a country and its people. It encourages you to travel in an engaged way—as opposed to the disengagement of seeing places packaged for tourists through a coach window or the viewfinder of a camera. And by witnessing other lives, we open up to possibilities that we were once blind to.

Never before had I appreciated so much that the real rewards of travel are not seeing transcendentally beautiful buildings or breathtaking landscapes, but enjoying the simple friendship and trust of strangers.

On the short walk back to the hotel I was propositioned by a gaggle of prostitutes.

'You married?'

'Yes.'

'That's okay. You can call me your wife's name, so there's no confusion.'

One woman, who was acting as a pimp for her daughter, tried to cajole me back to her place.

'I'm not interested.'

'It's okay,' she said. 'You can sleep on the couch.'

A couch? Hmm?

'Thanks anyway,' I said, 'but I think I'm done with couches for the moment.'

EPILOGUE

The couch surfing wave just keeps getting bigger and bigger. When I made my trip there were 150 000 members from 20 000 cities on CouchSurfing.com with around 1000 new members joining each week. By the time I'd finished writing the book there were 700 000 members from 45 000 cities and 10 000 new members joining every week. By the time you read this the membership will have probably have hit the million mark.

In July 2008 couch surfing passed the mark for one million positive experiences. Out of the eighteen people I stayed with on my trip I gave seventeen an 'extremely positive' (and one 'neutral' for Vikram and his Marble Emporium—which may have been a tad generous). Since my return I've also had a few couch surfers crash on my couch and I've enjoyed that every bit as much as staying with someone else. It has opened up my own city to me. I've taken my surfers out to tourist attractions (and lots of bars) that I didn't know existed until I'd searched them out on the net and showing them around has made me feel proud of my own city.

From my own couch surfing experiences I think the most amazing thing about the concept is that hosts and guests can really get to know each other. When you visit a place while couch surfing it's mostly the people you remember. By reaching out to travellers and hosts around the globe couch surfing has crossed social barriers and bridged cultural differences to create this unique experience where we share our homes, stories, inspirations and lives. I now consider my couch surfing hosts good friends and we all agree that the relationships formed through couch surfing are what matter most. I still keep in touch with most of my hosts and a few have threatened to come and surf on my couch in the near future.

It's actually been a while since I left my surfing friends, so I thought I'd give you an update on what they've been doing since I moved on:

Miguel hasn't changed at all. He is still cooking, riding, skiing, fighting off pumas and sleeping later from time to time.

Jose will be designing new vortex flanges for Nestlé for many more years to come. Last time I heard from him he was couch surfing, and comparing pipes, with another engineer in El Segundo, California.

Juan achieved the maximum score for his thesis and created 'a little revolution inside the university'. 'People stopped me just to say how wonderful and incredible was my project,' Juan told me in an email. It was so good that he won the 'Thesis of the Year' prize, then married Katya in Moscow and is now living there. They've started up a website promoting the Spanish language (www.spanishclass.ru) for Russians. Juan told me that he is the 'webmaster, designer, editor, redactor, moderator, journalist, philologist and translator'.

I get no response from my emails to Mariano, so I can only assume that he's been eaten by one of the roaming packs of dogs in Valparaíso.

Pedro finally finished recording his band's CD, and his dad did the cover illustration. I told him that I'd look out for it in the charts. Pedro and Nathalia are coming to surf on my couch in Australia in 2009.

I was Mariana's somewhat nervous first couch-surfing guest, but since then she has embraced the couch surfing concept (and one lucky Portuguese couch surfer). Mariana has had 31 people from 23 different countries stay with her, and they all say that is she the coolest *carioca* in Rio.

A few months after I left Bob he put an ad on Craigslist asking for budget travellers who wanted to see North America:

> *I will be touring the US, Mexico, and Central America for the next year. I have a 15 passenger van loaded with quality camping and cooking gear, 4 bicycles, a kayak, a computer with WiFi, a DVD player and movies, a radio, music for any situation, books on tape, a National Parks Pass, a frisbee,*

binoculars, field guides and anything else you can think of bringing on a prolonged road trip.

The last I heard from Bob he was in Nebraska with seven passengers. What surprised me the most was that with all the stuff he was taking there was any room left for people.

Jeremy emailed me recently and wrote: 'I am still employed at the same place despite my best efforts to slack off and get canned. In fact I was promoted a few months ago and am now a Tactical Development Systems Analyst.' He explained the job to me, but I still have no idea what he does. Jeremy has also been very busy dating a couple of women who live in his apartment building plus a woman he works with. 'It keeps me on my toes,' he said. 'I had a close call the other night when one of my romantically inclined neighbours dropped by while I was entertaining my romantically inclined work colleague.'

Smári moved into a bigger place with a friend (more room for empty Pepsi bottles) and is still studying and writing complicated mathematical equations. Smári has a blog that he regularly updates, although mostly I have no idea what he is talking about:

Ah, yes. The good news is that The Random Number has been found out to be 4. All other random numbers are actually less random than 4, irrespective of the distribution they are taken from. This can be seen by calculating the respective entropy of 4 on the one hand, and the respective entropy of all other integers on the other.

Let's remember that information entropy is defined as:

$$H(X) = \sum_{i=1}^{n} p(x_i) \log_2 \left(\frac{1}{p(x_i)} \right) = \sum_{i=1}^{n} p(x_i) \log_2 p(x_i)$$

The rest is obvious.

Joris emailed me recently to see if I was interested in buying Belgium. The entire country was up for auction on eBay. The initial bid was one euro ($A1.67). I put in a bid for ten euros then there were 26 subsequent bids culminating in a 10 million-euro offer before the auction was halted by eBay. The last time I heard from Joris he was in Mali doing research for a thesis. He'd gone back to university to do a Masters degree in Conflict and Development. When he has resolved the conflict he still plans to finish his Grand Bicycle Tour of Africa.

Cecile is still living in Luxembourg and still doesn't have any Luxembourgish friends.

On the day that James and Aylin got married it snowed. It was the first time in more than 30 years that snow had fallen in Istanbul in October. At least it made a perfect prelude to their icy honeymoon in Iceland. 'We couldn't afford to drink or eat much,' James told me. 'And my credit card was on fire.'

Mutisya has turned his 'couch surfing bedroom' over to volunteers working for the 'African Child Initiative &

Community Development Forum'. Mutisya set up the organisation to help a local orphanage, but has since expanded the initiative to help those affected by the 2008 post-election violence in Kenya that displaced over half a million people. In partnership with local community groups Mutisya started the project 'YOU CAN SAVE, YOU CAN HELP'. Mutisya is no longer a member of couch surfing as he wants to 'reserve his couch' for volunteers.

Walindah is still nursing and she even managed to get Elijah a job at the hospital. The last I heard from Walindah she was waiting for a response to an application to be a 'house member' on South African *Big Brother*.

Penelope and Sarah finished their call centre contract and travelled around India for a month before coming home to Australia to 'get a real job'. Sarah tells me that she now likes curry. Her belated conversion occurred within one week of their departure from India.

Vikram is no longer on couch surfing. I think he may have just pushed his Marble Emporium a bit too much and was politely asked to leave the site.

Jude is now the editor of two magazines. The latest one is called *Expat Travel & Lifestyle* magazine. At least his Masters degree in Spanish is coming in handy—he's been to Spain twice since I stayed with him.

Elvie is still living in paradise. The lucky thing.

Finally, I'd just like to give a few thanks. First of all a big comfy couch gracias, obrigado, thanks, takk, Dank je, merci, sagol, enkosi, shukriya and salamat to my hosts Miguel, Jose, Juan, Mariano, Pedro, Mariana, Bob, Jeremy, Smári, Joris, Cecile, James and Aylin, Mutisya, Walindah, Penelope and Sarah, Vikram, Jude, Elvie, Leika and Zane. If it wasn't for you guys I wouldn't have a book! A beautiful chaise longue thanks to my wife Natalie who never rolls her eyes even once when I tell her about my new madcap travelling idea for a book. A large ottoman of thanks to James Richardson with his red pen and wordsmith wizardry. And lastly a big chesterfield of thanks to my agent Pippa Masson at Curtis Brown and Jo Paul at Allen & Unwin.

If you'd like to view photos of my couch-surfing hosts (and their couches) you can check out the photo album of my trip at www.brianthacker.tv. Or drop me a line—I'd love to hear from you.

Brian Thacker
East St Kilda, October 2008